5 **PLAYS** 5

5 PLAYS 5

JAMES SCHEVILL

SWALLOW PRESS / OHIO UNIVERSITY PRESS

ATHENS

© Copyright 1993 by James Schevill

Permission to produce these plays must be obtained from Helen Merrill, Ltd., 435 W. 23 Street, #1A, New York, N.Y. 10011

Printed in the United States of America

Swallow Press/Ohio University Press books are printed on acid-free paper ∞

Library of Congress Cataloging-in-Publication Data

Schevill, James Erwin, 1920-
    [Plays. Selections]
    5 plays 5 / James Schevill.
       p.   cm.
    Contents: Lovecraft's follies — The ushers, or Lies,
accusations, curses, exorcisms — Mother O, or, The last American
mother — Shadows of memory — The last romantics.
    ISBN 0-8040-0967-8 (acid-free paper). — ISBN 0-8040-0968-6 (pbk. :
acid-free paper)
    I. Title.   II. Title: Five plays five.
PS3537.C3278A6   1992
812'.54—dc20

                                                    92-39580
                                                      CIP

TABLE OF CONTENTS

INTRODUCTION

Towards a New Poetic Realism in Contemporary Theatre

In his autobiography, *Entrances,* Alan Schneider, the director of the American premieres of most of Beckett's plays, stated his belief in a certain kind of poetic theatre: "I have always favored the poetic over the prosaic, siding with instinct over reason, swayed by the power of symbols, images, metaphors, all of the substances lurking behind the closed eyelids of the mind. To me, these are more faithful signs of essential truths than all those glossy photographs that seek to mirror our external world. I've always preferred Chekhov to Ibsen, Tennessee Williams to Arthur Miller, and Dostoyevsky to Tolstoy; but Beckett's metaphors reach deepest into my subconscious self."

Let us consider these points closely, both as a way to praise and argue a little with the living spirit of Alan Schneider, who did so much to promote and challenge the nature of American theatre. Also, I hope, in this way, to define more closely what I mean by advocating a theatre of "poetic realism."

First, the power of the poetic over the prosaic. The dominant form of American theatre today is the small-scale, television-influenced play with a few characters focused on a family crisis. Usually, such plays have one naturalistic setting, and are written in a prosaic, clipped, pseudo-colloquial tone that reflects the jumpy urban pace of our time. Two factors have created this kind of play. The first is the malaise of our inflated economy that, for the past ten years, has been dedicated to an unprecedented peace-time military build-up. Together with this military expansion has gone a national emphasis on money-making, characterized ironically by the word *yuppie,* which is really a play on *Yippee!* as well as *hippy.* What this ironic title really means is a successful participant in the new technology, as opposed to those who cannot cope and end up in the new service class, or as drop-outs, homeless and destitute. Trapped in this perilous moral and economic crisis, theatre has almost eliminated the production of new experimental, large-scale plays in the commercial and regional stages. The second factor that has caused our restrictive theatre today is the social dominance of the visual media, which is helping to change sharp ears into visually jaded eyes. Perhaps the chief cause of our disturbingly high rate of illiteracy today is the fact that a distorted visual specialization of our senses has been occurring in the last fifty years of the twentieth century. Compare this with the Grecian or the Elizabethan belief in the unity of the senses and the problems of our artistic and educational predicament become clearer. Reading, writing, and arithmetic, as simplistic educational solutions to our current problems of illiteracy, will not do. Because the arts represent sensual experience, they will always remain crucial to any real education. Unfortunately, our recent specialization of the senses has pushed theatre further and further into the background with the result that rock concerts have become the dominant form of the arts.

At its most clever, commercial peak of success, the small-scale family plays that we have developed move quickly through a sequence of conventional, tightly knit dramatic scenes. The power of poetry, on the other hand, lies in its ability to employ deep, suggestive images, and rhythms that have a unique power to match the emotional rhythms of the body and mind. Needless to say, all of the great world theatres have been based on poetic concepts and visions. They open up in a theatrical, presentational way that is impossible in our restricted American theatrical scene today. This is true not only of the classical Greek verse plays and those of the Elizabethans, but also of the outstanding playwrights of our time, particularly Beckett and Brecht, who wrote mainly in prose but with the eyes and ears of dedicated poets tuned to unusual images and new rhythmical structures to suit the changing times.

The change in poetic concepts of theatre today is illuminating. Shortly after World War II, verse drama became a lost concept. The turning point for this change in English and American drama occurred when T. S. Eliot rejected the exciting pulse of *Sweeney Agonistes,* which he could not finish to his satisfaction. In many ways, *Sweeney* turned out to be his most original play, far more exciting and promising than his formal later drawing room comedies. At that moment, completed in late 1948, Beckett's *Waiting for Godot* burst like a nuclear bomb upon the playwriting scene, followed by Brecht's opportunities to stage his own plays with his own Berliner Ensemble large-scale productions in East Berlin. Poetry in the theatre took a new direction. These productions marked indelibly our contemporary theatre, although many American plays today seem to exist in ignorance of what Beckett and Brecht accomplished. Written with a patina of thin, materialistic, Yuppie-satirical ideas, these new American plays show a revealing lack of ambition and raise the question: what has happened to the ambition of our playwrights? Are we playwrights willing to settle for some illusion of success when the American commercial theatre has failed almost completely to maintain even its former standards? Are we willing to sacrifice all of the hard-won advances achieved in the last fifty years to a false, misunderstood concept of "entertainment"? Entertainment, after all, is derived from the Latin "enter into," which means, basically, an encounter between actors and audience. It is sad in our society how entertainment has been reduced by the moguls who dominate the media into the idea of a brief relaxation followed by instant forgetting. Indeed, we are taught that the essence of entertainment is easy understanding, easy enjoyment, easy forgetting, as if anything easy can produce lasting entertainment—as if easy actions can give us greater emotional satisfaction than the mastery of difficult actions. Poetry in the theatre has always had a nobler purpose—the idea of grappling with language and ideas and myths that will have a deep, lasting impact on our minds and bodies.

Alan Schneider's next words, "siding with instinct over reason, etc." require more careful consideration. While theatre with its mimicking power aims for the emotional sources that instinct creates, we live in a time when we should be increasingly wary of sacrificing reason. In the waning months of 1989, distinguished Polish, Czech and East German theatre people showed us how the power of art in relationship to the social scene must harness reason and instinct together. Theatre in these countries is not divorced from society as it tends to be in the United States, where we must keep struggling to discover the roots of realism that have always been concerned in the theatre with social problems, historical or contemporary.

When we come to the problem of realism, we come to a difficulty. When Alan Schneider says that "symbols, images, metaphors . . . are more faithful signs of essential truths than all those glossy photographs that seek to mirror our external world," I don't think he is negating realism, any more than Brecht did when he wrote similar thoughts. Rather Schneider is scorning the slick surface of literal details that are so often used in playwriting to describe significant events. Trying to look deeper into the nature of realism, we seem to come to a certain kind of veiled truth. As Brecht showed in his famous essay, "The Street Scene," every witness of a street accident is likely to give a different account of that accident. So it is not enough for a playwright to describe the literal details. Let me use a personal example. Recently, walking home from work, I witnessed two cars in a collision at a dangerous intersection. Fortunately, both drivers were uninjured. They climbed out of their battered cars and began to argue angrily about who was to blame. The police arrived and began to measure the skidmarks and write out their official reports. I myself saw one car run the stop sign, but the other car was clearly driving too fast down the narrow street. The police officer correctly assigned blame to both parties. What happens now if I begin to transform the scene into a play? Immediately, I have to deal with motivation. Why does one driver run the stop sign, and the other speed too fast? The police officer's report describes only the literal facts, one kind of truth. As a playwright I must probe into the veiled truths that always exist in life, truths that usually remain invisible and unknown. What motivates the drivers to be in such a hurry? Now we begin to uncover the psychological features, the relationships between the individual and society, that make characters so fascinating. In the case I am discussing, I happened to learn that one driver was a habitually absent-minded driver, always thinking about something else when he was driving, and, continuously, running stop signs as a result. The other driver, believe it or not, was on his way to a late afternoon rendezvous with a woman whom he was courting. Immediately, a wide range of options opens for a playwright in portraying these characters. Most likely he or she might tackle a satirical, psychological portrayal of the two characters trapped in their particular family situations. Or, if more venturesome, the playwright might relate the drivers more closely in epic narrative fashion to their dependency on an automobile society. In 1990, the playwright might even use a car as the narrator, played by an actor, to describe the urban crisis caused by cars in our society. In any case, the playwright of this street accident now faces various ways to extend reality into the veiled truths of his own poetic perceptions.

Realism, then, becomes a matter of dimensions, not merely literal facts. The poetic realism that has dominated all great playwrights from the Greeks, the classic Chinese and Japanese writers, through the Elizabethans, Molière and the other great French dramatists, the Italian Commedia dell'Arte masters, down to Pirandello, Brecht, Beckett and other contemporary playwrights, is an elaboration of language and myth. At the end of his life Brecht was beginning to think that narrative is the most important element of theatre. How does one tell a story in theatrical terms? If language is the gift that determines individual style, social observation is the quality that creates myth. A poetic sense of language furnishes far more than distinctive verbal images and rhythms. It perceives also, if the senses are not splintered, unusual visual effects, revealing sequences of dramatic action, absorbing sounds that lead to a new sense of the function of music in theatre. This is why Alan Schneider's favorite playwright came to be Beckett. Take, for example, a passage in Beckett's late short piece, "Theatre I," in which a blind man confronts a man in a wheelchair:

B (the man in the wheelchair) Why don't you let yourself die?
A (the blind man) I have thought of it.
B (irritated) But you don't do it!
A I'm not unhappy enough. (Pause) That was always my unhap, unhappy, but not unhappy enough.
B But you must be every day a little more so.
A (violently) I am not unhappy enough!

Unhap indeed, the *unhap* of shattered senses and sensibilities that Beckett shows so well in his unique poetic, realistic style, which helps us to understand why he became Alan Schneider's favorite playwright. What we hear and see in this Beckett excerpt from "Theatre I" is a paradox: the ironic portrayal of our time's shattered sensibilities by a playwright with a rare sensual unity. Without this sensual unity that is inherent in the art of poetry, a playwright is sadly limited. One of the greatest sequence of poems, Rilke's *Sonnets to Orpheus,* begins with the line, "A tree grew there. O pure transcendence!" If the appearance of the tree is the first aspect of reality, the literal detail, the next perception is the veiled truth, the problem of how we transform our visions to achieve transcendence, to feel the transformation of the tree throughout its seasonal cycle, through its ability to sing in the wind like Orpheus. In this way, poetry as the essence of narration, leads to myth.

How does myth apply to our contemporary American theatre? Great plays—name any one you wish—have always depicted man or woman against the gods, against the forces of society, against tyranny of any kind. In such plays, the hierarchy of the family is set against invisible powers; the family is not reduced to its own self-centered structure as is so often the situation in American drama today. When the novelist Salman Rushdie was in the United States three years ago, he said that American writers are focused inwards on their own problems; they are psychologically oriented, while European and Latin-American writers seek to express the political and social forces that surround them. If this equation is too simplified, is there not a strong veiled truth behind it? The American playwright and historian Charles Mee Jr. said recently in *American Theatre:* "What I think of when I think of political theatre is theatre that is *consciously* political—theatre that understands human life within the larger context of history and economics and the flow of time and the shaping of character by forces other than psychological ones."

What is missing, then, so often in our self-centered plays is the reality of history. We Americans are trained to live in the present moment, the *instant* moment. Our theatre is humiliated and deprived of deep emotional power by the aura of *instant entertainment*, the necessity for theatres to scramble for money even on the regional and university theatre levels. Historical plays do not interest us very much because, to us, the past does not live; it consists of nostalgic facts to recollect briefly in museums or on dead historical days such as the Fourth of July. Imagine if Shakespeare had thought this way. He would have written none of his plays, all of which are based on historical and mythical material. What is needed then is a sense of history *now*. We need playwrights, and much of my work has been an attempt in this direction, who will try to show how history lives on to haunt and shape our lives today. Our pasts are not only the environments and genes that have shaped us; our pasts contain the mythological narratives out of which we struggle to shape our futures. Alas, only a few of our playwrights like John Guare, Adrienne Kennedy, Romulus Linney, and Maria Irene Fornes seek to examine how the myths of our past influence us today.

Finally, if theatre is to achieve a new kind of poetic realism that will suit our rapidly changing technological time, it must find a new reality of style. Michel Saint-Denis writes in *Theatre: The Rediscovery of Style:* "You cannot interpret the past in terms of the language and style of today. From your modern standpoint you must assimilate the reality of past styles. There are not two worlds; there is not a world of the modern and a world of the classic theatre. There is only one theatre, as there is only one world. But there is a continuity which slowly changes and develops from ancient to modern style." Through the ambiguous, poetic dimensions of veiled truths, through a dedicated renewal of myth and history, to a new style—these are the essential directions and tasks of a new poetic realism in the theatre. The new style must be contemporary in its comprehension of images and rhythms, and yet have a continuity from the past. It doesn't have to depend on dazzling stage effects, but it must be aware of the new technological age that we live in and which is changing us every day.

Those of us who have lived through the last fifty years have lived through the most tumultuous times in the history of the world. No other age has witnessed such great disasters and such incredible technological discoveries. We have seen the age of extreme nationalism debased and destroyed forever. In our hearts and bodies we know that modern technology has created a new international world. No country can survive today by clinging merely to its own language and customs. In the same way the theatre, which is the most social of all the arts, must adopt a new international vision without losing its cultural roots. This requires the development of a new sense of history, as in the plays of Heiner Mueller—how the past relates to the present, history that is not merely a pseudo-patriotic recognition of ancestral holidays.

The playwright, Vaclav Havel, now amazingly President of Czechoslovakia, wrote in one of his perceptive essays which contributed so much to the recent drastic changes in the eastern European countries: "The civilization of the new age has robbed old myths of their authority. It has put the full weight behind cold, descriptive Cartesian reason and recognizes only thinking in concepts." Certainly Havel does not mean that reason and realism can be bypassed in society and in the theatre. Instead, playwrights and all citizens of our shrinking world must reclaim and renew the authority of myths that confront the deep irrational, unconscious forces that have always sought to condition human destiny. We can no longer pretend that rigid, pragmatic systems of thought and institutional structures can guide us safely through the perilous times that we continue to face. As the new technology changes society, it tends to wash out history and myth with its bureaucratic ordering; it tends to make everything contemporary. This means that we must make a new effort to understand the deep, complex relationships between history and myth and how they affect the way we think and act. As August Wilson, the black American playwright, puts it: "In all my plays, I point toward reconnecting with the past. You have to know who you are, and understand your history in America over more than 300 years, to know what your relation is to your society."

Our society is exposed to constantly new visual stimuli and changing urban rhythms. Rock concerts have taken over the wonder of theatrical spectacles. A recent one hundred minute show by Madonna in Massachusetts was divided roughly into three acts, each with its own incredible set that New York Broadway theatres could not afford. The first set depicted a factory with huge rotating gears, the second set a temple/church for the display of Madonna, the troubled Catholic girl, and the third set was an enormous 1930s style ballroom for a scene that was devoted to a preview of Madonna's film based on the old detective cartoon, *Dick Tracy*. Such productions, combined with the technological performance art productions of George Coates and Laurie Anderson and similar figures, must make those of us who are working in theatre question how we can create our own original forms. Such a new style in theatre, I believe, will come from a new mastery in the visual arts combined with a new sense of poetic language. Perhaps such a theatre of poetic realism and visual wonder is only a dream at the moment—a dream of sensual unity in an age of specialization—but it is a dream to which everyone who believes in the eternal power of theatre to renew itself must aspire.

NOTE

This introduction was first given as a talk at the Alan Schneider Drama Conference at the University of Wisconsin in Madison in March, 1990. It was printed by Joel Schechter, the editor of *Theater,* published by the Yale School of Drama/Yale Repertory Theater, in the January, 1992 issue.)

LOVECRAFT'S

LOVECRAFT'S FOLLIES

FOLLIES

*To Adrian Hall and The Trinity Repertory Company
who commissioned this play.*

CAST OF CHARACTERS

Actors
Actress
Julie
Paul
Millsage
Boy
Mother
Father
Merchant
First Officer
Second Officer
Hippie Harlequin
Hippie Columbine
Von Braun
Nazi Official
Hitler
Eva
American Troops
Capcom
Astronaut
Charlie Brown
Snoopy
Minister
Second Astronaut
Space Official
Chorus
Second Space Official
Houston
Eagle
Columbia

Singer
Newsman
Tarzan
Ape
Lovecraft
Green Goddess
Green Guard
Green People
First Wife
Second Wife
Third Wife
Physicists
Housewives
Woman
Lawyer
Hunters
Physicist Slotin
Oppenheimer
Scientists
Authority
Black Inmate
George W.
Security Officer
Crew
Mr. Fat Cat
Burner of Cities
Guards
Movie Star
Black Lovecraft

PROLOGUE

(Torches are lit and flicker in the extreme distance. The actors appear at the back of the theater, behind the stage, as if emerging from history. MILLSAGE *is leading his cart of "follies," containing various props.)*

ACTOR *(The actor who plays Lovecraft acts as narrator. He appears suddenly from a trap door):*
Look you! They're coming. Look!
On the wild roads of the world
The actors wander with their carts
Through time, the timeless world of actors . . .

> *(The procession of actors moves forward onto the raked, circular stage. They are in ancient, colorful, tattered costumes of their profession except for a few like* MILLSAGE *in modern dress.)*

See how they come with their masks, props,
Costumes of their trade, the gypsies of pleasure . . .

> *(An actor appears with a small puppet show in which there is a sudden flash of light as the puppet appears writhing in Hell-Fire.)*

Everyman writhes in his morality play,
Burning in the hell of his decisions . . .

> *(The light on the puppet is extinguished. The actor puts on a clown mask and departs.)*

He departs tomorrow to play the clown at a village fair . . .

> *(Enter* HARLEQUIN *and* COLUMBINE *to Renaissance music. They knock at a door. A* SERVANT *looks at them suspiciously.)*

At the King's court, the actors enter
Through the servant's door to entertain . . .
Harlequin and Columbine laugh through their bitterness . . .

> *(*HARLEQUIN *and* COLUMBINE *gird themselves, laugh, do a turn, and enter through the servant's door.)*

Trade and commerce begin to transform the cities . . .

(On rides the BOURGEOIS GENTLEMAN *in a cart pulled by other actors. The* BOURGEOIS GENTLEMAN *is played by* PAUL MILLSAGE *in his modern suit, with briefcase, but also with a luxurious, colorful seventeenth-century headpiece.)*

The Bourgeois Gentleman is mocked to great applause . . .

(The BOURGEOIS GENTLEMAN *is rolled off in his cart.)*

Be careful of this motley crew wandering through history.
Like mirrors on their singular journeys,
They reflect the follies and delights of their time . . .

(The HUNTERS *appear as hunters from an older time, trespassers on forbidden territory.)*

They are dangerous!

(The HUNTERS *laugh, change into actors, and go to their positions.)*

No, they are merely entertainers . . .

(Another actor from the company moves forward. The rest of the actors who speak in the prologue are different actors from the company.)

ACTOR:
Tonight we bring you a play about a physicist named Stanley Millsage.

ACTOR *(a young, ironic actor):*
This is a play about physics!

ACTOR *(severely):*
It is a play about a scientist-artist named Stanley Millsage.

ACTOR:
Well, science and art used to be the same thing.

ACTOR *(another actor from the company speaks to the audience):*
Like you we are confronted with the problems of our time,
A secret technology that rules our lives.
Tonight we bring you a play based
On the hidden contradictions of our time.

ACTOR *(the young, mocking actor again):*
Our central character is a scientist-artist named Stanley Millsage.

ACTOR *(another actor from the company):*
Haunted by absurd visions of horror fiction,

Millsage has suddenly left his job in Huntsville, Alabama,
At the Marshall Space Center . . .

ACTOR *(another actor):*

He is trapped in Rhode Island
Where he follows his fantastic visions with his fourth wife . . .

(He motions to the actress who plays JULIE. *The actresses who play the
other three wives begin to protest.)*

ACTRESSES:

What? Four wives? That's too many . . . That's a bit much . . . Too
much . . .

ACTOR:

In the fashion of the theater,
Exaggeration breeds reality . . .

ACTOR:

Listen, then . . . We actors, and you, the audience,
Are the folly-specters of our protagonist, Stanley Millsage . . .

ACTOR:

For tonight we play the game of follies,
We play them with love and hate . . .
We call them truth or lies . . .

ACT I

SCENE 1

JULIE, *a young, attractive woman, the wife of* STANLEY MILLSAGE, *enters with* PAUL MILLSAGE, *Stanley's brother. Paul is an intelligent, jovial well-dressed lawyer in a modern suit, shirt, and tie. On stage, the actors are now in place in* Lovecraft's Follies, *the statue* MILLSAGE *has been creating. The head is a grotesque, enormous, lavishly painted representation of H. P. Lovecraft, the horror fiction writer. To portray the body, the actors group themselves tightly into the statue and hold up placards derived from various* Weird Tales *covers.*

JULIE *(pointing to the statue):*
There it is, Paul.

PAUL:
What the hell is it?

JULIE:
Stanley calls it "Lovecraft's Follies."

PAUL *(walking around the statue gingerly):*
Why this is . . . this is full of Weird Tales . . . Well, it's very unusual . . .

JULIE:
After we left Huntsville and came here, your brother has been awfully strange, Paul. I can't reach him. That's why I asked you to come.

PAUL *(sceptically touching the statue):*
It's dusty and greasy too . . . *(turning to her)* Maybe I'll be able to help in some way. You know I've always liked you best of his long-suffering wives.

JULIE:
Thank you, Paul. Considering the number of wives he's had that's quite a compliment.

PAUL *(looking at the statue):*
No wonder the security people are worried about him . . . I think Stan should go back to Huntsville and serious scientific work.

JULIE:

After what happened to him, Paul, he's not sure about going back. We keep hearing of people we know that have been questioned.

PAUL:

Now, Julie, let's not get all alarmed about this. Stanley is a very big man in the space program. Like most scientists, Stanley lacks what I call breadth. But he is a very big man. They have cleared him again for his return.

JULIE:

Just because you get a clearance doesn't mean they don't keep checking on you.

PAUL (*He rolls a letter out of the typewriter where* MILLSAGE *has been writing*):

Holy Toledo, listen to this . . . "The problem of this materialist technology is the loss of mystery. For years we have learned nothing but a false objectivity. We believe only in the practical object that cures, produces, entertains, and feeds. The scientist in the laboratory has become just another technician, another bureaucrat. Baskets like fences rise in his office marked *File* and *Hold, Out* and *In*. Over his desk hangs the motto: *If you do not act, then you cannot sin.* All of us, scientists, business men, lawyers—that's directed at me I suppose—are becoming Little Officials of Maybe, singing our last ballad from the inhuman bureaucracy that threatens to overwhelm us . . ."

(*As* PAUL *reads the letter,* STANLEY MILLSAGE *appears on a platform behind and above* PAUL. MILLSAGE *is an impressive, grey-haired, disheveled figure, middle-aged, in a rumpled sport coat and slacks. The actors in the statue begin to sing the ballad of "The Little Official of Maybe." The effect is as if the ballad is occurring in* MILLSAGE'S *mind satirizing his brother.*)

THE ACTORS (*singing the melody and chanting the effects of the sound poem*):

The Little Official of Maybe	Brrr
Who never says "Yes" or "No"	Brrr
Has a head the size of a ping-pong ball,	Brrrr
A stare as blank as snow.	Burroh
He wears a prim, anonymous suit	Booroh
Of neutral, washed-out grey,	Boooroh
And drapes around his flabby chest	Buuuro-crack
A clean white shirt every day.	Buuuro-cracky
Baskets like fences rise in his office,	Crat

8

Marked *File* and *Hold, Out* and *In;*
Over his desk on the wall hangs the motto:
If you do not act, then you cannot sin.

Cratchy
Crack
Buuuro-Cracky

At night he prays to his wife, "Perhaps . . ."
Then she tucks him in bed like a baby
Where he tosses and teases the tickling thought,
"I am the Little Official of Maybe."

Buuuro-Scratchy
Buuro-Cratchy
Rat
Bureau-Crat!

PAUL:
You know whom he's writing to?

JULIE:
No.

PAUL:
The new Chief Justice of the Supreme Court, Warren E. Burger.

JULIE:
Oh, god.

PAUL:
This is not good. You just can't write to the Chief Justice . . .

MILLSAGE *(interrupting as he walks up behind* PAUL*):*
Hello, Paul . . . What a surprise to see you! What are you doing in Rhode Island?

PAUL *(taken by surprise, he puts on his heartiest manner):*
Oh, Stanley! Well, hey boy, good to see you! Why the hell didn't you meet me at the airport?

MILLSAGE:
I didn't even know you were coming . . .

PAUL *(chuckling):*
I guess you were busy writing to the new Chief Justice. You always were a great letter writer, Stan.

MILLSAGE:
I see you've been reading my mail already.

PAUL *(sarcastically):*
I thought they were open letters to the world.

MILLSAGE:
They are. They are open to the world and to my brother. They are not open to Security.

PAUL:

There are some people who don't think anything should be "open" to Security.

JULIE:

Stop it you two!

YOUNG ACTOR (*ironically to the audience*):

This is a melodrama about two quarreling brothers.

PAUL:

All right, I'm sorry. What is this Lovecraft monster you're working on?

MILLSAGE:

H. P. Lovecraft, next to Poe the greatest writer of horror fiction in the country.

PAUL:

Horror fiction, for christ's sake . . .

MILLSAGE:

Why did you let her talk you into coming anyway?

JULIE:

That's not fair. He came here to help . . .

MILLSAGE:

Help! We've got to get out of this world and live somewhere else. We've got to live somewhere else. Don't you see?

PAUL (*gesturing at the statue*):

Is that the latest fashion in sculpture nowadays?

MILLSAGE:

Be careful. He's made of rare things.

JULIE:

Rare, secondhand things. We spend a lot of time at the Salvation Army and junk places . . .

MILLSAGE:

Rhode Island is full of antiques, living and dead. That's why we came here.

PAUL:

Is there a real letter embedded in here? The writing is so small I can't make it out . . .

MILLSAGE:

It's an actual letter of Lovecraft's. He was maybe the last, great corre-
spondent in this country who believed in the power of the letter to create
feelings and connections between people. He had an enormous family of
letter writing friends who called him "Grandpa Theobold."

PAUL:

I hate to say it, Stan, but this is the paraphernalia for sadism . . . or
maybe worse.

MILLSAGE:

I'm building a metaphor for life.

PAUL:

Horror fiction is a metaphor for life?

MILLSAGE:

Lovecraft wrote most of his stories for the magazine, *Weird Tales*. He
used to walk around carrying a copy with the cover torn off . . .

PAUL:

Stan, I wouldn't defend H. P. Lovecraft. But no one wants to be seen carrying a book with a pornographic cover.

MILLSAGE:

Don't you think it's a time for weird tales?

JULIE:

Let's all sit down and talk quietly about this thing.

PAUL:

No, you can keep the fantastic. You can't go on like this. You're a fine
physicist. You know you're already riding the borderline. They'll with-
draw your clearance.

MILLSAGE:

Lovecraft's Follies, Paul . . . It's a way of searching maybe . . .
   (A picture of an old man is projected on the screen.)

PAUL:

That's dad. Where did you get that picture? *(A picture of an old woman appears.)* It's Mother! She looks so sad there. That's not the way she was!

MILLSAGE:

Lovecraft's Follies, Paul. They're Lovecraft's parents, that's who they
really are. Lovecraft was brought up by his grandfather, a wealthy real

estate broker, but his father, a salesman for the Gorham Silver Company of Providence, was a syphilitic . . . They kept that secret, of course . . .

PAUL:

What the hell does that have to do with our parents?

MILLSAGE:

H. P. Lovecraft, Gentleman of high social position and gentility which he so greatly admired. When Lovecraft was only two years old, a child prodigy, his parents made him stand on a table and recite Mother Goose . . . You remember how our parents used to put me up on a table and make me recite too? . . .

(Now the actors come from behind the projections playing the part of the mother and father. Another actor plays the part of the child. The action is highly stylized as though the generation gap images are exaggerated in grotesque details in MILLSAGE'S *mind.)*

BOY *(beginning to slap father on the leg):*
Papa, papa, you look just like a young man!

MOTHER:

Leave your father alone. Why don't you recite for us?

BOY:

I don't want to!

MOTHER:

Come on, dear. You know how much we want to hear you recite. Climb up on the table.

BOY *(climbs up on table):*
Why do I always have to do it from up here?

MOTHER:

It's always easier to project from the top of a table, dear.

FATHER:

Don't you think it's time to cut his hair?

MOTHER:

No, it's so pretty . . . Go ahead and recite, dear.

BOY *(declaiming "Old Mother Goose and the Golden Egg"):*
Old Mother Goose,
When she wanted to wander

Would ride through the air
On a very fine gander . . . Mother, what's a gander?

MOTHER:
It's a male goose, dear.

BOY *(continuing):*
Mother Goose had a house,
It was built in a wood . . .

MOTHER:
'Twas, dear, not it was . . .

BOY:
'Twas built in a wood,
Where an owl at the door
For sentinel stood . . . *(An actor puts on an owl mask and begins quiet, owl sounds.)*
She had a son Jack,
A plain-looking lad,
He was not very good,
Nor yet very bad . . .

FATHER *(to mother):*
Don't you think we should build up his ego more? He ought to be independent . . .

MOTHER *(savagely):*
Like you? Go out and consort with loose women? Get yourself a terrible disease no one can mention?

FATHER:
Someone has to be loose in this world. *(Pointing to boy)* Send him to the market. Make him independent like all constitutional Americans except myself . . .

BOY *(reciting):*
She sent him to market,
A live goose he bought;
See, mother, says he,
I have not been for nought . . .

Jack found one morning
As I have been told,
His goose had lain him
An egg of pure gold . . .

13

MOTHER:

I told you he'd be a real success. He tells stories so beautifully. He's such a
pretty boy.

FATHER:

The frontier may be lost but we've got him. Eureka! He's discovered gold.
He's going to be a banker, merchant, lawyer, scientist. He'll discover a
cure for my syphilis. We'll be able to make love again.

MOTHER:

Never.

BOY:

Jack sold his gold egg
To a merchant untrue,
Who cheated him out
Of half of his due . . .

MERCHANT (*As Jack approaches with egg*):

Son, I'm glad to see that you have a college degree and have produced this
gold egg in your laboratory. We need more and better research in this
country, especially if it produces gold. Why do we make gold keys and
give them to the benefactors of our cities? Because all that glitters is not
gold. Only the real thing can open the doors of opportunity. In the future
we're going to make all the keys to our missiles out of gold. That's what we
mean by military-industrial complex. More beautiful gold keys, like the
Greeks used gold. That's why we call our missiles Jupiter, Titan, Poseidon, Spartan—because we send 'em off underground and under the sea
with golden keys! (*Two officers appear as if underground holding missile-
launch keys. They wear anonymous, white-faced masks and hold gold keys.*)

FIRST OFFICER:

Got your gold key around your neck, Merv?

SECOND OFFICER:

Yeah, Pete.

FIRST OFFICER:

Beautiful keys aren't they?

SECOND OFFICER:

Real good craftsmanship.

FIRST OFFICER:

You got it tight around your neck on the cord?

SECOND OFFICER:
Yeah, the cord fits real well . . .

FIRST OFFICER:
I never thought I'd be wearing a gold key around my neck on a cord . . .

SECOND OFFICER:
You're right . . . It feels real good . . .

FIRST OFFICER:
When you look at a gold key this far underground it really glitters . . .

SECOND OFFICER:
Yeah, there's nothing like a missile silo to look at gold.

FIRST OFFICER:
All you have to do is put the gold key in the slot . . . That took a real sculptor . . .

SECOND OFFICER:
But I have to put mine in too . . .

FIRST OFFICER (*waving his gold key*):
I'm watching you, Merv . . . These long-haired kids had better keep those geese laying gold eggs . . .

SECOND OFFICER (*waving his gold key*):
I'm watching you, Pete . . . We'd better help the merchant get those kids . . .

BOY (*shrieking as the* MERCHANT *and* OFFICERS *belabor him*):
Then Jack went a-courting
A lady so gay
As fair as the lily,
And sweet as the May.

The merchant and the squire
Soon came at his back,
And began to belabor
The sides of Poor Jack . . .

MERCHANT (*belaboring the* BOY):
Gold, gold, gold! Don't you understand anything about the International Bank? What'll happen to the value of gold? What'll happen to Fort Knox if you start screwing around with long-haired girls? Stick to your geese, boy!

OFFICERS *(as they belabor* BOY*):*
What about our gold keys? We can't just wear cords around our neck. We need our gold keys underground. You can hump your hippie girls some other time! Let's get a little security on your goose, son.

BOY:
Then old Mother Goose
That instant came in,
And turned her son, Jack,
Into famed Harlequin.

She then with her wand
Touched the lady so fine,
And turned her at once
Into sweet Columbine.

MOTHER:
I'll save him, I'll save him. He'll be my lover forever!

FATHER:
Cut his hair! Cut his hair!

(Actors come out as HARLEQUIN *and* COLUMBINE, *modern hippie-type kids wearing classical masks. The lighting and mood change to a quiet love scene.)*

HIPPIE HARLEQUIN:
Look, Columbine, it's a gold key!

HIPPIE COLUMBINE:
No it's not. It's a coin . . .

HIPPIE HARLEQUIN:
We can buy some pot from the Mafia!

HIPPIE COLUMBINE:
No it's gold . . . Throw it away . . .

(They continue on their barefooted dance through life.)

HIPPIE HARLEQUIN:
Look, it's a gold penny!

HIPPIE COLUMBINE:
No it's not silly, pennies are made out of copper.

HIPPIE HARLEQUIN:

They are? Oh well, pennies don't buy anything nowadays. What good is money?

HIPPIE COLUMBINE:

You can buy anything you want with it, that's what.

HIPPIE HARLEQUIN:

Come on, let's jump over the money.

(They sing "Jumping for Love over the Money.")

HIPPIE HARLEQUIN:

I jump over the battered penny
    in sudden spring
for love and not for money;
    penny, penny, penny, penny
where is my love, and where is my money?

HIPPIE COLUMBINE:

Barefoot down the melting road,
    hot in the sun,
I prance the asphalt with dirty feet,
    penny, penny, penny, penny
jumping for love over the money.

HIPPIE HARLEQUIN:

Girl in jeans, with hanging hair,
    come jumping near
for love and not for money;
    penny, penny, penny, penny
Here is my love and there is my money.
    I pick up the penny
    and jump for love.

MOTHER:

Come home! Come home!

FATHER:

Come back to your American suburb, son. We need you. *(He falls dead.)*

MOTHER:

Your father is dead from that horrible disease. Come home, son!

BOY (*kicking* FATHER):

He's not dead . . . Papa, you look just like a young man . . . You look just like a young man . . . You look just like a young man . . .

(The mother puts on black.)

BOY (*slowly turning*):

Mother, why are you all dressed in black?

MOTHER:

I'm in mourning . . .

BOY:

For whom?

MOTHER:

For myself.

BOY:

No, I can't stand your black clothes.

MOTHER:

What are you doing?

BOY:

I'm going to pin bright things all over you. (*He starts to pin bright bits of cloth to her clothes.*)

MOTHER:

It's no use . . . I have to mourn . . .

BOY:

But for whom?

MOTHER:

For the loss of my son.

BOY (*desperately*):

Mommy! I'll recite for you again. Listen! I'll recite for you again!

(He climbs up on the table and begins feverishly reciting, "Old Mother Goose, when she wanted to wander, would ride through the air on a marvelous gander . . ." As he recites, the MOTHER *takes off her black mourning and listens; the* FATHER *comes back to life and nods approvingly; the* HIPPIE COLUMBINE *watches sadly from the distance; the* OFFICERS *wave their gold missile keys; and the* MERCHANT *walks up and slaps the* BOY *on the back with congratulations.*)

MILLSAGE:

How'd you like it, Paul? That's Scene 1 . . .

PAUL:

I think the whole thing is pretty silly. Maybe you do have a problem that's not easily solved and maybe you were a mama's boy but I get damn sick of blaming everything on Mother.

MILLSAGE:

I'm not blaming her, Paul. Forget our parents for now. This is Lovecraft's Follies, his way of looking at things.

JULIE:

Is it meant to have some connection with your lives? Is this our lives? When Jack grew up and his father died, why did he give the girl up?

MILLSAGE:

Because he was two years old!

PAUL:

Stanley, you're going to have to get better control of yourself. I don't appreciate this in front of me.

MILLSAGE:

Would you prefer it behind your back? She didn't have to bring you here.

PAUL:

We haven't seen each other for a long time. I thought I could help. That's the only reason I came. Stan, I have to be honest, some of your superiors came to see me.

MILLSAGE:

Who came to see you?

PAUL:

Two of your bosses at the Marshall Space Center in Huntsville . . .

MILLSAGE:

Who were they?

PAUL:

I can't mention names. They spoke to me in confidence.

MILLSAGE:

Damn them.

PAUL:

They admire your work. They want to keep you if possible.

MILLSAGE:

Admire my work! Oh, brother, what a funny man you are!

PAUL:

You're an important peg. You work on a key team. You've written important studies in Huntsville.

MILLSAGE *(bitterly):*

I'm mentioned in *Who's Who* too.

PAUL:

Is that all space means to you? We've landed on the moon. I was glued to television watching that amazing landing. And you know what? I was proud, proud that you helped. You must have watched too . . .

MILLSAGE:

Yes I watched, Paul . . . The watched watching. We live in a moon hypnosis.

PAUL:

Well, for God's sake man.

MILLSAGE *(mockingly):*

Well, for God's sake . . .

PAUL:

Don't just keep repeating everything I say. We're on the moon—stand tall man. We've mapped it, we've landed there, it's ours.

MILLSAGE:

Ours? What does that mean?

PAUL:

Aren't you proud that we got there first instead of the Russians? Who knows what's next—Mars? Don't you want to be a part of that?

JULIE:

Over your desk, Stan, you used to keep the words of the astronomer, Whipple. Remember how much that meant to you? . . .

ACTOR *(speaking Whipple's words from the side of the stage as if the words are echoing in* MILLSAGE'S *memory):*

Man has broken the tyrannical bounds of gravity that confined him so long to earth. Now man's machines and devices travel across the gravity barrier of a universe so vast that it defies comprehension. No longer are man's eyes blinded by the black curtain of atmosphere that closes out most of the incoming messages of radiation from outer space . . .

PAUL *(interrupting excitedly)*:
You're damned right boy, and what I'm here for—the reason I've come all the way to Rhode Island is to let you know—that I—your brother—your wife—all the boys on the team want you to go back to your job at the Marshall Space Center, stop your letter writing, forget about your fantastic visions, your Lovecraft's Follies, get back to work under Wernher von Braun . . . *(They move off stage and remain watching for a time under the spell of* MILLSAGE'S *next vision.)*

VON BRAUN *(He appears on the high platform, smoking a pipe, answering an unseen reporter. A projection of* VON BRAUN *is shown on the screen)*:
Are we ahead of the Russians or are they ahead of us? A couple of years ago you could answer the question in very simple terms. For example, right after Sputnik it was pretty clear they had something in orbit. We didn't. So they were ahead in the space program . . .

ACTOR *(As a projection of McNamara is seen, an actor speaks the words of Robert McNamara)*:
Robert McNamara . . . has said ". . . Man is a rational animal, but with a nearly infinite capacity for folly . . . There is a kind of mad momentum intrinsic to the development of all new nuclear weaponry . . ."

VON BRAUN:
But today the space program has so many facets that it may be impossible for all eternity from now on to be ahead of them in all fields. And, equally, it will be impossible for them to be ahead of us in all fields . . . The Russians may put their emphasis in other areas of space exploration. They have always expressed great interest in manned space stations in earth orbit. The same type of hardware,

MILLSAGE *(They speak simultaneously)*:
Hardware. Did you get that word?

PAUL:
What's the matter with that word?
It takes a lot of stuff . . .

MILLSAGE:
Scene 2, Lovecraft's Follies,
Paul . . .

VON BRAUN *(cont.)*:
the same rockets, the same type of spacecraft can be used to assemble space stations in orbit . . .

(Actors enter as NAZI OFFICIAL *and as* HITLER. *An enormous swastika banner drops down, hanging over the stage.)*

NAZI OFFICIAL:
Mein Fuehrer, Herr Doktor von Braun is here to see you.

HITLER:
I don't want to see any more scientists unless they produce.

NAZI OFFICIAL:
But he's at Peenemunde, Mein Fuehrer . . .

HITLER:
What's at Peenemunde, Schweinehund?

NAZI OFFICIAL:
You put it there, Mein Fuehrer . . .

HITLER:
You mean it's going to work, the Ultimate Hardware?

NAZI OFFICIAL:
Yes, Mein Fuehrer, the Ultimate Hardware . . .

HITLER:
What's the last report from Russia?

NAZI OFFICIAL:
Four thousand tanks lost, 2,005 airplanes, 1,500 guns lost—that's how-itzers and mortars of all calibres—3,300 rifles, 952 trucks . . .

HITLER:
That's a lot of hardware. We need the Ultimate Hardware. Bring him in. *(Enter* VON BRAUN. *He salutes.)* Stand up, von Braun. You don't have to salute if you've got the Ultimate Hardware.

VON BRAUN:
It works, Mein Fuehrer, it works! It's the pure Ultimate Hardware!

HITLER:
I don't give a swastika if it's pure or not so long as it works.

VON BRAUN: *(He gives a long, pure, ecstatic, technical statement of which* HITLER *doesn't understand a word and shows his impatience increasingly.* VON BRAUN *ends with):*
It's the first unmanned Hardware!

HITLER *(suspiciously)*:
Unmanned Hardware is not so good. If it's unmanned, who watches it?

VON BRAUN:
The Hardware watches the Hardware, Mein Fuehrer! It's ideal! It whizzes off little platforms that can be camouflaged easily. Then it buzzes off over the channel and goes boom!

HITLER:
Where does it go boom?

VON BRAUN:
Wherever you want it. Inside it there's a piece of adjustable hardware that guides the hardware. It's all self-adjusting. All you have to do is set the hardware before it buzzes off. The only problem is, it needs to be a little more self-adjustable . . .

HITLER:
Speak plain German. What do you mean a little more self-adjustable?

VON BRAUN:
Sorry, Mein Fuehrer, I've been studying English for recreation. My plain German is a little rusty. The problem is the hardware adjusts itself approximately so there's maybe a slight margin of error in the target . . .

HITLER:
How much of a margin of error? You know, von Braun, we don't have camps for nothing . . .

VON BRAUN:
Only a little margin of error, a trivial distance . . . If you aim at an airfield, maybe you hit the city ten miles away instead. We get around that by building lots of Ultimate Hardware.

HITLER:
Too late, von Braun. Germany has betrayed me! You Germans didn't give me enough hardware. You were polluted by the Jewish and Slavic races. I'm going to take Germany with me, von Braun. You're all going to die with me! Eva! *(Enter* HITLER'S *wife in exaggerated Nordic costume with a Valkyrie helmet.)*

EVA:
Yes, Mein Fuehrer?

HITLER:
You're the only one who hasn't betrayed me.

EVA:

I will never betray you, Mein Fuehrer.

HITLER:

I'm going to shoot you. We're going to Valhalla. *(Wagnerian music.)*

EVA:

Yes, Mein Fuehrer. It is a privilege to die with you, Mein Fuehrer.
(HITLER *shoots her and then himself, pulling down the swastika banner as he falls. Blackout. A wild short interlude of chaos to indicate the occupation of Berlin. Whirling lights, sirens, shots, actors rushing around. Then lights up on the* AMERICAN TROOPS *as they enter singing and marching.)*

AMERICAN TROOPS *(singing):*

Where is the man with the Ultimate Hardware?
We want him to fly to the moon.
We'll give him a piece of Alabama
And workers from night until noon,
    Building the Hardware, the Ultimate Hardware,
    The Master of nuts, bolts, and screws,
    Towers, rockets, and all the spare parts
    Building Hardware, the Ultimate Hardware!
When the Doctor puts us on the moon,
    the moon, the moon, the moon, the moon,
When on TV the stars and stripes we see,
    we see, we see, we see,
Wave over the sea of Serenity,
    -nity, -nity, -nity
We'll give him part of Alabama
    We'll give him *part* of Alabama
We'll give him *half* of Alabama
    We'll give him *half* of Alabama
We'll give him *all* of Alabama
    We'll give him *all* of Alabama
Alabama,   Alabama,
        Alabama,   Alabama
Ala-   Ala-
    -bama,   -bama,
Give him Alabama—
    For building the Hardware, the Ultimate Hardware,
    The Master of nuts, bolts, and screws,
    Towers, rockets, and all the spare parts

Building Hardware, Hardware, Hardware, Hardware,
Building the Ultimate Hardware.

VON BRAUN (*emerging cautiously from a trapdoor*):
If you give me Alabama for the Ultimate Hardware I will come. Good
thing I studied English. Besides Alabama is not in Russia. I will come to
Alabama if you promise me I can develop my Ultimate Hardware. I will
bring all my scientists with me. You have liberated us from that madman
Hitler. He never understood hardware. We had to obey him. You had to
get along with the military and the industrialists. You Americans don't
know what it was like in Nazi Germany. I tried to protect my Jewish colleagues even if there weren't any left. I will give you Americans the moon
. . . Because the moon is mine. I will show you how to build all the different kinds of hardware. I will show you the chains of mountains on the
moon like iron jaws—the Appenines, the Caucasus, the Alps, the Carpa-
thians. I will show you the great parallel crevasses around the Mare
Humorum . . .

AMERICAN TROOPS:
Huh?

VON BRAUN:
I will teach you the Latin names. I will show you the wasteland of lunar
craters, hundreds of thousands of them. I will show you the ghost craters.
Give me Alabama and I will come to the United States. We will go to the
moon together!

AMERICAN TROOPS (*singing enthusiastically as they march out with* VON
BRAUN):
We've got us the man with the Ultimate Hardware,
The Master of nuts, bolts, and screws,
Towers, rockets, and all the spare parts
Building Hardware, Hardware, Hardware, Hardware . . .

VON BRAUN (*turning back to the audience*):
When I escape from Huntsville and go to Washington, D.C., we Americans will conquer space together. (*He exits with the American troops as they
all sing the final line together, "Building the Ultimate Hardware."*)

(*The lights come up immediately on* CAPCOM, *an actor representing the
Houston Space Center. The astronauts, in their glistening, metallic-looking
suits, have climbed up ladders at the side of the theater into the spacecraft.
The spacecraft and the lunar module ride and separate on a track over the
stage. Actors below in the darkness pull the spacecraft and the lunar module*

by ropes. CAPCOM *is seated speaking into a microphone on the platform at the back of the stage.)*

CAPCOM:

Good morning, Charlie Brown.

ASTRONAUT:

Good morning, Smiling Jack.

CAPCOM:

You boys have been up a while I see.

ASTRONAUT:

Yeah, we tried to sneak up on you.

CAPCOM:

We thought you'd like to hear your horoscopes now before you start work, right?

ASTRONAUT

Sure, might as well have something to do while we're eating this plastic stuff you call—food.

CAPCOM:

John's horoscope's kind of interesting this morning. It says: "Everybody you know has something helpful to offer. Put in a busy day and assemble your results in the evening."

ASTRONAUT:

Make sure you do that, John, assemble your results in the evening.

CAPCOM:

All right, let's get down to business. Time for the nitty-gritty. Climb into Snoopy . . .

ASTRONAUT:

Roger . . .

VOICE OVER:

At 3:36 p.m., Snoopy, the lunar module, separated from Charlie Brown, the spacecraft . . .

CAPCOM *(glued to the panels):*

Big Brother is watching . . . *(The spacecraft and the lunar module separate.)*

CHARLIE BROWN (*the astronaut left back in the spacecraft*):
Keep up the good work, boys. You'll never know how big this thing gets when there ain't nobody in here but one guy.

SNOOPY (*one of the astronauts in the lunar module*):
You'll never know how small it looks when you're as far as we are.

CHARLIE BROWN:
OK, separation . . .

SNOOPY:
OK, configure thrust for us in there, John, we're moving away . . . OK, José, say Adiós and see you back in about six hours.

CHARLIE BROWN:
Roger.

CAPCOM (*Watching the big tube*):
Snoop and Charlie Brown, we see you separating on the boob tube!

SNOOPY:
Have a good time while we're gone, Babe. And don't get lonesome out there, John. Don't accept any TEI updates.

CHARLIE BROWN:
Don't you worry . . . Until you get back, I ain't copying any more pads.

SNOOPY (*As the lights dim*):
OK, John, we're out here in earthship. How about turning on your flashing light? (CHARLIE BROWN *begins signals with a powerful flashlight. This should have the quality of a game.*) Beautiful, you've got a nice one. It looks like the old Gemini Agena . . . Go ahead, kill the tube any time you want and put the cover over it.

(*Blackout in the theater*)
Boy, I'll tell you that's black out there, isn't it?

CHARLIE BROWN:
No other color to describe that . . .

(*A projection behind the astronauts of the actual lunar module descending towards the moon's surface*)

SNOOPY (*exuberantly*):
Hello, Houston, this is Snoopy. We're down here among the rocks, rambling along the boulders right now.

SNOOPY:

Roger, Snoopy, go ahead.

SNOOPY:

We is going. We is down above the pavement, Charlie.

CAPCOM:

Roger. I hear you weaving your way up the freeway.

(A burst of light)

SNOOPY:

Oh, Charlie, we just saw a BEEP damn earthrise. It's just got to be magnificent. Tell Jack there are enough boulders up here to fill Galveston Bay.

CAPCOM:

Snoop. Houston. There will be no update on the phasing pad. Everything is looking real good.

SNOOPY:

OK, it's a fantastic sight. They do have different shades of browns and greys here. The moon is not colorless.

CAPCOM:

OK, Snoop, it is time to go up and rejoin Charlie. All right, let's jettison the descent stage . . .

SNOOPY *(sound — crash):*
Roger. Here we go . . .
BEEP of a bitch BEEP . . .

CAPCOM:

Hello Snoopy, what's the BEEP'S going on? BEEP . . . BEEP . . .

(Black out)

MINISTER *(storming on, waxing furious):*
Millions of innocent American children have been subjected to filthy indecencies by the astronauts' flight to the moon. Through the heaven of our Lord, they mouthed the obscene slogans scribbled on the walls of latrines! Instead of planting the cross of decency and righteous living on the moon, they humiliate decent Christians with gutter talk and sexual blasphemies. We demand respect for the family, the flag, and for our Lord, Jesus Christ. If the Federal Government, sitting complacently there in Washington, is going to permit this outrage to our great religious traditions, the Christian people will rise and protest with fire and sword. The

Lord will not permit this blasphemy of His heavenly body, the moon! *(Lights up on the* ASTRONAUTS *who are submitting uneasily to a press conference.)*

ASTRONAUT *(uncomfortably):*
What happened was that about twenty seconds before the scheduled separation of the lunar module's ascent and descent stages, the LM moved slightly. I had to use maneuvering jets to get it back into its proper position. Then both stages of the module started to gyrate . . .

SECOND ASTRONAUT:
It was—uh—slightly upsetting, because we were coming down backward. We pitched downward, down to ten miles from the moon's surface. All of a sudden the thing takes off!

ASTRONAUT *(smiling wryly):*
I can see why he would say, "What the heck BEEP was that?

SECOND ASTRONAUT:
What you heard was just three men trying to do a job in a new world . . . a new environment . . .

ASTRONAUT:
We want to thank the vast majority of the American people for their very sincere understanding. To those who were offended, particularly some of those whose prayers were with us, I can only sincerely say from all of us, "We're sorry . . ."

SPACE OFFICIAL *(to another* SPACE OFFICIAL *as the* ASTRONAUTS *leave the press conference and stand by the ladder preparing to become the new crew of Apollo* 11*):*
No excuses, god damn it. Their profanity may cost us a $100,000,000 cut in the space program. Next time when we really hit that moon, we scrub it. Any idiot knows you can't use those words on television, damn those squareheads. The next Apollo crew has to be cleaner than a hound's tooth. I want the right image, understand. The whole world will be watching. No more of their stupid swear words! This is not a game!

(A rock song begins for the final moon landing, the "song of Magnificent Desolation"—Aldrin's words in describing the moon.)

Have you ever walked
on Magnificent Desolation?
Have you ever talked
to Magnificent Desolation?

CHORUS *(everyone joining in):*
That's what you see
when you're weightless at noon;
That's what you know
when you reach the moon.

(The ASTRONAUTS, *now the new crew of Armstrong, Aldrin, and Collins, begin to ascend the ladder again while the music continues in the background.)*

SPACE OFFICIAL:
Another thing, let's get rid of the comic book names. Snoopy and Charlie Brown may be all right for Apollo 10, but we need something more serious, more international for Apollo 11.

SECOND SPACE OFFICIAL:
How about Columbia?

SPACE OFFICIAL:
Great idea. It's a play on Columbus too. Say, I've got the name for the lunar module . . .

SECOND SPACE OFFICIAL:
What's that?

SPACE OFFICIAL:
Eagle.

SECOND SPACE OFFICIAL:
Ego?

SPACE OFFICIAL:
Eagle, Eagle, you know, our national bird . . .

(Blackout on the SPACE OFFICIALS. *The ''Lem'' with the two* ASTRO-NAUTS *aboard begins to separate again from the spacecraft. The rock song is heard louder.)*

All those craters in your eye,
they're Magnificent Desolation.
When you reach Tranquility Base
it's Magnificent Desolation.

CHORUS:
That's what you see
when you're weightless at noon;
That's what you know
when you reach the moon.

HOUSTON (CAPCOM *again with tremendous excitement as the actual landing begins. The astronauts are seen descending in a balloon-like basket*):
You are go for landing. Over.

EAGLE:
Roger, go for landing . . . 35 degrees, 750, coming down to 23; 700 feet, 21 down, 33 degrees; 350 feet, down at 4; 300 feet, down 3 and a half, 47 forward . . . 50, down at 2 and a half, 19 forward; 4 and a half down, 5 and a half down, 6 and a half down, 5 and a half down, 9 forward; 75 feet, looking good, down 2 and a half, 6 forward.

(During this search, a film of the real moon landing is projected on the screen.)

HOUSTON:
Sixty seconds.

EAGLE:
Lights on *(they switch on the lights);* down 2 and a half; forward, forward; shadow; 4 forward, 4 forward, picking up some dust, drifting to the right a little.

HOUSTON:
Thirty seconds.

EAGLE:
Contact light. Okay, engine off.

HOUSTON:
We copy. You're down, Eagle.

EAGLE:
Houston, Tranquility Base here. The Eagle has landed.

HOUSTON:
Roger, Tranquility. You've got a bunch of guys about to turn blue. We're breathing again. Thanks a lot.

COLUMBIA:
How do you read me?

HOUSTON:
Columbia, he has landed Tranquility Base. Eagle is at Tranquility.

COLUMBIA:
Yes, I heard the whole thing.

HOUSTON:
Well, it's a good show.

COLUMBIA:
Fantastic . . .

> (*The rock song again as the* ASTRONAUTS *throw out a ladder and begin to descend from the module to the moon's surface*)

When you're in lunar orbit,
put down on Magnificent Desolation,
walk near the Module's golden leg
into Magnificent Desolation.

CHORUS:
That's what you see
when you're weightless at noon;
That's what you know
when you reach the moon . . .

ASTRONAUT: *(on the ladder):*
Well, I'm looking head-on at it. OK, my antenna's out.

ASTRONAUT:
Your visor.

ASTRONAUT:
Yep.

ASTRONAUT:
Your back is up against the porch. Now you're clear. Straight down to your left a little bit. You're lined up nicely. Now you're clear. You're catching the first hinge.

ASTRONAUT:
The what hinge?

ASTRONAUT:
All right, move. Roll to the left. Put your left foot to the right a little bit. Okay, that's good. More left. Good.

ASTRONAUT: *(on the last rung of the ladder):*
Okay, Houston. I'm on the porch.

HOUSTON:
Roger, we're getting a picture on the TV.

ASTRONAUT:

You've got a good picture, huh?

HOUSTON:

There's a great deal of contrast in it and currently it's upside down on monitor. But we can make out a fair amount of detail.

ASTRONAUT: *(about to step on moon):*

I'm going to step off the LM now. *(He steps onto the moon)* That's one small step for a man, one giant leap for mankind . . .

SINGER:

Have you ever walked
on Magnificent Desolation?
Have you ever talked
to Magnificent Desolation?

CHORUS:

That's what you see
when you're weightless at noon;
That's what you know
when you reach the moon.

> *(The* ASTRONAUT *puts up a plastic flag and salutes awkwardly. On the screen the film shows the real action of the astronauts on the moon. Then the* ASTRONAUT *on the stage takes out a pogo stick and bounces around triumphantly.)*

NEWSMAN *(as the lights change):*

Dr. von Braun, now that we've put an American flag on the moon, what's next . . .

VON BRAUN *(puffing on his pipe, his calm, documentary self):*

If the space program continues to be supported at the present rate, it would appear to me we would have the capability to land a man on Mars by 1982 or 1985, something like that. But the moon is a pretty large place, remember. Just by visiting one *mare*—that's Latin for sea—we don't know the moon. By visiting a number of places with essentially the same hardware we can get more scientific return. We have worked out a rather detailed plan on how to explore Mars after we get through with the moon. We start out with a series of unmanned flights to answer the basic questions about Mars and get some good maps of that planet. On the basis of all this data, the space agency will have to make up its mind whether Mars is interesting enough to be visited by man. I think we will find it interesting. The round trip would take over a year, so you have to plan it on a somewhat grander scale than Apollo. You need a much more sophisticated kind of hardware. We don't want just three men. You would probably want to send along, for instance, a doctor and a cook. Then we need really big hardware, two or three ships flying in a convoy . . .

(Towards the end of this interview, strange chanting sounds are heard from the actors around the theater. Eerie musical sounds are heard. The chanted sounds are based on the actors improvising syllabic sounds from Lovecraft's cryptic chants "Ph iglui mglw'nafh cthulhu r'lyeh wat 'hagl fhtagn." The Lovecraft statue lights up in its grotesque pop art way. Masks of terrifying, ancient, mysterious stonelike faces are held high by actors near the statue. The actors stand or crouch below in darkness, holding up the masks, which are illuminated in eerie, green light.)

MILLSAGE *(crouching in the shadows at the front of the stage as he begins his vision of Lovecraft's horror fiction):*
. . . For the Old Ones are forever ready, waiting. Dead and yet undead, they can be revived by certain arts when the stars are in the right position in the cycle of eternity. A bloody sacrifice on a hidden tumulus, some cryptic chant, may yet be the means by which they can surmount all checks, and out of space and time sweep down and regain their lost dominion . . . The sciences, have hitherto harmed us little . . . But some day the piecing together of disassociated knowledge will open up such terrifying vistas of reality . . .

ACTOR *(as the actors begin to act out* MILLSAGE'S *vision of Lovecraft's horror fiction):*
(scream) Something bumped into me, something soft and plump . . .

ACTOR:
It must have been the rats; the viscous, gelatinous, ravenous army that feed on the dead and the living . . .

(Actors as beasts and carrion birds appear. Flapping sounds of giant wings and strange, chanted cries are heard.)

ACTOR:
Why shouldn't rats and the Old Ones eat forbidden things? Why shouldn't rats and the Old Ones eat forbidden things?

(At the climax of this swift scene—the sense of a terrifying horror fiction sacrifice is evident, a woman is being eaten alive by a society that has regressed into beasts and carrion birds.)

PAUL *(appearing in the midst of* MILLSAGE'S *nightmare):*
Jesus, you are sick! Don't you see, Stanley, what you're doing to yourself?
This is a nightmare. You know von Braun well. He's a great scientist.
Probably you would have done the same thing in Germany to save your
skin. We'd better talk more about this tomorrow. I'm tired and I'd like to
get to bed.

JULIE *(worried):*
Come, I'll show you to your room, Paul.

PAUL:
And all that stuff about the rats in the walls—you've got to stop playing
around with Lovecraft's Follies.

> (PAUL *and* JULIE *exit.* MILLSAGE *sits at typewriter and types letter.*
> JULIE *reenters.)*

MILLSAGE *(savagely):*
Have you got Big Brother the Spy tucked safely in bed? Blood may be
thicker than water, but your target is not bloody or watery.

JULIE:
If you don't want to go back to Huntsville, don't go. I'll do anything you
want.

MILLSAGE:
It's not just Huntsville.

JULIE:
What is it then? What are you doing?

MILLSAGE:
Writing a letter to Security about my brother.

JULIE:
Don't be childish.

MILLSAGE *(reading):*
"Gentlemen, I take back my opinions expressed in our recent exchanges
about your inefficiency. While, in my opinion, the bureaucracy of your
secret administration is still overloaded, I confess that you do occasionally
get to the heart of the matter. Specifically, my heart. Your ability to enlist
the services of my brother and now my wife . . .

JULIE:

They didn't enlist my services.

MILLSAGE:

How'd Paul get here then?

JULIE:

I asked him. I told you that.

MILLSAGE:

I suppose you didn't know he was in contact with security at the Space Center. And God knows where else?

JULIE:

No, I didn't. You have to believe me. He is your brother, Stan.

MILLSAGE:

Why'd you want him here?

JULIE:

We need help.

MILLSAGE *(blowing up):*

Bring 'em all in. Record everything from birth to death. Dig into the school records, doctor's files, psychiatrist's notes, credit-card status, divorce suits, photographs, and fingerprints. Run them all through the computer. Turn our lives into an open book.

JULIE:

Stan, I know how you feel about spying into your private life. But what I'm talking about is our private lives.

MILLSAGE:

Julie, I want to be part of things. I don't want to be just another outsider. That's what it's turning into. I want to devote my whole life to it. I want to live in the center of discovery. In the greatest age of science there's ever been—we commute from decaying cities to hidden suburbs. Huntsville, Houston, and the other installations—they're hidden, secret suburbs outside decaying cities.

JULIE:

Why go back then? We can make out somehow.

MILLSAGE:

The machines, the laboratories, are in Huntsville. Down at the bottom of the ant heap, the action is there.

JULIE:

Stan, you know it's not my idea of paradise—that German colony with its isolation, the scientists' wives with their tea parties . . . But I'll go back if you want . . .

MILLSAGE:

I want a decision as much as you do, Julie. That's why I'm consulting the oracles.

JULIE:

You could go into teaching and do your research on the side.

MILLSAGE (ironically):

I'm a research genius, not a teacher.

JULIE (defensively):

All science isn't under the government.

MILLSAGE:

How many laboratories are not somehow connected with defense? Listen to tonight's paper (He picks up a newspaper lying by the typewriter.) "American science is shaken by a national controversy that could alter the main thrust of technology in this country for many years. The scientific community and one of its biggest allies, the U.S. Military Establishment, are being charged with too great a complicity in each other's affairs. Each is accused of having feathered—and shared—the other's nest for so long that the Pentagon's influence is overextended and science is now distorted and misdirected. Forces are at work that could reduce science's role as handmaiden to military technology and turn more of its attention to the country's domestic problems . . . But the Defense Department has no intention of seriously reducing its basic ties to the scientific community . . ."* I want some unity of vision again. I want science as the art it once was.

JULIE:

But, Stanley, you let this interfere with us. You are running away . . .

MILLSAGE (impulsively):

I'll show you how much I love you . . .

JULIE:

Oh no, don't go off into your fantasy world.

*The Evening Bulletin, Providence, R. I., by Douglas C. Wilson, Feb. 28, 1970.

MILLSAGE:

Not just fantasy, exploration . . .

(*The* GREEN GODDESS *appears, half naked, from a trap door.*)

JULIE:

My god, she's green.

MILLSAGE:

The Green Goddess of Love . . . (*The Lovecraft statue lights up and a muscular man in a loin cloth steps out of it. He lets out a jungle screech. He is accompanied by an ape, played by an actor.*)

JULIE (*hitting him*):

Oh Stanley, no, *Tarzan and the Green Goddess*. Please don't do this.

MILLSAGE (*holding her as they struggle*):

Lovecraft's Follies . . . You'll see . . .

TARZAN (*to the* APE):

We must find it, Cheetah, we must go in search of the sacred, lost empire of the Green Goddess.

APE:

This place doesn't look safe for an ape.

(*Another actor, playing* LOVECRAFT, *steps from behind the statue.* LOVECRAFT *is dressed in a white suit and pajama hat; he carries an umbrella.*)

LOVECRAFT:

Lord Greystoke, I presume?

TARZAN:

Here in the jungle I am Tarzan of the Apes.

LOVECRAFT:

Then luck is certainly with me for I have come all the way from Rhode Island to find you.

TARZAN:

Who are you and what do you want of Tarzan of the Apes?

LOVECRAFT:

My name is H. P. Lovecraft of *Weird Tales*.

APE:

Careful, Tarzan. we've got a much bigger following than he does. Don't forget we've been translated into thirty-two languages, including Braille.

LOVECRAFT:

It is my mission to accompany you to the empire of the Green Goddess. You may be in need of my scientific help. *(Rolls of green paper, jungle images, drop down.* LOVECRAFT *pushes through them with his umbrella, as they begin their journey.)*

APE:

Watch it Tarzan. He's an odd one.

TARZAN:

I go there to free my woman, Jane. The Green Goddess has kidnapped her.

LOVECRAFT:

You have to be careful of these primitive green savages.

TARZAN:

Are they more dangerous than man who alone of all creatures brings dissension and strife wheresoever he first sets foot?

APE:

Watch it, Tarzan, that's not ape language. You're getting to speak like Lord Greystoke.

LOVECRAFT:

Why did the Green Goddess kidnap your wife, Jane?

TARZAN:

The Green Goddess wants to color me green and make me her Green God.

LOVECRAFT:

That would ruin the white race.

APE:

It wouldn't help the apes either. Think of a green ape swinging through the trees . . .

LOVECRAFT:

I shudder when I think of the fate of the white race if we are overrun by green people.

APE:

But we don't know whether they're so bad yet. Maybe Tarzan can fake making love to the Green Goddess until we can rescue Jane and make our escape.

TARZAN:

Tarzan does not make love to green woman, only white woman, Jane. Come, we waste time . . . *(They go off. The* GREEN GODDESS *signals to her companions.)*

GREEN GODDESS *(to various people):*

Go and fetch the captive white woman, the mate of Tarzan . . . Go fetch Tarzan. *(They go and grab* JULIE *who struggles and protests to* MILLSAGE.*)*

JULIE:

Stanley, please! Don't do this. You're insane!

GREEN GODDESS *(as* JULIE *is brought before her):*

Bring her closer. So you are the mate of Tarzan.

JULIE:

The hell I am.

GREEN GODDESS:

To Love, everything is clear. In our world green is the color of love. We see everything through a green light. You do not love Tarzan?

JULIE:

I am not Jane.

GREEN GODDESS:

Clothe her in the green sacrificial clothes and chain her. Soon we will make you a secondary green goddess. When Tarzan arrives we will transform him into a Green God. Then we will see whether he loves you or me. My power of love will conquer! (TARZAN, LOVECRAFT, *and the* APE *are brought in as prisoners)*

GREEN GUARD:

My goddess, we have caught Tarzan and these strangers.

GREEN GODDESS:

Who are these strangers?

TARZAN:

This is Cheetah, my friend, the ape, and H. P. Lovecraft from *Weird Tales.*

GREEN GODDESS:

Love-craft? With such a name he may be eligible for our kingdom if he will accept the color green.

LOVECRAFT:

You don't understand. I am H. P. Lovecraft, Gentleman of Providence.

GREEN GODDESS:

What is gentleman? There are no green gentlemen.

LOVECRAFT:

That's because you're too primitive to understand. I'm talking of a white gentleman, the enthusiastic champion of total abstinence and cultivation of the higher senses; of moderate, healthy militarism as contrasted with dangerous peace-preaching; of the domination by the English and kindred races over the lesser divisions of mankind such as you green people.

GREEN GODDESS (to TARZAN):

Does this white gibberish make sense to you, Tarzan of the beautiful body? Think what you could do if you were green.

TARZAN:

Well, I like apes better than people, but after all I am Lord Greystoke. The English race has to stick together.

APE:

What about us apes?

TARZAN:

Don't worry, friend, I'll fight to preserve wild life sanctuaries.

GREEN GODDESS:

Then you both must die and be transformed. Prepare the sacrifice. Begin with Tarzan.

TARZAN (to LOVECRAFT as the GREEN PEOPLE advance on him):

Don't worry. I'm the strongest jungle man in the world. I know all about beasts and primitive men. They can't hold me with any of their primitive bonds. (He breaks his bonds and roars his jungle cry.) You can't enslave a free, white jungle man!

APE:

Master is as strong as an ape!

LOVECRAFT:

I'm with you, Tarzan! If something happens to your white strength, I've got my white *Weird Tales* weapons. (He puts up his umbrella inside out and screams at the GREEN GODDESS.) You can't stand up against the white race. We come from the Western factories of money and weapons!

GREEN GODDESS:

What is money? With your puzzles you dry the magic out of your bodies. Do you not think we green people have studied time? We have learned how—what do you call it?—tight-assed the white man is with his money. We know of your curious, psychological scientists who speak of the withdrawal of love and the creation of vast machines through money that you have dared to color green. Learn now of the Green Power of Love!

(Song and ritual action of the "Green Power of Love." All of the green people sing this as TARZAN *is prepared for the sacrifice. The sacrifice should use all kinds of weird primitive masks and phallic, sacred sexual objects. The ceremony is akin to all of the tribal ceremonies of excremental magic. Behind the ritual action is heard the changing and singing of the chorus, the rhythm of magical instruments.)*

GREEN GODDESS *(singing)*:

Green power to the people,
Green is the power of love.
Enter the soft world of green,
You can give,
     you can feel,
         you can live!

GREEN GODDESS:

Let the green power of love move through you. Come, Tarzan. *(Slowly,* TARZAN *turns toward the* GREEN GODDESS.)

APE *(alarmed)*:

Wait a minute, Tarzan, what are you doing? Let's get back to the trees!

LOVECRAFT:

Tarzan, you must think white!

GREEN GODDESS *(singing)*:   GREEN PEOPLE *(chanting)*:
Lie down on the altar of love   *Mo-huh-money.*
Where all sacrifice is made,   *Rub the money out of him.*
Where each thing flowers   *Mo-huh-money.*
Green in love's eternal time.   *Rub in green love.*

*(*TARZAN *lies down on the altar. A roar of triumph is heard from the* GREEN PEOPLE.)*

Green power to the people,
Green is the power of love.
Enter the soft world of green

You can give,
    you can feel,
        you can live!

GREEN GODDESS:

Lord Greystoke, you must die. The end of the British Empire has come. The myth of white supremacy is doomed. Green Tarzan shall live forever. Out of the old white age flowers the new, green age. Out of the dirty paper green, let the essence of green sea, sky penetrate into waiting flesh. Green Tarzan shall live forever!

GREEN PEOPLE *(they have been chanting):*

Mo-huh-money.
Rub the money out of him.
Mo-huh-money,
Rub in green love.

APE *(watching, suddenly enchanted by the ceremony):*

Wait! I want to be green too! *(He climbs onto the altar and lies down beside* TARZAN.*)*

GREEN PEOPLE *(chanting):*

Green power to the people,
Green is the power of love,
Enter the soft world of green,
You can give,
    you can feel,
        you can live!

(Two GREEN MEN *approach* JULIE, *take her to the altar, and put her on top of* TARZAN *and the* APE.*)*

JULIE:

Save me, save me! The green people are going to rape me!

LOVECRAFT *(calling in his weapons over a bullhorn):*

Come in Air Force! The Air Force is on its way. Come in *Weird Tales,* come in . . . Call in napalm strike against green people. Let 'em have it on target. Open up the underground caves. Planes go, ray guns, Titan, Poseidon, Spring, Spartan, Mirv, Mirv! Wipe 'em out. Pave their country over with white cement!

(Actors appear as weapons, imitating planes and missiles. The GREEN PEOPLE *are wiped out, but* TARZAN *and the* APE *escape.)*

LOVECRAFT (*emerging again after the slaughter*):
Long live the white race! The green people are dead. We'll create the eighteenth century again, the Age of Reason. I've saved you, Jane.

(JULIE *climbs down slowly from the altar.*)

JULIE:
They're dead. The Green Goddess is dead. The green people are dead.

LOVECRAFT:
I saved you for Millsage. He's waiting for you. Good-bye, Jane . . .

(*He exits, stomping over the bodies of the* GREEN PEOPLE.)

JULIE (*turning to* MILLSAGE):
What were they going to do to me?

MILLSAGE:
Rape you with love maybe? Isn't that what you said you wanted?

JULIE:
I hate this, Stanley! I hate Lovecraft! He's a racist. What are you trying to do? Why are you doing this?

MILLSAGE:
He's gone. It's only a play. Why are you crying, Julie? Didn't you want Lovecraft to protect you?

JULIE:
I didn't know what he was like . . .

MILLSAGE:
I'm sorry. It's all over now. The Hollywood game, the money game, is over . . . (*The actors playing the* GREEN PEOPLE *get up and leave. Three actresses remain lying on stage; they will play the* GHOSTS OF MILLSAGE'S FORMER WIVES.) Julie, you've got to forget the ghosts of my ex-wives.

FIRST WIFE:
Goodbye to the apartment in Los Alamos.

SECOND WIFE:
Good-bye to the life of the physicist's wife.

THIRD WIFE:
Good-bye to science and the big machines.

ALL THREE WIVES:
The wives of scientists make the best ghosts.

(The sound of high-energy physics machines is heard echoing in MILL-SAGE'S *mind.)*

FIRST WIFE:
You betray . . .

SECOND WIFE:
Betray . . .

THIRD WIFE:
Betray . . .

FIRST WIFE:
You betray your hope to the military-industrial money complex.

JULIE:
I'm not one of them. Why do you humiliate me with them?

MILLSAGE:
Don't you see I'm giving you a chance to leave. I don't want you to stay and be hurt.

JULIE:
Do you want me to leave?

MILLSAGE:
Julie, is the green world so impossible, so frightening? Why are you afraid? What of? Trust? Naivete?

JULIE:
Your green world is not us. It's not our life.

MILLSAGE:
Science has gone through a fantastic world to find its reality.

JULIE:
Stanley, I don't even understand the point you're making.

MILLSAGE:
We killed thousands of yellow men at Hiroshima and Nagasaki.

JULIE:
That's not us Stanley; that is not our guilt.

MILLSAGE:
I have no argument for my innocence that even makes sense. What I am trying to say to you is that maybe we have to go through the fantastic world to get to our own reality.

JULIE:

We don't seem to be able to travel together. I don't know what to do, Stan. We need help. That's the only reason I asked Paul to come, believe me. *(She goes out.* MILLSAGE *stares after her, then turns as the ghosts of the wives come forward mockingly.)*

FIRST WIFE:

Good-bye to the apartment in Los Alamos.

SECOND WIFE:

Good-bye to the life of the physicist's wife.

THIRD WIFE:

Good-bye to science and the big machines.

ALL THREE WIVES:

The wives of scientists make the best ghosts.

(The sound of high-energy physics machines is heard again and MILLSAGE *reacts.)*

FIRST WIFE:

You betray . . .

SECOND WIFE:

Betray . . .

THIRD WIFE:

Betray . . .

FIRST WIFE:

You betray your hope to the military-industrial-money complex.

FIRST WIFE:

Betray . . .

SECOND WIFE:

Betray . . .

THIRD WIFE:

Betray . . .

(The WIVES *exit.* MILLSAGE *stares after their ghosts for a long time, then walks off slowly.)*

END OF ACT I

ACT II

SCENE I

Toward the end of the intermission, MILLSAGE *enters and begins typing. Facing him is an empty chair. At the side of the theatre the four actors, who have changed openly into the costumes of hunters from various historical periods, begin the ritual clothing of the actor who plays* OPPENHEIMER. *They dress him as an Indian shaman, lift him up deep in his trancelike state, and parade him across the stage before seating him in the chair facing* MILLSAGE. *The* HUNTERS *leave the stage as* MILLSAGE *continues to type.*

> NOTE: At this point, in the premiere performance of the play by the Trinity Square Repertory Company, a short, documentary film of the bombings of Hiroshima and Nagasaki was shown. This sequence lasted three to four minutes and consisted of excerpts from a documentary film made by Japanese cameramen. After being suppressed for many years, the film was released and distributed by the Columbia University Film Library. The narration to the film, consisting of simple, direct, factual comments about the nature of the bombs and what happened to the inhabitants of Hiroshima and Nagasaki, was spoken directly to the audience by the actor who played Lovecraft. After the film sequence ended, the lights went up and the action continued as follows with the shaman still sitting motionless in his chair.

PAUL *(entering):*
Another letter, Grandpa Theobold?

MILLSAGE:

Just finishing my letter to Security about you . . . *(He reads)* "All right, gentlemen, you win. I will talk to my brother. I'll try to tell him what happened to me at Los Alamos. After all he is my blood, my name, if not my kind of chromosomes . . . If you want to know, the real truth is that I've always envied him. He sleeps better at night. He doesn't have so much trouble with women. He is never bothered by dreams and nightmares the way I am. He gets along better with people . . .

PAUL:

What happened to you and Julie last night?

MILLSAGE:

I'm tired of being a security target . . .

47

PAUL:

Are you being fair to her?

MILLSAGE:

No.

PAUL:

At least you admit it.

MILLSAGE:

I'm a scientist—reasonable, unreasonable . . . What do you want me to say? That I'm not very good with women?

PAUL:

Then why'd you get married again?

MILLSAGE:

Because I don't happen to be the kind of person who can live alone. I don't like to look at myself in the mirror. I like to look at a woman. It's a softer reflection.

PAUL:

You don't see where you are, in the middle of the desert.

MILLSAGE:

That's where I began, at Los Alamos.

PAUL:

If you lose your security clearance, you'll never get another job. Even the universities won't have you.

MILLSAGE:

Is that what they told you to tell me? That I might lose my security if . . .

PAUL:

They made no threats. All they did was to point out the options. They're eager to keep you at Huntsville, but they can't ignore all the security rules. We're at war in Viet Nam. Fifty thousand American boys have been killed. The Chinese have the bomb now; the Russians are building up their missiles. We can't afford to lose our superiority in nuclear weapons.

MILLSAGE:

Your answer is always . . . more technology, more technology. You're a lawyer, Paul. How does security look to you?

PAUL:
Ugly, but necessary.

MILLSAGE:
That is a contradiction, Paul. The duality and the contradictions facing man today . . . It is a difficult premise, but let's see . . . *(Slide: The Shaman and the Hunters)* Ladies and gentlemen, H. P. Lovecraft presents *The Shaman and the Hunters.*

LOVECRAFT *(appearing suddenly, mockingly, he carries a black cat):*
In the age of true science fiction we have created a shaman in the desert, a medicine man. His name is Oppenheimer.

MILLSAGE:
A medicine man. His name is Oppenheimer.

LOVECRAFT *(mocking* MILLSAGE*):*
A medicine man. His name is Oppenheimer.

PHYSICISTS *(entering, they circle* OPPENHEIMER *and kneel around him):*
Depressive . . .
  Lonely . . .
    Poetic . . .
      Unnatural . . .
        Isolated . . .
          Jewish . . .
            Emaciated . . .
              Glittering . . .
                Proud . . .
                  Ambitious . . .
                    Administrator . . .
                      Magician . . .

LOVECRAFT *(to* OPPENHEIMER*):*
You once said, "I have two loves, physics and the desert. It troubles me that I don't see any way to bring them together." You brought them together when you moved from Berkeley to Los Alamos. You also brought the military hunters.

(The HUNTERS *appear high on the platform, illuminated from below, and the* PHYSICISTS *shrink back.)*

PHYSICISTS *(singing):*
Praise to the Shaman
Cursed and blessed is he,

49

Leader of our secret team,
Master of the explosive flame.

LOVECRAFT (*ironically, while stroking the cat*):
On a desert mesa named after the poplar trees, Los Alamos, the shaman and the hunters created a secret, suburban city, a city of weapons research and housewives breeding, raising children in the Indian-haunted, red desert soil under the shadow of the Sangre de Cristo mountains.

(*Square dance begins, increases to a frenzied, distorted tempo.*)

HOUSEWIFE:
We were having the time of our lives.

HOUSEWIFE:
The mere thought of returning to a sane and prosaic civilian life sounded flat and dull.

HOUSEWIFE:
Of course, we didn't see much of Oppenheimer. When he did come to our parties, he left early. But once, in a production of *Arsenic and Old Lace,* we got Oppenheimer to play the corpse. (*All laugh.*) We were having the time of our lives. (*Laughter.*)

LOVECRAFT:
The shaman worked his magic to supply the hunters with their killing materials. The hunters were content for a little while. Busy but happy. The shaman submitted himself to their demands and cut himself off from the world. But one night . . .

HOUSEWIVES:
One night . . .   One night . . .   One night . . .

LOVECRAFT:
. . . he received a demand from his past, a woman he had once loved. He went to her and spent the night at her house, while the hunters waited in the bushes outside. (*The* HUNTERS *spring into watching positions around the stage.*)

WOMAN (*an accusing, suicidal ghost*):
Why don't you speak to me? You never say anything. You never tell me anything. Stay with me, please. You don't know what it's like. I can't sleep any more. A cold moon comes and sits on my eyes. Insects with their metal legs crawl across my face. I'm alone. Nobody comes to visit me. I'm a doctor, but when a patient tries to speak to me I don't hear anything.

Stay with me tonight. What difference does it make if you're married? Stay with me. All those formulas in your head . . . is that all you care about? Why can't you talk to me? Why doesn't your magic work? (PAUL and MILLSAGE *enter on platform.*)

MILLSAGE:

The woman was strong, Paul. His magic did work for a little while longer. But the hunters had grown suspicious. It was the beginning.

(*In* MILLSAGE'S *vision reflections of* OPPENHEIMER'S *security hearing are mixed into the action. A* GOVERNMENT LAWYER *is questioning one of the* HUNTERS.)

LAWYER:

The woman he spent the night with was a Communist.

HUNTER:

We know now that she was a Communist.

LAWYER:

Did the security officers' definition of good discretion include spending the night with a known Communist woman?

HUNTER:

Our impression was that his interest was more romantic than otherwise.

LAWYER:

Just how cooperative are the scientists?

PAUL (*pressed by* MILLSAGE'S *vision into the role of another lawyer, a security official at* OPPENHEIMER'S *hearing*):

The scientists en masse present an extremely difficult problem. The reason for it, as near as I can judge, is that they lack what I call breadth. They are extremely competent in their field, but this competence leads them falsely to believe that they are as competent in any other field.

LAWYER:

Just how cooperative are the scientists?

HUNTER:

They think that they can handle the administrative aspects of an Army post better than any Army officer.

LAWYER:

Just how cooperative are the scientists?

HUNTER:

We know now that she was a Communist.

LAWYER:

Just how cooperative are the scientists?

PAUL:

I hope my scientist friends will forgive me, but their very nature made things pretty difficult. *(Music.)*

LOVECRAFT:

After the suspicion had begun, the scientists soon became divided. The practical physicists and those lost in a mystical world. The shaman had a protégé. The shaman's friend was named Louis Slotin. He suffered from nightmares. Slotin worked on the critical assembly of the bomb, pushing together the two hemispheres with a screwdriver to find the ultimate climax. He called this "tickling the Dragon's tail." The practical physicists protested against Slotin's guilty visions. The shaman struggled for peace in his doman, but one day . . .

PHYSICIST SLOTIN *(manipulating the two hemispheres of the bomb at a table)*:
Come closer. Watch me tickle the Dragon's tail . . . It's a little Dragon, right, a beautiful Dragon . . . All that invisible force . . . Come watch me tickle the Dragon's tail . . .

PHYSICIST *(protesting to* OPPENHEIMER*)*:
Stop him. There's something about that man that outrages me.

PHYSICIST *(also protesting)*:
You can't trust him. I don't like the way his eyes gleam when he talks about tickling the Dragon's tail.

PHYSICISTS *(protesting)*:
It's indecent,
    anarchical,
        reckless,
            disturbing . . .

SLOTIN *(holding up his screwdriver and pointing with it)*:
Don't you see the faces there? Can't you see them? They belong to the Dragon, German faces, Japanese faces, human faces . . . Come watch me tickle the Dragon's tail . . .

(With his screwdriver, he pushes the two hemispheres too close together and a blue ionization glow fills the air. As the PHYSICISTS *flee,* SLOTIN

52

flings himself forward over the two parts to separate them and receives a killing dose of radiation.)

THE PHYSICISTS *(singing as a model of the Hiroshima bomb, "Little Boy," is lowered into* OPPENHEIMER'S *hands):*

Praise to the Shaman,
Cursed and blessed is he,
Leader of our secret team,
Master of the explosive flame . . .

The father of "Little Boy,"
The birth of nuclear joy
And the power to destroy . . .

LOVECRAFT:

August 6, 1945, at Hiroshima, "Little Boy" killed 100,000 . . . *(A model of "Fat Man" is lowered into* OPPENHEIMER'S *hands.)*

LOVECRAFT:

On August 9, 1945, "Fat Man," the plutonium bomb, exploded at Nagasaki. In a single instant 50,000 people died. "Little Boy" and "Fat Man" were awkward, primitive weapons compared with the hydrogen bomb that was to emerge from the shaman's arsenal, its force equal to 31,000,000 tons of TNT.

(A model of the slim technologically more "efficient" hydrogen bomb is lowered and OPPENHEIMER *shrinks away from it, crying out.)*

The guilty shaman recoiled and began to agonize in his mind . . .

OPPENHEIMER *(tormented):*

I find myself profoundly in anguish over the fact that no ethical discussion of any weight or nobility has been addressed to the problem of atomic weapons . . . What are we to make of a civilization which has always regarded ethics as an essential part of human life . . . What are we to make of a civilization which has always been dedicated to Ahimsa, the Sanskrit word that means doing no harm or hurt . . . What are we to think of such a civilization which speaks of the prospect of killing their fellow man only in the sporting term of winning?

LOVECRAFT:

The shaman speaks his magic in complex sentences, the tortured utterance of mystery while his disciples chant and decipher his ritual meaning . . .

PHYSICISTS AND HUNTERS (*accusingly to the Shaman, as he seeks to escape them*):

Myself in anguish . . .	Ahimsa . . .
Atomic weapons . . .	. . . doing no harm . . .
Civilization . . .	. . . doing no hurt . . .
Ethical discussions . . .	Ahimsa . . .
They talk about killing . . .	Ahimsa . . .
Killing everybody . . .	. . . doing no harm . . .
Ahimsa . . .	Ahimsa . . .

(*One by one, the scientists testify against* OPPENHEIMER *as the lights come up on the interrogating* LAWYER *and the witness stand. As the scientists enter, they are ushered in by the* HUNTERS *to maintain the ritual ceremony.*)

LAWYER:

What did Dr. Oppenheimer tell you?

PHYSICIST:

He said that he did not think the United States should build the hydrogen bomb. The main reason he had for this was that, if we built a hydrogen bomb, then the Russians would build a hydrogen bomb, whereas if we did not build a hydrogen bomb, then the Russians would not build a hydrogen bomb. I found this such an odd point of view that I don't understand to this day . . . (*He moves off the stand and another physicist moves up mechanically to occupy the witness chair.*)

LAWYER:

Doctor, is it or is it not true that, in the case of a scientist as influential as Dr. Oppenheimer, a failure to lend his enthusiasm and vigorous support to the hydrogen-bomb program might constitute hindrance or even opposition to the program?

PHYSICIST (*cautiously*):

There is a certin element of semantics in that question, but I would say . . . yes. (*He moves off the stand and another scientist moves up to the witness chair.*)

LAWYER:

Was there any discussion between you and Dr. Oppenheimer about your views on his loyalty?

SCIENTIST:

I have fogotten the details, but I believe at one point Dr. Oppenheimer asked me if I thought he was pro-Russian, or whether he was just confused. As near as I can recall, I responded that I wish I knew.

LAWYER:

Did Dr. Oppenheimer say anything further in that context?

SCIENTIST:

He asked me if I had impugned his loyalty to high officials of the Defense Department and I believe I responded simply, yes.

LAWYER:

Do you recall that he had any comment to make on your mental process?

SCIENTIST:

Yes, he said that I was a paranoid. *(He moves off the stand and another scientist moves to the witness chair.)*

LAWYER:

Would you care to give the Board, Sir, any comments you have, upon the basis of your knowledge of Dr. Oppenheimer, about his character, his loyalty, and his associations in that context?

SCIENTIST:

That is a rather large order.

LAWYER:

I know it is, Doctor.

SCIENTIST:

There were elements of the mystic in his apparent philosophy of life that were very difficult to understand. He is a man of tremendous sincerity and his ability to convince people depends so much upon this sincerity. A whole series of events started happening immediately after he left Los Alamos. Many of our scientists came back from it pacifists. I think this was due very largely to his influence. He objected to the Security clause in the Atomic energy contracts. Then there were the arguments he used for not working on the H-bomb. For four years we twiddled our thumbs. All these things seemed to fit together to give a certain pattern to his philosophy.

LAWYER:

I will put it in very simple terms, Doctor. Having in mind all that you have said, and you know, would you trust him?

SCIENTIST:

You mean in matters of security?

LAWYER:
Yes, Sir.

SCIENTIST *(hesitatingly)*:
I would find—trust, you know, involves a reasonable doubt . . .

LAWYER:
That is right.

SCIENTIST:
I would say . . . On that basis I would find it difficult to do so. *(He moves off the stand and another physicist walks to the witness chair.)*

LAWYER:
Do you or do you not believe that Dr. Oppenheimer is a security risk?

PHYSICIST *(with a heavy accent)*:
In a great number of cases, I have seen Dr. Oppenheimer act—I understood Dr. Oppenheimer acted—in a way which for me was exceedingly hard to understand. I thoroughly disagreed with him on numerous issues and his actions frankly appeared to me confused and complicated. To this extent, I feel that I would like to see the vital interests of this country in hands which I understand better, and therefore trust more.

(The WOMAN *appears again, ghostlike, gliding around* OPPENHEIMER.*)*

WOMAN *(mockingly)*:
Trust! Trust! Trust! . . . After I killed myself, a friend at Los Alamos told you of my suicide.

(An actor approaches OPPENHEIMER *and talks to him confidentially.)*

OPPENHEIMER *(blankly)*:
Thank you . . .

WOMAN *(bitterly)*:
Thank you for what? The dead do not die so easily. You couldn't sleep that night and began to read John Donne's sonnets . . .

OPPENHEIMER *(starting to read mechanically)*:
"Since she whom I lov'd hath payed her last debt
To Nature . . . and to hers, and my good is dead . . .

THE WOMAN *(mockingly)*:
I can't hear you, Shaman!

OPPENHEIMER:
"Since she whom I lov'd hath payed her last debt
To Nature, and to hers, and my good is dead . . .

WOMAN *(echoing him):*
". . . and my good is dead . . .

OPPENHEIMER:
". . . And her Soul early into heaven ravished.

WOMAN:
Am I ravished into heaven? Did the red glow of the Mesa cliffs really merge physics with the desert, with the austere love of your Sanskrit ideal, Ahimsa?

SCIENTISTS *(chanting mockingly):*
Ahimsa
    (Doing no harm)
Ahimsa, Ahimsa
    (Doing no hurt)
        Ahimsa!

WOMAN:
Why did you call the first atomic bomb, Trinity?

OPPENHEIMER *(muttering in agony):*
"Batter my heart, three-person'd God." . . . Trinity . . . Trinity . . . Trinity . . .

WOMAN:
How could you bring a poet's sense of God to the fire of an atomic explosion?

OPPENHEIMER *(crying out in anguish):*
"Batter my heart, three-person'd God, for you . . .
    As yet but knock, breathe, shine, and seek to mend; . . ."

(A projection of the first Trinity explosion in the desert flashes on the screen.)

WOMAN:
Shine!

OPPENHEIMER *(rising):*
"That I may rise, and stand, o'erthrow me, and bend
Your force, to break, blow, burn, and make me new."

(As the screen lights up with the Trinity explosion, the ACTORS *and the* WOMAN, *like a Greek chorus, move around* OPPENHEIMER'S *shaman figure, chanting and speaking.)*

Batter my heart, three-person'd God . . .
Trinity . . . Trinity . . . Trinity . . .
O'erthrow me and bend your force to break . . .
Blow, burn, and make me new . . .

OPPENHEIMER *(feverishly):*
Make me new!

(The screen goes dark abruptly and the HUNTERS *move forward in the stark light.)*

WOMAN:
You delivered science into the hands of secrecy, into the power of the Hunters!

OPPENHEIMER:
No, I sought to keep it under civilian control. That was my whole desire.

WOMAN *(bitterly):*
Civilian control . . . When the scientists began to petition to prevent the use of the bomb against Japan, you refused to sign. Did you really believe that was the way to keep it under civilian control?

OPPENHEIMER *(agonized, withdrawing as the* SCIENTISTS *confront him with the petition):*
The matter is being dealt with at a higher level . . .

THE WOMAN AND THE SCIENTISTS *(chanting):*
Higher level . . . Hunters . . .
The higher level of Hunters . . .

HUNTER *(as narrator to the audience):*
The official minutes of the Interim Committee on the use of the bomb . . .

ANOTHER HUNTER:
"After much discussion, Secretary Stimson expressed the conclusion, on which there was general agreement, that we could not give the Japanese any warning; that we could not concentrate on a civilian area; but that we should make a profound psychological impression on as many of the inhabitants as possible . . ."

THE WOMAN AND THE HUNTERS *(chanting and moving around* OPPEN-
HEIMER*):*
Don't warn the Japanese . . .
Make a profound . . . profound . . . profound . . .
psychological . . . psycho-logical . . . *psycho-logical* . . .
impression . . .

PROFOUND PSYCHO-LOGICAL IMPRESSION

PHYSICIST *(to* OPPENHEIMER*)*:
What does that jargon mean?

OPPENHEIMER *(agonized):*
Maximum civilian slaughter . . .

WOMAN:
The Hunters used you and discarded you when they pleased.

OPPENHEIMER:
Washington became the plague of Thebes! *(A* HUNTER *repeats this line
mockingly over a bull horn.)*

THE WOMAN AND THE SCIENTISTS *(with increasing intensity to* OPPEN-
HEIMER*):*
The plague of Thebes . . .
    The plague of Thebes . . .
        The plague of Thebes . . .
            Your plague!

(The ritual ceremony of humiliation begins in which the HUNTERS *and the*
SCIENTISTS *strip the shaman of his magic. The ceremony begins on the
platform at the back of the stage. Then* OPPENHEIMER *is spun down onto
the stage along the line of his accusers as they embrace him and strip him of
his magical ornaments. As in the tribal relationship of the shaman and the
hunters, there is a strange, deeply rooted relationship of fear, respect,
hatred, and love in this ritual ceremony of humiliation. The following lines,
mainly from the official transcript of the* OPPENHEIMER *security hearing,
are spoken during the ritual ceremony. The Shaman remains silent during
the ceremony, accepting his humiliation with a strange mixture of humility
and evident pride.)*

LAWYER *(breaking the Shaman's magic stick over his knee):*
This office is of the opinion that Oppenheimer is not to be fully trusted
and that his loyalty to a nation is divided.

HUNTER *(ripping off the Shaman's beads):*
J. R. Oppenheimer is trying to secure, by espionage, highly secret information which is vital to the security of the United States.

HUNTER *(tearing off the Shaman's headdress):*
Oppenheimer has allowed a tight clique of known Communists to grow up
about him within the project.

HUNTER *(stripping off the Shaman's jacket):*
It is the opinion of this officer that Oppenheimer is deeply concerned with
gaining a worldwide reputation as a scientist.

SCIENTISTS *(as a* HUNTER *tears off the Shaman's magic pouch and sprinkles
the contents over the stage):*
Depressive . . . Lonely . . .
Poetic . . . Unnatural . . . Administrator . . . Magician . . . *(They
fall back in awe at the contents of the magic pouch.)*

HUNTER *(through a bull horn):*
The United States Army and the Security officials of this country are in
the position to destroy your name, reputation, and career.

LOVECRAFT *(resuming his role as narrator):*
Some time after J. R. Oppenheimer was condemned to lose his security
clearance, he was honored at the White House by the President of the
United States. The President gave Oppenheimer the Fermi Award, the
highest award of the Atomic Energy Commission. But no one restored
Oppenheimer's security clearance . . .

(The SCIENTISTS *and* HUNTERS *celebrate* OPPENHEIMER'S *award in
a satirical circus parade as they carry him high on their shoulders around
the stage. Acrobatic and juggling acts are performed in this mock parade as
the participants sing a quick-time version of the earlier chorus):*

Praise to the Shaman,	Mr. Shaman of the bomb,
Cursed and blessed is he,	You are our sickness and our health
Leader of our secret team,	Our clean and dirty wealth,
Master of the explosive flame.	Mr. Shaman of the bomb.
Praise to the Shaman,	Mr. Shaman of the bomb,
Cursed and blessed is he.	You have unlocked our wealth
In the cosmic furnace	Our clean and dirty health,
Shines his haunted face.	Mr. Shaman of the bomb.

(After the award is presented to OPPENHEIMER, *he turns to the audience
and speaks. The* HUNTERS *and the* SCIENTISTS *have lined up in a*

V-shape behind him. Again OPPENHEIMER'S *manner of speaking is oddly formal, tormented.*)

OPPENHEIMER:
It is our hope that in years to come we may look at this scroll and all that it signifies with pride . . . Today that pride must be tempered . . .

CHORUS *(mockingly):*
Tempered . . .

OPPENHEIMER:
. . . tempered with a profound concern. If atomic bombs are to be added to the arsenals of a warring world. . . .

CHORUS:
. . . arsenals . . .

OPPENHEIMER:
. . . Then the time will come when they will be used and mankind will curse the names of Los Alamos and Hiroshima . . .

CHORUS *(they begin to chant with a rising intensity that ends with a woman's voice screaming the word Hiroshima):*
Los Alamos . . . Los Alamos . . . Los Alamos . . . Hiroshima . . .

(*The* HUNTERS *and the* SCIENTISTS *carry* OPPENHEIMER *back to the platform at the rear of the stage, singing "Praise to the Shaman, etc."* OP-PENHEIMER *either dies high on the platform in a glowing, red light, or, if technically possible, he is lifted in a cage high over the stage. The cage lights up as the chorus sings. The effect of the cage is a cosmic furnace, the image sung by the chorus. In the cage,* OPPENHEIMER *is possessed by the energy of the sun. Submitting to it, he dies.*)

LOVECRAFT:
On February 18, 1967, Oppenheimer died, still an official security risk . . .

(*The chorus of* SCIENTISTS *and* HUNTERS *honor* OPPENHEIMER *in a final funeral procession for the Shaman. They carry his body off and sing again:*)

CHORUS:
Praise to the Shaman,
Cursed and blessed is he,
Leader of our secret team,
Master of the explosive flame.

Mr. Shaman of the bomb,
You are our sickness and our health,
Our clean and dirty wealth,
Mr. Shaman of the bomb.

Praise to the Shaman,
Cursed and blessed is he . . .
In the cosmic furnace
Shines his haunted face.

LOVECRAFT (*alone on the stage after the funeral procession has exited*):
In the cosmic furnace, shines his haunted face . . .

SCENE 2

(This scene follows immediately.)

PAUL (*accusingly to* MILLSAGE):
You distort everything with your half truths. It was tragic what happened
to Oppenheimer, but we have to protect freedom. Even Julie knows what
would happen to Lovecraft if he lived in Russia . . .

MILLSAGE:
Lovecraft was an obsolete romantic.

JULIE:
Stan, please, I admire Oppenheimer as much as you do. I understand how
you feel, but Lovecraft's world is a dangerous fantasy. I want to help you
get rid of him, Stan.

PAUL:
What would happen if we abolished all security? We'd lose our freedom in
a moment.

MILLSAGE:
Do you really believe that, Paul?

PAUL:
What about the Russian agents? It's not only CIA all the time. Security is
necessary.

MILLSAGE:
What *about* the Russians?

PAUL:

We do have to fight for justice and civil rights. I'm a lawyer. I know what happens in Russian courts. What about the Brodsky case?

MILLSAGE:

The Brodsky case . . .

PAUL:

The trial of the poet, Josef Brodsky in Leningrad, 1964. The judge was a woman. He was sentenced to five years of hard labor in Siberia because his poetry was politically unacceptable.

JULIE:

It's the same thing, Stan. It really is the same thing. I'll play the Woman Judge. We'll get rid of Lovecraft . . .

PAUL (taking on his brother's role as master of follies):

H. P. Lovecraft will appear tonight as Brodsky the poet . . . (A projection of Brodsky with the inscription "The Trial of Josef Brodsky" is shown on the screen.) H. P. Lovecraft will appear tonight as Brodsky the poet.

LOVECRAFT (suddenly):

No, not tonight. I won't play Brodsky the Jew. Everyone knows that secret regulations contaminate the Soviet Union as well as the United States. (Accusingly to MILLSAGE) You Stanley Millsage are a coward—afraid, afraid to examine your problems in the open . . . What are you afraid of? . . . Bryce?

(The Brodsky projection vanishes abruptly and in its place appears a photograph of the Alabama state asylum at Bryce with a newspaper headline: NIGHTMARE AT BRYCE—SCIENTIST IS LOCKED UP IN MENTAL HOSPITAL. Inmates of the hospital shuffle forward, their hospital pajamas over their basic acting costumes.)

MILLSAGE:

Maybe I am afraid . . .

(As if in MILLSAGE'S vision, the inmates sing and perform part of the ballad of "The Silent Majority." While they sing, other inmates shuffle in and assume their silent positions. Immense silences punctuate the song. Some of the inmates carry on a curiously painted boat.)

Join the Silent Majority,
Ride with the common crew;
Don't rock the ship of state
By trying things too new.

Join the Silent Majority,
Don't listen to the lonely voice.
Don't rock the ship of state.
By shouting to rejoice.

Join the Silent Majority,
Learn to be silent and free.
Don't rock the ship of state
Join the Silent . . .
    Join the Silent . . .
        Join the Silent Majority . . .

SCENE 3

(Follows Without Break)

MILLSAGE *(shouting):*
Afraid?

JULIE *(alarmed):*
What is it, Stanley? Because of your arrest? . . .

PAUL:
What about your arrest?

MILLSAGE *(to PAUL):*
Didn't your friends tell you what happened?

PAUL:
Yes. I know that you had some unfortunate run-in with the city and state authorities in Alabama.

JULIE:
We don't have to go over all of this with Paul. Stan, that's all over. It's part of the past.

MILLSAGE:
No Julie, you're wrong. This is my affair now. Lovecraft is right. I don't need him anymore. I've got to do this myself. How was I arrested, Paul? I was walking downtown in Huntsville one night, thinking nothing—doing just that—walking. I walk at night some times . . .

PAUL:
Everybody knows it's dangerous, Stan, to walk around in the dark. That's not just in Huntsville, that's everywhere—even right here in Rhode Island.

MILLSAGE:

I took a shortcut through a construction site—somehow I stumbled and fell.

PAUL:

You're lucky! The police might have shot you. The civil authorities have more problems than you could imagine.

JULIE (*turning to* PAUL):

Please, Paul, he's right. Let him go on.

MILLSAGE:

When I stumbled I was quickly surrounded by police. They immediately assumed that I was drunk and took me to the station to be booked for trespassing. Since I hadn't been drinking, I was sure the drunk charge wouldn't stick. But I underestimated the Alabama police. What seemed to confuse them was that I was not drunk, that I was a physicist and that I worked at the Space Center. They sent me to the state asylum for mental observation.

PAUL:

That was inexcusable, but you can't blame the Space Center for the behavior of primitive local authorities.

MILLSAGE:

I entered the asylum sane. The whole test procedure was geared to prove I am not. Only by great effort can I beat their tests. The others pass the time playing cards. I don't know how to play cards—so I pass the time painting the wall. It's something I know, paint and brushes. How to paint a wall with my own kind of art . . . But I am marked for so knowing. It is compared to card playing an odd, insane kind of thing to know . . .

(*Projection: The Follies of Stanley Millsage*)

AUTHORITY (*an official at the asylum*):

What are you painting, Mr. Millsage?

MILLSAGE:

It's a wall.

AUTHORITY:

What are you painting on the wall?

MILLSAGE:

I'm painting it white.

AUTHORITY:

Is that a solid white?

MILLSAGE:

No, I don't like solid white. I'm a physicist. I like invisible things. Did the Space Center confirm that I'm a physicist?

AUTHORITY:

Yes, of course. You're a fine physicist.

MILLSAGE:

When will I be able to leave?

AUTHORITY:

Soon. Soon enough. Well, if you're not painting the wall solidly, would you tell me why you're painting it?

MILLSAGE:

Why or how?

AUTHORITY:

Whichever you prefer.

MILLSAGE:

Why I'm painting it is because it's there and I'm here. How I'm painting it is with the minimum amount of white paint that's needed. Look closely. What do you see?

AUTHORITY:

Lines on a white wall.

MILLSAGE:

Only lines?

AUTHORITY:

White lines.

MILLSAGE:

But that's what you're supposed to see.

AUTHORITY:

Yes, well, go ahead, Mr. Millsage. Good luck with your painting.

BLACK INMATE (*appearing suddenly*):

Don't let him bug you, man.

MILLSAGE:

Are you black?

BLACK INMATE:
  Yes, I'm black.

MILLSAGE:
  I thought this was a segregated asylum.

BLACK INMATE:
  You see what you see.

MILLSAGE:
  Have you been here long?

BLACK INMATE:
  I'm the first black heart transplant.

MILLSAGE:
  Black heart transplant?

BLACK INMATE:
  Some doctor gave me the heart of a seventeen-year-old kid who got shot in
  a burglary. The kid was white.

MILLSAGE:
  They put you in here for that?

BLACK INMATE:
  It's not just Alabama. The whole world's screwed up.

MILLSAGE *(as inmates bring the boat to the front of the stage):*
  What are they doing?

BLACK INMATE:
  It's like you and your white painting. White on white, huh? Are you painting the history of the white race?

MILLSAGE:
  Perhaps.

BLACK INMATE *(mockingly):*
  Well, perhaps I'm the new history teacher, you know.

MILLSAGE:
  History teacher?

BLACK INMATE *(waving):*
  Black studies in the soulship. I call this the *Folly Ship.*

MILLSAGE:
  The what?

BLACK INMATE:

The *Folly Ship* . . . *(He sings.)* "Pack up your follies in your old kit bag . . ."

MILLSAGE:

Will you have any passengers on your ship?

BLACK INMATE:

We got the first president, George W.

MILLSAGE:

George W.?

BLACK INMATE:

The old captain of the *Folly Ship*.

(An inmate as GEORGE W. *comes forward. A tri-cornered hat is tossed to him. He puts it on and stands by the ship in the pose of the captain.)*

GEORGE W.:

Are we ready to sail? It's been a long trip, but our ship is in good shape. What is our destination? *(One of the guards now a* SECURITY OFFICER *with briefcase chained to his wrist, moves forward.)*

SECURITY OFFICER:

The destination is secret, Mr. President.

GEORGE W.:

But I'm the captain of the ship. We've been sailing for a long time. I ought to know.

SECURITY OFFICER:

The codes are locked in here, sir. *(He pats his briefcase)* I can make them available on a moment's notice. But we must be careful.

GEORGE W. *(looking around at the* GUARDS):

Who are these people watching us?

SECURITY OFFICER:

Guards, sir.

GEORGE W.:

Why are they staring at me?

SECURITY OFFICER:

They're guarding your place in history.

GEORGE W.:

I prefer small ships of state. Why can't we keep things agricultural, the
way Jefferson wanted?

SECURITY OFFICER:

He's dead, sir. After all he wasn't the real father of his country. Here's
your new crew. (MR. FAT CAT, *the* BURNER OF CITIES, *the* MOVIE STAR,
and the SCIENTIST *come forward as the new crew. The* GUARDS *check them
in, examine their papers, etc.)*

CREW: *(singing):*

We're the new crew for your ship of state,
       Mr. President, Mr. President.
We'll sail with you on the *Folly Ship,*
       Mr. President, Mr. President.
We count on you to unify the present and the past.
Where we sail is up to security,
       Mr. President, Mr. President.
We offer ourselves to you, to you
We offer ourselves to you, as your new crew.

MR. FAT CAT *(climbing into the boat):*

You've got nothing to worry about, Mr. President. We've got plenty of
food for anyone who works. All we have to do is eat. Eating is just a matter
of the right kind of alliances. Our suburbs are full of eating. We've got the
machines, we've got the goods, we've got the real estate. We pile them in
our ship of state, protect it with a few carriers and nuclear subs, and off we
row to the underdeveloped countries for our markets. *(Starts to row.)*

GEORGE W.:

Who is that?

CREW *(singing):*

That's Mr. Fat Cat
Who's never met defeats;
That's Mr. Fat Cat who occupies two seats.
Because we've got the goods
and the machines,
Mr. Fat Cat eats and eats.

GEORGE W.:

But he looks awfully fat to me. How can he row very fast or very far?

SECURITY OFFICER:

If he gets too fat, we'll put him on an anti-inflation diet. *(The* SECURITY

GUARDS *move up menacingly.* FAT CAT *rows faster, more fearfully. The* BURNER OF CITIES, *dressed as a black revolutionist in dark glasses, swings forward.*)

BURNER OF CITIES:

I'm your man, Daddy W., me, the Burner of Cities. You taught me the scene, man. Remember how the Redskins called you "The Burner of Villages?"

GEORGE W.:

That was a long time ago in the Indian Wars. We were outnumbered, on the edge of the frontier. It was a matter of self-preservation.

BURNER OF CITIES:

Sure, Daddy, you don't have to draw pictures. I dig your scene. You're my President, man, even if I couldn't vote for you. Only it's a city thing now . . .

GEORGE W.:

A city thing?

BURNER OF CITIES:

Yeah, like the beat is different. You gotta flow more. You gotta stop more. You gotta swing with the hammer.

GEORGE W.:

The hammer?

BURNER OF CITIES:

Hammer, drill, the smashing beat, man. Like noise, the music of noise.

GEORGE W.:

What about silence?

BURNER OF CITIES:

That's groovy too when you can get it. But they got us jammed in there. You can't hear too much silence when you got five to ten in a room, man. It don't matter. If we don't get what we want, we're gonna burn the cities down.

GEORGE W.:

You will burn too. Violence will achieve nothing.

BURNER OF CITIES:

Oh yeah, Daddy? What about your American Revolution? Violence is as American as cherry pie. You know how it is. You were a slave-owner too.

GEORGE W.:
That was a long time ago in the Revolutionary War.

BURNER OF CITIES:
If we get that fire to glowing hot enough, maybe it'll burn out the past. Freedom in the fire, man, freedom in the fire *(The inmates react as the* GUARDS *spring to attention. Gayly, the* BURNER OF CITIES *dances a few steps, leaps into the Ship of State, and starts to row against* FAT CAT. *A ferocious, comic pantomine ensues as the two row against each other.)*

GEORGE W. *(alarmed):*
What are they doing? They're rowing against each other. The ship will sink! Help!

(SECURITY AGENTS hurry forward to straighten out the rowing. A fanfare is heard. The MOVIE STAR *sways up glamorously to the ship and is ushered reverently to her seat by the* GUARDS *as she poses for the cameras.)*

CREW *and* GUARDS *(singing praisefully):*
She's so lovely, she's our dream
She's the goddess of our team.
She's our cool queen of the movie screen,
The dream that we all can screw.

(All the GUARDS *and* AGENTS *begin to make love to her. She pushes them away and they collapse on the stage.)*

MOVIE STAR:
In secret, gentlemen, please. Remember your jobs. Secrecy! You must love me secretly. I am everyone's private passion. You worship me in the dark. In the dark I am the doll for your fantasies. I sail across the sea to foreign countries and teach them about American glamour. I am the eternal mistress and bride. Sail on, America! *(She climbs into the ship.* GEORGE W. *kisses her hand as the* SCIENTIST *comes running, an energetic, hopping technologist waving his invention.)*

SCIENTIST:
Wait!

GEORGE W.: ·
What do you want?

SCIENTIST:
The technology is waiting outside. You can't sail without the technology.

GEORGE W.:

Who are you? What is the technology?

SCIENTIST:

Say, who's been briefing you? *(He looks at the* GUARDS *and* AGENTS *around the ship and draws* GEORGE W. *aside.)* Mr. President, I think your security is maybe a little too tight. They aren't giving you the right briefing. You don't think this ship runs on sails any more, do you? *(He pulls down a panel in the side of the ship to reveal a tangle of wires and switches.)* What kind of current are you on?

GEORGE W.:

I am an old general who cannot die.

SCIENTIST *(assuringly)*:

Don't you worry about that. Nobody's going to die. We're building machines to take care of that. Leave the machines to us. All you have to do is guard the peace.

GEORGE W.:

But what about some machines for peace? I'll need them too.

SCIENTIST:

Sure, the whole object of making weapons is not to kill people.

GEROGE W.:

It isn't?

SCIENTIST:

It's to find time for somebody to find other ways to solve these problems. That somebody is you, Mr. President. Let's all row together. *(He salutes and climbs aboard. With* GEORGE W. *at the bow, guiding the ship into the future, the ship begins to rock violently back and forth as the* CREW *and the* GUARDS *sing.)*

ALL *(singing as red, white, and blue lights spin around reflecting on the walls of the theatre)*:

Sail on, oh *Folly Ship;*
We've got a world to win;
While flames envelop the earth
We'll plant our flag on the moon.

Sail on, oh *Folly Ship,*
We face a whole new frontier;
Forever sailing in secrecy
We have all been cleared to be free.

(MILLSAGE *rushes around the ship, tormented by his vision.*)

Sail on, oh *Folly Ship,*
Sail on through violent seas,
For the pursuit of happiness
Is still the goal we bless!

MILLSAGE (*Struggling to stop the rocking motion of the ship as* GEORGE W. *hammers at him with his tri-cornered hat*):
That's not what science is! (*Sudden black out. The lights come up on a black inmate who climbs on a table and bows to* MILLSAGE.) Who are you?

BLACK INMATE:
H. P. Lovecraft at your service, sir.

MILLSAGE:
You're not Lovecraft. He was a prim New Englander, a white man. (*The* WHITE LOVECRAFT *appears behind the* BLACK INMATE *as a mute, mocking reflection of the American racial split that* MILLSAGE *sees in his vision.*)

BLACK LOVECRAFT:
What's skin color? Can't H. P. Lovecraft, the inheritor of Poe's fantastic visions, show you your follies in a black skin? I'm an eerie magician, man. (*He puts on a white mask.*) What's the black revolution about today if it can't show you your white follies? And now for your final folly . . . You think your ship of state is about to sail off into the wild red, white, and blue? *The* WHITE LOVECRAFT *continues silently throughout this scene to mock and contradict the* BLACK LOVECRAFT'S *actions.*)

MILLSAGE:
You *are* mad . . . This *is* an asylum . . .

BLACK LOVECRAFT:
Everyone has to judge that for himself. Answer my question . . . What's the name of your ship of state?

MILLSAGE:
You called it the *Folly Ship* . . .

BLACK LOVECRAFT:
Are you crazy, man? What Ship? You're looking at the *Mirv-Medusa.*

MILLSAGE:
The what?

BLACK LOVECRAFT:

The *Mirv-Medusa.* The way you scientists name things is weird, man. Like I can't even pronounce *Mirv,* to say nothing of what it means . . .

MILLSAGE:

M.I.R.V. Multiple Individually-targeted Reentry Vehicle . . .

BLACK LOVECRAFT:

Real clear . . . Like maybe it's some kind of game . . .

MILLSAGE:

It's a game to destroy the world. A little space bus rides through the sky and spits out doom from its many nuclear warheads.

BLACK LOVECRAFT:

Right on the target—Medusa heads . . . You see? It's not a ship, it's a superpower! It's a missile! The *Mirv-Medusa! (From the ship the actors emerge slowly. They wear ancient grotesque masks and wave missile heads back and forth menacingly. The* BLACK LOVECRAFT *rushes at the ship and tries to strike off the missile heads.)*

BLACK LOVECRAFT *(crying out):*

Old myths never die. You cut one head, another grows in its place. *(He smashes another* Mirv *head and calls:)* Help me, man! One head's off. Don't you hear 'em? The other heads are growing. Don't you hear me? Help! Help! *(The* GUARDS *subdue him, drag him back to the platform, and put on his white mask. At the same time the* WHITE LOVECRAFT *follows the* BLACK LOVECRAFT *back to the platform, puts on a black mask, and sits motionless beside his mirror image.)*

BURNER OF CITIES *(to* MILLSAGE):

Go back to your painting, man. White on white. *(The inmates all look at* MILLSAGE, *laugh, and exit.)*

MILLSAGE:

After two weeks of observation, I was released. I had to sign a paper saying that I wouldn't sue the state for false arrest. As for the asylum, Paul, to me this means that all scientists are in it—there by the very nature of spying, the continuous molding of our thoughts toward the military, the industrial-money-profit complex. As a physicist, I have this knowledge which could help—like painting the wall white on white. Unlike card playing, it is not natural *(Turning to* JULIE) Do you think I'm mad?

JULIE *(going to him):*
No, I don't think you're mad. I love you Stanley, that's all I know. I believe in you . . .

MILLSAGE:
In science? I don't know . . . Technology is the new politics that runs the world in all major powers.

ACTOR:
After the first nuclear explosion, Oppenheimer said . . . *(Projections of the Trinity explosion and* OPPENHEIMER. *The actor who played the shaman appears in his traditional actor's costume and speaks* OPPENHEIMER'S *words:)*

OPPENHEIMER:
In some real sense which no humor, no overstatement can quite extinguish, the physicists have known sin; and this is a knowledge which they cannot lose . . .

ACTOR:
Another physicists, Dr. Percy Bridgman, answered Oppenheimer. *(Slide of Dr. Percy Bridgman)*

ACTOR *(another actor speaks the words of Bridgman):*
Scientists aren't responsible for the facts that are in nature. It's their job to find the facts. There's no sin connected with it—no morals. If anyone should have a sense of sin, it's God. He put the facts there.

PAUL:
They're both right. Can't you see that, Stan? Pure science can exist side by side with technology. That's what this country is all about, permitting the free expression of all ideas.

MILLSAGE *(turning from* PAUL *to* JULIE *as he speaks):*
Science isn't just a matter of gadgets and facts. It's a matter of mysteries too. In the end we have to respect the private, as well as the public celebrations of life. Any aspect of science that does not serve man's needs and hopes cannot be called science.

JULIE:
I understand, Stanley . . .

PAUL:
Does this mean you won't go back to Huntsville?

MILLSAGE *(slowly):*
Somehow it's not just my choice . . .

(The actors, now in their basic, traditional acting costumes as at the beginning of the play, have been moving again slowly onto the stage, humming the ballad of "The Silent Majority." The projection reading The Follies of Stanley Millsage *is flashed on the screen again.)*

PAUL:
Well, at last we can admit that this has all been your own follies.

MILLSAGE:
For me the follies have been a journey. I wanted to take some wild, lonely voyage of discovery to find myself, to find my country, to heal my marriage. I wanted to show you my love, Julie.

(He stands holding JULIE *as the actors pile the props on the carts and make the final arrangements for their departure. They sing the ballad of "The Silent Majority":)*

Join the Silent Majority,
Ride with the common crew,
Don't rock the ship of state
By trying things too new.

Join the Silent Majority.
Don't listen to the lonely voice,
Don't rock the ship of state
By shouting to rejoice.

Join the Silent Majority,
Learn to be silent and free.
Don't rock the ship of state.
Join the Silent . . .
　　Join the Silent . . .
　　　　Join the Silent Majority . . .

(As this song rises to its climax in MILLSAGE'S *vision, it is sung contrapuntally to the final verse of* Folly Ship: *"Sail on, oh Folly Ship, sail on through violent seas, for the pursuit of happiness is still the goal we bless!"* MILLSAGE *kisses* JULIE *and helps her onto the cart. As he leads the cart out, he turns to* JULIE, *smiles, and promises her:)*

MILLSAGE *(waving):*
Well, that's the end of Lovecraft's follies . . .

(The actors wind off into the distance, their torches blazing, their song fading away slowly. The eerie figure of LOVECRAFT *appears from the trap door. He looks around sharply at the audience and watches the actors disappear into time and space. Then he says mockingly to the audience:)*

LOVECRAFT:
Maybe! *(And he runs after the actors . . .)*

THE END

NOTE

Our fantasies today are half-comic, half-tragic. When the computer makes an error, we smile wryly, but we are also afraid of becoming mechanical men. We feel something extraordinary in the scientific achievements of the moon landing, but there is also a sense of terror as well as joy in Aldrin's description of the moon, "Magnificent Desolation." We are caught in the trap of science versus technology, the central theme of my play.

Two key experiences lie behind this play. I was born and grew up in Berkeley, California, in the midst of the exciting, major discoveries in nuclear physics. E. O. Lawrence, the head of the Radiation Laboratory and the inventor of the cyclotron, was a neighbor, and Oppenheimer lived on the hill above our house. In the Army during World War II, as an officer in a secret program concerned with German prisoners of war, I witnessed the growing problems of governmental and military security and how these problems affected our technology. After my discharge from the Army in 1946, my first books of poems and plays were published by a physicist, Bern Porter, who had worked on the atomic bomb project and who resigned his position when the bomb fell on Hiroshima. I have had Porter's important work in the relationships between science and art in mind in my play, although, of course, my protagonist, Stanley Millsage, is an imaginary projection from the characteristics of many different scientists and artists whom I have met.

When Adrian Hall asked me to write this play, I was grateful for the opportunity to work with a director who has achieved a unique reputation for his exploration of space relationships in the theatre. In *Lovecraft's Follies* we have tried to explore the way our lives move suddenly today from our private family affairs into the rapidly changing world—one moment comic, the next moment grotesque—of American power. And I have tried also to celebrate through the music of Richard Cumming and rare theatrical ritualistic opportunities, the unified ensemble and special abilities of the Trinity Repertory Company.

Grateful acknowledgment for help and advice on this play is made to Bern Porter, Hugo Leckey, Barton St. Armand, and Edwin Honig. The premiere of this play took place in Providence, Rhode Island, in March, 1970. Adrian Hall directed with settings designed by Eugene Lee, lighting by Roger Morgan, costumes by John Lehmeyer, and music by Richard Cumming. The cast included James Eichelberger, William Cain, James Gallery, Elizabeth Ann Sachs, Ruth Benson, Robert Black, Robert J. Colonna, Bree Cavazos, Cynthia Craig, William Damkoehler, Ronald Frazier, Ed Hall, David C. Jones, Richard Kavanaugh, David Kennett, Marguerite H. Lenert, George Martin, Barbara Meek, Martin Molson, Dan Plucinski, Donald Somers and Richard Steele.

THE USHERS

or *Lies, Accusations, Curses, Exorcisms*
To James Barnhill and John Emigh

(The characters in this play are not characters in the traditional sense of depth, roundness. They are images, mirages, fantasies of American experience. Their presences transform constantly, merge dream-like, play through and around the audience if possible so they become shadows of the audience. The central, mysterious, ritualistic presence is that of ushers—cast and audience alike—wandering actively and passively on singular American voyages, voyages that never end.

What are ushers? Who are ushers? Are all of us middle-class Americans ushers of some strange kind? Young, inexperienced, yearning for experience? Experienced, older, accustomed to dreamworlds, bruised by reality?

Ushers are accustomed to ushering themselves and other people on dream-journeys. Ushers have a certain distinction, even pride in their profession although their destiny is never certain. They acquire names, they travel in search of discoveries. Their basic fear is that because of the nature of their profession, they will never arrive; they will never participate finally in any goal; they will merely usher. Yet, in their fear, they practice optimism. They yearn to be ideal Americans, to usher, if not to command American experience.

On their voyages, the ushers participate actively in their dreams of destiny. They dream of ushering every possible kind of journey, of ushering so strongly, so powerfully, that they will become the action that they usher. They are convinced that every American can become the action he desires, even if this action of equality is impossible. The ushers dream and pursue no matter what farce or nightmare they encounter, no matter how they are changed by their strange voyages.

The play takes place in a unique space. The audience enters through a special environment composed of American waste products, secondhand tires, battered kitchenware, garbage cans, posters, traffic warning signs, etc. The ushers usher them mysteriously, courteously, to their seats. Some of the seats are set aside; they have a sense of status to them.

As the audience walks through the special environment, they witness various unusual actions focused mainly around cooking and eating images. An ESKIMO *is chanting over a walrus skin. A* MEXICAN *mutters, "Alma, Alma," over a mound of rising dough. Two* INDIANS *chant, "The corn grows up, etc." over a pile of corn and meal. A* BLACK *cooks Soul Food . . . An American institutional* COOK *with a tattoo on his forearm and a white cook's hat cooks eggs on a greasy pan.*

As the audience is ushered in in small groups, the SENIOR USHERS *are slowly more and more evident, giving instructions to the* JUNIOR USHERS, *greeting members of the audience, assigning seats, and warning all of the other ushers to keep the spectators away from the cooking activities and anything that may seem unsafe.*

After everyone is seated and the ushers are standing in prominent positions, USHER 3 *claps his hands loudly and all of the ushers pivot and stare at the audience. The procession of the cast enters. First, come two* ACTORS *bearing the head of the Statue of Liberty. They sing the first verse of the final hymn of the play,* "Oh Goddess of Liberty, etc."

Next comes the MASTER COOK *with* HUSBANDS *and* HOUSEWIVES, *their arms full of frozen food packages.*

Next comes the AMERICAN INQUISITOR *with several ushers whispering and pointing to the many names lettered on his jacket.*

Then the athletic-looking CURSEMASTER *around whom several athletes and dancers prance as they lead brief yells, bounce, throw, and catch tennis balls, etc.*

Next comes the NATIONAL CRIER *with his megaphone. He calls through it to the ushers and audience,* "Marriage Licenses, Births, Divorces Asked, Divorces Granted, Bankruptcy Petitions, Driving Charges, Deaths and Funerals, Arrivals and Departures . . ." *He repeats these as he moves through the environment and the audience.*

Two INDIANS *and the* OGRE KACHINA *follow. They are accompanied by the* BELLY-DRUM PLAYER. *One* INDIAN, *dressed as a Koshare clown, with an alarm clock strapped to his wrist, circulates among the audience, tapping the alarm clock, and crying out mockingly,* "What time is it? What time is it?"

Next comes the DEER MOTHER *with one or two dancers, dancing to their own mysterious music, flute and drum.*

Last in the procession is the REVOLUTIONARY FIGUREHEAD *in his ragged, bloody costume. He cries out occasionally some of his furious lines from his last speech in the Statue of Liberty.*

During the procession, the four USHERS *have become more evident, particularly the two* SENIOR USHERS. USHER 3 *is the most prominent of the* SENIOR USHERS, *worn and paranoid in his successful mask of aggressive certainty.* USHER 4, *his wife, is equally aggressive and sure of herself, defensive of their ushering and homemaking privileges. The two young* USHERS, 1 *and* 2, *are selected from the other ushers in a brief ceremony that takes place before Scene* 1. *This occurs after the procession has entered and all of the ushers are seated before the audience. The* SENIOR USHERS *officiate at this silent ceremony. They circulate among the* USHERS, *select the two young* USHERS *for office, and motion them to prominent seats.* USHER 3 *finally claps his hands, indicating that the ceremony is to begin. All of the* USHERS *turn and stare at the audience. An empty table lit with candles is in a central position. The four* USHERS *survey the candlelit table with a sense of awe and fear.*)

(1) CEREMONY OF THE FREEDOM EGGS

USHER 1: *(slowly)*
The table is empty.

USHER 2: *(looking at the audience)*
Someone is going to eat.

USHER 3:
It's late. They've eaten already.

USHER 4: *(nervously)*
You can't be sure. Someone is always hungry.

USHER 3: *(with authority, pointing at the empty table)*
Of course. That's why we begin with the threat of dinner. *(With veteran ushering authority, he gestures and calls offstage.) Bring on the Freedom Eggs! (The* USHERS *freeze in close relationship to the audience. Silence.)*

USHER 4: *(with a nervous, wifely pluck at his sleeve)*
You've made a mistake, dear. Don't you mean Freedom Omelette if it's dinner?

USHER 3:
I said Freedom *Eggs.*

USHER 2:
No one seems to be coming for dinner.

USHER 3:
That's why it's a threat.

USHER 1:
Really? I don't feel scared.

USHER 3: *(staring at him scornfully)*
You will. If you can feel anything.

USHER 2:
You have no right to speak to him like that.

USHER 4: *(with indignant authority)*
Who are the Senior Ushers here? You young people think you know everything.

USHER 3:
Well, you don't need to ride her. She's just a beginner.

USHER 4: *(snapping)*
They need more discipline these days. Anybody thinks he can usher.

USHER 3:
Don't worry. They'll learn what part's an art and what part's a science.

USHER 1:
In Usher's College, they never taught us. Sometimes, you know, I just dream we're condemned to usher. Crazy I know.

USHER 3:
Condemned? I saw you ushering those people in. You liked it. You didn't have to do it.

USHER 1:
I know. I like to do it. I like the company. You never know who you'll see next.

USHER 2:
It keeps you from getting too lonely.

USHER 3: *(expansively)*
Now you're beginning to see. That's why I wanted to become an Usher. To show people marvelous journeys. Jolt them away from their everyday jobs. I dreamed of showing them to the best restaurants, giving them the best entertainment and food, introducing them to mysterious smells and tastes.

USHER 2: *(staring at him with excitement and recognition)*
That's why we're here.

USHER 3: *(impatiently)*
Don't be too young, too starry-eyed. Don't forget everyone is condemned to eat, to watch people eating. It's the major thing everyone does with infinite variations. That's all we're doing. *(He calls.)* Bring on the Freedom Eggs!

(Silence)

USHER 3: *(sneering)*

You're a young fool. Don't you see they've already eaten? They'll never bring them. We're just supposed to usher people to food. They don't want us to eat it.

USHER 2:

But that's not fair. We should be able to participate too. When we were trained, everybody said we'd get a chance to work, to find the surprising action.

USHER 1: *(supporting her)*

That's what they said, that's why we went to the Usher's College.

USHER 3: *(with harsh authority)*

They sold you a bill of goods. You kids always think there's a free menu everywhere.

USHER 4: *(trying to smooth things over)*

Don't be so harsh on them. You can't be so sure what will happen.

USHER 3: *(dogmatically)*

I've got a good idea of what will happen. Haven't I been an Usher for thirty years? Something has happened every time. I didn't get to be a Senior Usher for nothing.

USHER 2:

Will something exciting really happen?

USHER 4:

Don't worry, my dear. But I don't think we'll get the . . . *(Suddenly, on a frenzied impulse, she shouts.)* Bring on the Freedom Eggs!

USHER 3:

Don't waste your breath. Food should be non-verbal.

USHER 4: *(sighing)*

It never is. People love to name favorite sauces. I've got a lot of cookbooks with fancy names myself. It's a great way to live.

USHER 3: *(reflecting)*

Particularly if we can burn things, make them flame with brandy.

USHER 1: *(slowly)*

Do you think we've made them angry?

USHER 3:

Made who angry?

USHER 1:
Whoever's in the kitchen.

USHER 4: *(breaking into laughter with* USHER 3*)*
Did you hear him? "Whoever's in the kitchen."

USHER 3:
We don't know who's in the kitchen.

USHER 4:
Of course we don't know. We're not supposed to know. That's what makes ushering exciting. *(Then romantically)* When we're up here, we're immortal.

USHER 3: *(seizing on this, to the* YOUNG USHERS*)*
Get it through your green heads. You understand what she means? Up here we can dream anything we eat. We can eat anything we dream.

USHER 2: *(She is not reassured and looks around scared.)*
I don't think we're going to get anything to eat.

USHER 1:
Don't show them you're afraid.

USHER 2: *(turning on him, pouring out her fears)*
Is it so bad I'm afraid? Why do we always eat in darkness? Why do we like candles so much if we're not afraid of what we eat? Why do we always have to usher people to food if there isn't a sense of danger?

USHER 1: *(urging her)*
Go on then. Ask them.

USHER 2:
Do I have to?

USHER 1:
What have we got to lose?

USHER 2: *(timidly after a long hesitation)*
Bring on the Freedom Eggs.

USHER 3: *(with contempt)*
That was terrible. They aren't even listening any more.

USHER 4:
You need more authority if you're going to learn how to be an usher.

86

USHER 3:

An usher should know where everything is. You haven't got a clue.

USHER 1: *(flaring up)*

That's not fair. We're just beginning. You want us to do everything right. You don't know how to teach any more. You want us to lead the way.

USHER 3:

You lead? You can't even lead the way to the kitchen.

USHER 4: *(growling at the* YOUNG USHERS)

They don't even have any religion any more.

USHER 3: *(pointing to the* YOUNG USHERS)

No spirit, no patience. That's what you need—patience! Sit down and wait.

(The four USHERS *sit down to wait; the* YOUNG USHERS *try to relax.)*

USHER 4: *(whispering, trying to make something happen)*

I feel it starting. It's happening. Can't you feel the table moving?

USHER 3:

Forget about it. You're imagining things.

USHER 4:

But you know it does happen.

USHER 1:

What happens?

USHER 4: *(to* USHER 3)

Should I tell them?

USHER 3:

Go on, tell them. It's better they know now.

USHER 4: *(slowly)*

Sometimes they force us to eat.

USHER 3: *(Sharply)*

Not like that. You're too old. *(looking at the* YOUNG USHERS) They only force you to eat when you're a kid, a baby or a child.

USHER 4:

Or when you're sick or when you're insane. Don't forget that!

USHER 2: *(Suddenly)*

Wait. I feel as though I'm eating.

USHER 1:

What? There's nothing there.

USHER 2:

No, I'm eating.

USHER 3:

She's dreaming. She's crazy.

USHER 4:

Maybe they're forcing her to eat!

USHER 2:

No, they're not forcing me. I'm eating! They're feeding me.

USHER 1:

Who's feeding you? Stop it! There's no one here.

USHER 2: *(ecstatically)*

I'm eating my Freedom Eggs!

USHER 1: *(shaking her)*

Stop it, you're dreaming! Don't you see? If we get any real food, it'll be from real cooks, real people.

USHER 2:

No, I won't believe it. I won't believe there are no Freedom Eggs.

USHER 3:

Take it easy. Of course there are Freedom Eggs. We just haven't found the right way to usher them.

USHER 4:

He's right. We've got to find the right way. Ushering is meaningless if it doesn't lead to food.

USHER 3: *(reflecting)*

Food is the first action of life, but it's the toughest thing to usher. Every time you start to lead the way, it turns out a little different. Once I remember I dreamed about a Master Cook. I was really sweating. It was in a very hot country. I ushered this Master Cook into the steaming jungle. You know what he did? He tried to ignore where we were. He treated me as if my geography of ushering was absolutely wrong. In that hot, steaming jungle, he kept on raving about freezers and frozen food. Freezers and frozen food in a jungle. It was a nightmare I tell you.

USHER 4: *(after trying to interrupt him)*
We don't need your stories now. We need cooperation. Stop snapping at each other. We need a unity of ushers.

USHER 2: *(looking at* USHER 4 *with new admiration)*
I'm willing.

USHER 1:
Let's try it together.

USHER 3:
If you two get with it. Otherwise it won't do any good.

USHER 4:
We must try.

USHER 3: *(shrugging)*
All right. I'll lead the way. Follow my signal.

ALL OF THE USHERS: *(as they follow* USHER 3*'s mysterious tablerapping and handclapping ushering signals)* BRING ON THE FREEDOM EGGS! *(There is no answer and they all sag into silence.)*

USHER 3:
I told you. No answer. Food isn't what it used to be. You have to wait. You have to cook it, usher it yourself these days.

(2) THE MASTER COOK
AND THE EATING RITUALS

(An USHER *ushers in the* MASTER COOK *who appears in a glowing neon frame, as if on a television screen. He wears a surrealistic combination of a historical and a modern chef's costume, funny, threatening, and authoritative.)*

MASTER COOK:
Good evening, ladies and gentlemen. Welcome to your Master Cook. The nature of good eating is simplicity and economy. What is good for your pocketbook is good for your stomach and vice versa. Tonight we bring you our Freezer Program. How to freeze well. How to keep a well-stocked freezer on practically nothing. Remember the practical simplicity of the old Eskimo recipe for a frozen dinner.

(The ESKIMO *from the opening procession is seen muttering incantations over the body of a walrus.)*

ESKIMO: *(chanting)*

Kill and clean out the guts of a medium-sized walrus. Then catch in your net as many small migrating birds as you can. From the wing of each bird, remove only one small wing feather. Store the birds intact in the interior cavern of the walrus. Sew up the walrus and leave it to freeze in a convenient, safe place. Be very careful to indicate the place on a map. Hang the map in your igloo for safety. Wait two years or so. Take down the map, find the frozen walrus if you can. Notify your clan of a feast. Thaw walrus until tender and delicate. Slice and serve.

MASTER COOK:

Today, of course, when you visit your favorite supermarket, you must avoid frozen foods that have been stored too long. Be careful of bargain frozen foods—they've lost their nourishing flavors and vitamins. Be a quick-witted trader in your favorite market. Find the ripe time to stuff your freezer and profit.

(Two housewives, played by USHERS 2 *and* 4, *enter and begin to mime frantically "stuffing their freezers.")*

MASTER COOK:

Be careful. Your freezer is not designed for miserly hoarding. *(ashamed, they slow down)* Learn to manage your freezer on a definite season to season plan. Establish a chart control geared to your family's needs. *(The housewives mime struggling to establish a chart control.)* If you handle your chart control correctly, and stock your freezer with family favorites, you'll establish a strong suspense factor for your husband and children. They'll ask eagerly, "What's thawing?"

(Many voices, laughing children's voices first, then eager teenage voices, then more and more menacing adult voices repeat "What's thawing?" *until the two housewives hurl the control charts angrily offstage at the hidden voices.)*

MASTER COOK: *(as the housewives return to the freezers)*

Watch your space estimates. The average, hearty appetite requires three cubic feet per family member—that is if you schedule a turnover every six months. *(The housewives have been busy stuffing packages into the freezer.)* Never overload your freezer. *(They begin unloading packages.)* When you put in your new packages, place them against the freezer plates. *(The housewives insert new packages very carefully.) Stop! (They stop.)* Exceptions are sandwiches and baked items. Check all packages carefully. Sandwiches and baked items attract moisture if placed directly against the freezer plates. *(Frantically, the housewives remove the sandwiches and baked items and replace them.)* Now for the problem of condensation.

(The housewives and MASTER COOK *freeze in place as a Navajo incantation for rain is heard out of the darkness. Music accompanies this and the sounds of dancing.)*

"The corn grows up.
The waters of the dark clouds drop, drop.
The rain descends,
The waters from the corn leaves drop, drop.
The rain descends.
The waters from the plants drop, drop.
The corn grows up.
The waters of the dark mists drop, drop . . .")

MASTER COOK: *(resuming instructions)*
The build-up of condensation is affected by many factors—the number of times you open your freezer, the state of loading, and the care with which you wrap your food. *(Alarmed, the housewives inspect the food wrappings) Also, remember your freezer is not a plaything for children! (The housewives thrust away imaginary children.)* Back to con-den-sa-tion. Sound the defrost alarm in your mind whenever one-half inch of frost accumulates on the freezer plates. If the frost has not solidified into hard ice, scrape off the frost. *(The housewives scrape, but one encounters hard ice.)* If the ice is too hard, *turn off the current. (The* MASTER COOK *becomes more and more authoritative and urgent as the situation becomes more demanding. The housewives respond with increasing frenzy.)* Remove all food. Refrigerate it immediately. Sometimes you may use pans of hot water on the ice problem. The pans must be elevated on racks to insure that they do not come in direct contact with the freezer plates or walls. *(Disaster threatens the housewives and they give up on the hot water pans method.)* No matter how often you defrost, be absolutely certain to clean up any spillage that occurs. *(The housewives clean up the spillage frantically.)* At least once a year, wipe out your freezer thoroughly with a cloth dipped in a solution of one tablespoon baking soda to one quart lukewarm water. *(They follow instructions.)* Dry the freezer well, with a fresh cloth or better yet, *with a hair dryer. (One housewife plugs in a hair dryer as the* MASTER COOK *shouts instructions.)* Make certain the lining is thoroughly dry before you turn on the current again. Let the freezer run for half an hour before returning food to it. *(The housewives shut off the dryer, start the freezers again, and turn in relief to leave, when the* MASTER COOK *warns:)* Power failure! Power fail-

ure! *(The housewives scurry about in alarm as the freezers fall silent.)* Don't underestimate the serious power break. A 25 degree rise in temperature over a 24 hour period will ruin all of the nutritive values that you have struggled to preserve. If a long break is indicated, call your local dealer or favorite ice cream parlor for dry ice. *(The housewives rush to the telephones to put in emergency calls.)* This ice has a temperature of 100 degrees below zero—Fahrenheit, that is. Therefore, exercise extreme caution. Do not touch dry ice with your bare hands. Handle it only with heavy gloves. *(The housewives struggle to put on enormous, heavy gloves.)* If you act soon enough after a power failure, a 50 lb. cake of dry ice *(The housewives struggle to lift the heavy weight with their heavy gloves.)* will prevent thawing for 2 or 3 days. Do not attempt to chip or cut the block. *(One housewife has been doing this in her battle to make the block fit.)* A stray chip may cause injury. One caution—when the electricity resumes and your freezer is operating normally again, all meats, poultry, and fish registering more than 50 degrees must be cooked and eaten at once!

(The MASTER COOK *and the housewives freeze in place again as the slow, quiet, intense Navajo Rain Incantation is heard again:*

The corn grows up,
The waters of the dark clouds drop, drop.

The rain descends.
The waters from the corn leaves drop, drop.
The rain descends.
The waters from the plants drop, drop.
The corn grows up.
The waters of the dark mists drop, drop . . .)

(An early, anonymous nursery rhyme is acted out quickly to music:

Here sits the Lord Mayor,
Here sit his men,
Here sits the cockadoodle,
Here sits the hen,
Here sits the little chickens,
Here they run in,
Chin chopper, chin chopper, chin chopper, chin.)

MASTER COOK: *(annoyed)*
You are not paying attention. You are failing to master the modern techniques for food consumption. Pay attention! *(Two* MEXICANS *are bent over imaginary rising yeast doughs muttering entranced, "Alma! Alma!*

Alma!") Do not let yourselves be distracted by primitive magical spells or ideas that are nonsense scientifically. These Mexicans think that rising yeast doughs because they are so animated are possessed by spirits or "almas" as they call them. Go on with you. Out! *(He chases the* MEXICANS *out exasperatedly as they exit chanting, "Alma!"*) *(Then, to the housewives as their husbands come home eagerly, carrying their commuting briefcases, calling "What's for dinner, etc. We've got to get to the movies, etc."*) If you have a particularly busy schedule, dinner-in-a-hurry demands supreme planning, cautious supermarket shopping, and cooking in advance. Be sure to keep a well-balanced, tasty range of convenient foods on your Inspiration Shelf. They will inspire you when you need a Dinner-On-The-Run. *(The husbands are now seated, poised for their instant dinners, the bustling housewives ready to serve them.)*

USHER 2: *(bustling in with dish and serving grandly)*
Red-Flannel Hash.

USHER 1: *(eating greedily)*
Great.

USHER 4:
Chicken a la King.

USHER 3:
Great.

USHER 2:
Cranberry Ginger Relish.

USHER 1:
Tastes great.

USHER 4:
Fried Tomato Halves With Cream.

USHER 3:
Hm.

USHER 2:
Velvet Fudge Cake.

USHER 1:
Great dessert. *(He grabs her.)* Let's go! We're late for the movies! *(They rush out, the wife dragging, exhausted.)*

USHER 4:
Spicy Raisin Cupcakes!

USHER 3: *(devouring them)*

Great dessert. *(He grabs her.)* Let's go! We're late for . . . *(But she passes out, and he drags her off furiously in order not to be late for their appointment.)*

MASTER COOK:

Today we have of course the problem of vegetarianism—how to get the most from the least. Take eggplant for example.

OFFSTAGE VOICE: *(sighing the French word)*

Aubergine.

MASTER COOK:

Never mind the Frenchies. When eggplants are stuffed, they look so beautiful in their bright green caps against their polished purple cases. Remember in preparation that eggplant has a fatal, blotter-like capacity for butter and oil.

(An IMAM or PRIEST in the Near East has just eaten an eggplant dish prepared by his fiancee and is so entranced by it that he turns to her father and demands:)

PRIEST:

This aubergine is superb. Her dowry for our marriage must be the oil in which to cook the aubergine for the rest of our lives.

FATHER:

Agreed! Bring the Great Ali Baba jars of oil and store them in their new home!

(A sequence of comic servants stagger in under imaginary Great Ali Baba jars of oil.)

PRIEST: *(prepared to eat)*

My love, it is the first night of our marriage. Have you prepared the aubergine?

PRIEST'S WIFE:

Here it is, my husband, prepared from the Great Ali Baba jars of oil.

PRIEST:

Delicious. We will have the aubergine again tomorrow night.

PRIEST'S WIFE: *(desperately)*

Bring more Ali Baba jars of oil.

(Another quick sequence of servants stagger in under the weight of heavy jars.)

PRIEST:

My love, it is the second night of our marriage. Have you prepared the aubergine?

PRIEST'S WIFE:

Here it is, my husband, prepared from the Great Ali Baba jars of oil.

PRIEST:

Superb. We will have the aubergine again tomorrow night.

PRIEST'S WIFE: *(desperately)*

I must have more Ali Baba jars of oil.

(One comic servant staggers on with a last jar and spills it.)

PRIEST'S WIFE:

Fool, what have you done? That is the last Great Ali Baba jar!

PRIEST: *(calling impatiently)*

My love, it is the third night of our marriage. Have you prepared the aubergine?

PRIEST'S WIFE: *(wringing her hands)*

Alas, the first two nights have exhausted the supply of oil from the Great Ali Baba jars. There is no more aubergine.

PRIEST: *(crying out in anguish)*

It is the curse of God! *(and he collapses in a faint)*

MASTER COOK:

So much for the problem of vegetarianism. If you are careful with the science of planning, you can stretch your inflated dollars wisely in preparing what I call Thrifty Meals. *(Two seedy-looking housewives enter; they can be the same actresses.)* Be penny-wise and sprinkle your ideas through your dinner menus and you'll enjoy the results. *(Two tired worker-husbands enter in their filthy workclothes.)*

USHER 1: *(growling)*

For Christ Sake, isn't dinner ready? I'm starved.

USHER 3:

What the hell you been doing all day? I'm starving.

USHER 2: *(slouching in)*

Look, dear. You'll love it.

MASTER COOK:

Remember—many famous dishes have been created out of little or nothing. Existential food can be the salvation of your pocketbook.

USHER 1:

What the hell is this?

USHER 2:

Texas Hash.

USHER 4:

Easy Chili.

USHER 2:

Green Salad with Radishes.

USHER 4:

Orange-Grapefruit Pinwheel Salad.

USHER 3: *(gaping)*

I'll be goddamned.

USHER 2:

Molasses Crinkles.

USHER 1:

What?

USHER 4:

Quickie French Tarts.

USHER 3: *(enraged)*

Don't give me that!

(They advance on their wives and strangle them in rage. Then they turn and advance menacingly on the Master Cook.)

MASTER COOK:

Wait! To live we must eat. We must eat with intelligence and not with a simple stoking mechanism.

(They grapple with the MASTER COOK and rip off his outer garments revealing a Beggar underneath. There must be a remarkable transition here as the scene goes back in food through the anonymous 14th century ballad, "I cannot eat but little meat." The MASTER COOK as the Beggar becomes the central characer in this song, the Housewives revive and participate with

their Husbands. They all accompany the ballad on improvised instruments,
as the scene becomes a joyous celebration.)

BEGGAR:

    I cannot eat but little meat,
        My stomach is not good;
    But sure I think that I can drink
        With him that wears a hood.

    Though I go bare, take you no care,
        I nothing am a-cold;
    I stuff my skin so full within
        of jolly good ale and old.

ALL: *(joining in singing and playing on their improvised instruments)*
    Back and side go bare, go bare;
    Both foot and hand go cold;
    But, belly, God send thee good ale enough,
    Whether it be new or old.

BEGGAR:

    I love no roast but a nut-brown toast,
        And a crab laid in the fire;
    A little bread shall do me stead;
        Much bread I not desire,
    No frost nor snow, no wind, I trow,
        Can hurt me if I wold;
    I am so wrapped and thoroughly lapped
        Of jolly good ale and old.

ALL: *(joining in)*
    Back and side go bare, go bare:
    Both foot and hand go cold;
    But, belly, God send thee good ale enough,
    Whether it be new or old.

BEGGAR: *(as one of the women plays Tib)*
    And Tib, my wife, that as her life
        Loveth well good ale to seek,
    Full oft drinks she till ye may see
        The tears run down her cheek:
    Then doth she trowl to me the bowl
        Even as a maltworm should,
    And saith . . .

TIB:
              "Sweetheart, I took my part
Of this jolly good ale and old."

ALL: *(singing and dancing)*
  Back and side go bare, go bare;
  Both foot and hand go cold;
  But, belly, God send thee good ale enough,
  Whether it be new or old.

BEGGAR:
  Now let them drink till they nod and wink,
    Even as good fellows should do . . .

    (They have stopped dancing slowly and sink down.)

They shall not miss to have the bliss
  Good ale doth bring men to;
And all poor souls that have scoured bowls
  Or have them lustily trolled,
God save the lives of them and their wives,
  Whether they be young or old . . .

    *(Slowly, to a single, last, mournful, instrumental sound, the Beggar sings
    the last chorus alone.)*

Back and side, go bare, go bare,
Both foot and hand go cold;
But, belly, God send thee good ale enough,
Whether it be new or old.

(3) THE CALL FOR IDENTITY

USHER 1: *(appears dragging Usher 2 back into the audience)*
Come on, let's go. It's safer out there.

USHERS 3 & 4:
Stop! Where are you going?

USHER 1:
Back into the audience. I want my identity back.

USHER 3:
Are you crazy? An usher has no identity. That's why we came up here.

USHER 2:

At least you know what to do when you're an usher.

USHER 4: *(grandly striking a pose)*

Here you can become anything, you can play anything, you can acquire a name, you can perform any dream you please, you can become anyone you wish to be.

USHER 1:

No thanks. I'm happy just to be an usher.

VOICE: *(out of the darkness)*

Step forward, Ushers.

USHER 2: *(scared)*

What's that?

USHER 1:

Let's get out of here.

VOICE:

Step forward, Ushers, into the Chamber of Identity.

USHERS 1 & 2: *(stepping upstage reluctantly)*

Who are you?

VOICE: *(as he steps into view)*

The American Inquisitor. *(He is a powerful figure in a tall Uncle Sam hat, an ancient, grotesque mask, and a jacket lettered with names.)*

USHER 3: *(nervously)*

That's a laugh. There is no American Inquisitor.

INQUISITOR:

There is now. Are you prepared for the interrogation?

USHER 4:

What interrogation? What have we done?

INQUISITOR:

It is what you haven't done. As ushers you are accused of failing to establish an American identity. All you have done is try to eat.

USHER 1:

But our record is excellent, particularly these people with years of professional experience. They've ushered in burlesque shows, baroque movie theatres, opera houses, the best universities. No one has ever complained.

INQUISITOR:

No one has ever recognized you either. All you have done is usher people into the darkness, to the fate of their dreams. You have never revealed your identities.

USHER 2:

No one ever asked our names.

INQUISITOR:

Well, someone is about to. Line up, please, in American formation. The seniors first. *(The four* USHERS *line up together.)* Good. We shall begin. *(to* USHER 1) What is your name?

USHER 1:

Jonathan P. Edwards.

INQUISITOR:

That is an imitation name. What does the P stand for?

USHER 1: *(uneasily)*

I don't use the P much. That's for Parmenter, my mother's maiden name.

INQUISITOR:

Jonathan Parmenter Edwards, you stand in the shadow of a name. You are accused of failing to fulfill your American name. You are hiding behind the role of usher. *(to* USHER 2) What is your name?

USHER 2: *(anxiously)*

Judy, Sir, Judy Gordon.

INQUISITOR:

No middle name to suppress?

USHER 2:

My parents never thought I was worth a middle name.

INQUISITOR:

You are accused of hiding behind the nickname, Judy. What is your real name?

USHER 2:

Judith, Sir.

INQUISITOR:

Judith? You are accused of imitating the Old Testament.

USHER 2:

That's why I use Judy, Sir.

INQUISITOR: *(pointing to* USHER 3*)*
About face. What is your name?

USHER 3:
John Perkins Abernathy Johnson.

INQUISITOR:
You are accused of too many foreign last names. *(to* USHER 4*)* Your name.

USHER 4:
Rosemary Forsythia Johnson. I'm his wife, Sir.

INQUISITOR:
You are accused of Un-American botanical names. Are you ready for the sentence?

USHERS: *(They all protest, "What do you mean? You can't sentence us . . . etc.")*

INQUISITOR: *(impatiently, waving his arm)*
Your appeals are rejected. I sentence you to the Melting Pot of Names to learn your American identities. Place them in the Sounding Chairs.

(Two guards appear and strap the USHERS *into four chairs. The* AMERICAN INQUISITOR *starts his invocation over a large pot.)*

INQUISITOR:
Oh American names, I summon you out of the Melting Pot. Fly through the darkness of time, through revolutionary wars, out of the lost worlds into the new. *(He stirs the pot.)* I stir you together into a common brew. Teach us the eagle names, the buffalo names, the Big Sky names, the desert names, the skyscraper names, the factory names, the ocean spindrift names, the money names. Listen!

CHORUS OF NAMES: *(Out of the darkness, a counterpoint of men's and women's voices chant names to music.)*

MEN'S VOICES:
Solomon.
Jeremiah.
Saul.

WOMEN'S VOICES:
Ruth.
Naomi.
Leah.

MEN'S VOICES:	WOMEN'S VOICES:
Refugio.	Francesca.
Jaime.	Maria.

MEN'S VOICES:	WOMEN'S VOICES:
Mikhail.	Zoya.
Vaslav.	Vera.
	Romola.

MEN'S VOICES:	WOMEN'S VOICES:
Fortunato.	Consuela.
	Esperanza.

MEN'S VOICES:	WOMEN'S VOICES:
Francois.	Eugenie.
Henri.	Felicity.

MEN'S VOICES:	WOMEN'S VOICES:
Wilfred.	Rowena.

INQUISITOR: *(imploringly, with his arms raised)*
Change us! Change our names. Change us!

MEN'S VOICES:	WOMEN'S VOICES:
Michael.	Mary.
John.	Katharine.
Robert.	Louise.
Peter.	Nancy.
Gordon.	Margo.
Edwin.	Diana.
Ben.	Polly.
William.	Betty.
Henry.	Edith.
Charles.	Ann.
Joe.	Sadie.
Cliff.	Sally.
Kenneth.	Jane.
Sam.	Carrie.
George.	Ethel.

INQUISITOR:

Praise the tuning, the liberation of American names. *(to the* USHERS*)* Set them free. Let them walk through the streets in their new names. What are your names?

USHER 1:
John P. Edwards.

USHER 2:
Mary J. Gordon.

USHER 3:
J. Perkins Johnson.

USHER 4:
Rose F. Johnson.

INQUISITOR: *(a final blessing as they kneel)*
I brand you now with American identities. See with new eyes an expanding country, a soaring economy. Walk in your new baptismal faith through American streets. Fight your national wars with pride. Join your civic organizations. Study your Law and Order. You are now American names.

(4) THE IMMIGRANTS' CURSES

USHER 1:
We're changed!

USHER 2:
Freedom, independence at last.

USHER 3:
We don't have to watch any more. We're men of action.

USHER 4:
Women of equality.

> *(The* CURSEMASTER *appears. He is formally dressed like an official toastmaster, but with a long red sash labeled* CURSEMASTER.*)*

CURSEMASTER:
Wait! You have your names, but you must still cast off your past.

USHER 1:
Who are you?

CURSEMASTER:
Your Cursemaster.

USHER 2:
Cursemaster?

CURSEMASTER:

To win the present, to march into the future, it is necessary to curse the past.

USHER 3: *(muttering)*

Ushers never study much history.

CURSEMASTER:

Have you invented your curses?

USHER 4:

Too many young people are cursing. Cursing should be forbidden tasting.

CURSEMASTER:

Invention is greater than knowledge. To be American, you must become inventors.

> *(He signals and a garishly, Pop-Art painted panel with images from American history slides into place. The panel has a hole in the center through which a masked actor sticks his head. To spare the actor, masks can be held up in the hole. The masks represent various racial stereotypes to fit the curses. The effect is much like the old carnival act of customers throwing balls at a "boy" who falls into a tub of water when the target is hit. However, the purpose here is to draw the audience in, get them to throw balls at the masks too. The* CURSEMASTER *produces a box of balls—baseballs, golf balls, tennis balls—take your pick.)*

USHER 1:

Look at all those balls.

CURSEMASTER: *(passing them out to the* USHERS*)*

American balls—baseballs, golf balls, tennis balls—take your pick. When a face from the past appears in that hole, you utter your curse and throw your ball. Wham! *(he illustrates)*

USHER 2:

Straight at the face?

CURSEMASTER:

Of course! How else can you free yourself from the past?

USHER 3:

Can't you give us an example to set us off?

CURSEMASTER:

Gladly. Let us begin with the Revolutionary Curse of 1776. First, a toast to the Revolution! *(He raises his glass.)* A California frontier wine of course. *(The first mask, a British stereotype, appears in the hole.)* *(He throws balls at the target and utters the first curse alone. Gradually, as the curses build up, enthusiasm should grow. The entire cast should appear and join in the curses and, at last, the audience should be invited to participate in the throwing. The racial implication of the curses should be allowed to make its own effect.)*

  NOTE: *Music should play a strong role in the curses)*

Fe, fi, fo, fum,
I smell the blood of an Englishman;
Be he alive or be he dead,
I'll grind his bones to make my bread.

USHER 3: *(enthusiastically)*
  Good. I know that. *(He grabs some balls and begins to throw and invent a curse:)*
  Down with the Redcoats
  Stuff their tea down their throats,
  Shoot 'em down with snipers,
  Cut their bloody wind-pipers,
  Hit 'em with the Stars and Stripers!

CURSEMASTER:
  Excellent. Who's next?

USHER 2: *(getting into the spirit suddenly)*
  Make the British eat their taxes,
  Melt 'em into candle-waxes,
  Come on, all you Minute Men,
  General George, give the King a goose,
  We'll fly Old George in a noose!

  (The mask is raised high, dangling as if in a noose, to cries of triumph)

CURSEMASTER:
  On! Into the past!

  (Two masks, more grotesquely distorted racial stereotypes, appear alternating in the hole.)

USHERS: *(One starts with the familiar nursery rhyme, then the others all join in with the variations, and the cast comes out to join in, as the CURSEMASTER beats encouragement.)*

Ibbety bibbety gibbety goat,
Ibbety bibbety cut his throat,
Tragedy,
Down with the goatee,
Out goes YOU.

Ibbety bibbety gibbety frogs
Ibbety bibbety sink the wogs
Ibbety bibbety pole the Polacks
Ibbety bibbety give 'em their smacks
Almanacs, almanacs,
Down goes the Devil,
Out goes YOU.

Ibbety bibbety wops and kikes
Ibbety bibbety niggers and triggers
Ibbety bibbety spicks and micks
Ibbety bibbety give 'em their licks
Almanacs, almanacs,
Down goes the Devil
Out goes YOU.

CURSEMASTER: *(waving and dancing wild encouragement)*
Westward Ho! Climb into your pioneer wagons, your prairie schooners.
On to California!

(Racially stereotyped masks of Indians and Chinese wave in the hole.)

USHERS: *(Arms around each other they begin to sing like a barbershop quartet.)*
Yo, ho, heave ho
For California oh,
There's plenty of gold
So I've been told
In the land of California . . .

   (Burn the redskins out,
    Claim the gold that's ours,
    and send the yellowbellies back to China)

Yo, ho, heave ho
For California oh,
There's plenty of bones
So I've been told
In the land of California . . .

(Burn the redskins out,
 Claim the gold that's ours,
 And send the yellowbellies back to China)

(By now, with the cast participating enthusiastically in the curses, members of the audience have been drawn in.)

CURSEMASTER:
You have conquered the virginal west. The frontier is yours. Your missiles guard the Pacific Ocean. But a dangerous cancer grows within. Its poisonous cells burst all over America. Europe and Asia threaten again. You rally your patriotic squads against the foreign menace and utter your national curse:

(Masks of Russian and Chinese Communists, the Viet Cong too, alternate in the hole.)

USHERS AND THE ENTIRE CAST: *(grouped like football squads into cheering sections; after the first verse they can draw in the audience, give them balls to throw, etc. This final curse is, of course, based on the famous football yell and must build up with the appropriate rhythm and musical accompaniment.)*
Get those Reds, those Commies, those pricks,
Give 'em the axe, the axe, the licks,
Get those Reds, those Commies, those pricks,
Give 'em the axe, the axe, the licks;
Give 'em the axe, the axe, the axe
Give 'em the axe, the axe, the axe
Give 'em the axe
Give 'em the axe
Give 'em the axe—WHERE?

Right in the neck the neck the neck
(Get those Reds, those Commies, those pricks)
Right in the neck the neck the neck
(Get those Reds, those Commies, those pricks)
Right in the neck
Right in the neck
Right in the neck—THERE!

CURSEMASTER: *(final toast in the bedlam)*
Here's to the Victory of Curses!

(5) OFFICIAL PRONOUNCEMENTS

(The NATIONAL CRIER *comes on and meets informally with the* CURSEMAS-TER. *Worn out by their exertions in the cursing sequence, the* USHERS *are resting uneasily, waiting. The* NATIONAL CRIER *is wired for sound, with broadcasting set, and TV antenna. Out of him sprout images of all of the technological equipment to issue Official Pronouncements. He carries an enormous megaphone lettered with the words—*NATIONAL CRIER—OFFICIAL PRONOUNCE-MENTS.)

NATIONAL CRIER:
Is the time of cursing over?

CURSEMASTER:
They have entered the present. They are ready for the Official Pronouncements.

USHER 2:
What do we do now?

USHER 4: *(moaning)*
My feet ache. I want to rest.

USHER 1:
Sit down and wait.

USHER 3:
I hate waiting.

NATIONAL CRIER: *(mounting a stand)*
I am the National Crier. From my voice flows the official language. I mark the news, the final points of judgment. From the lost villages, the settlements, the countryside, I moved to the cities. I issued the proclamations of the states. When the states fought between themselves to settle the national destiny, I moved to Washington. There I became the National Crier. Through the air I issue the Official Pronouncements. *(He levels his enormous megaphone at the Ushers.)* As new American voyagers, you will learn to hear and ignore the Official Pronouncements.

Two ASSISTANTS *keep bringing long lists—officially stamped and typed documents, record books, etc. —from which the* NATIONAL CRIER *reads through his megaphone. As he reads, the following* simultaneous *actions take place:)*

NATIONAL CRIER: (reading officially)

Marriage Licenses:
Corinne Ellis, 22 to
Robert Marston, 24:
Elizabeth Schmitt, 20,
to Alexander Hanno, 21;
Estella Blea, 25, to
Jose Lucero, 24;
JoAnn Loomis, 38, to
Leo Blackstone, 31.

(An actor and actress embrace.)

ACTOR:
Do you really love me?

ACTRESS:
I'm not sure.

ACTOR:
That's a terrible thing to say.

ACTRESS:
You want the truth don't you?

ACTOR:
I want you to love me, that's all.

(Meanwhile other members of the cast are going directly to individual members of the audience and saying very directly to them the following lines.)

ACTOR:
"O love is the crooked thing."

ACTOR:
Marriage is the living end.

ACTRESS:
If I marry, it'll have to be a man who shares things. This is a selfish male-dominated society.

ACTRESS:
I like a sentimental movie like *Love Story.* It makes you realize that love doesn't last very long.

ACTOR:
Marriage should be permitted only between the age of 45 and 65. That would save a lot of problems.

NATIONAL CRIER:
Births
July 25, St. Joseph
Hospital, Mr. and Mrs.
Robert J. Cohen, boy;
August 2, Presbyterian
Hospital, Mr. and Mrs.
Wilfred L. Peters, girl;

ACTOR: *(as doctor)*
It's a fine boy, Mrs. Cohen.

ACTRESS:
What do you mean, *it?*
Isn't it all right?

August 15, University Heights Hospital, Mary Wilson, girl; September 3, Sandia Base Hospital, Capt. and Mrs. Terence O. Peterson, twins.

ACTOR:
It's a fine girl, Mrs. Cohen.

ACTRESS:
A girl, my god, my husband wanted a boy. Can't I ever have a boy?

(Overlapping, other members of the cast speak directly to individual members of the audience.)

ACTOR:
I can't remember anything 'til I was five years old, yet Freud says those are the crucial years.

ACTRESS:
I want to have eight children. Maybe that's not right, but I want to do it. I love children.

ACTOR:
I'm a Leo. What are you? Astrology's great, isn't it?

ACTRESS:
I won't have more than two children. I believe in birth control, don't you?

NATIONAL CRIER:
Divorces Asked
Mary Ellen vs. Narcissus Corona;
Herman R. vs. Patricia Knight;
Ruth Ann vs. Joseph Ortiz;
Earlene J. vs. Elbert P. Watson;
Manuel H. vs. Josephine Wilkins.

ACTRESS: *(screaming at actor)*
I never should have married you. You're the absolute bottom!

ACTOR: *(coldly)*
For sure you're not the top.

ACTRESS:
I want a divorce!

ACTOR:
I suppose you want all my money too.

ACTRESS:
Damn right, you're the meanest son-of-a-bitch I ever saw.

(Overlapping, other members of the cast speak directly to individual members of the audience.)

ACTRESS:

I threw my ring into the river when I got my divorce. I threw it as far as I could.

ACTOR:

In most states you still have to prove adultery.

ACTRESS:

What can you expect of a man who always treats you like a piece of burnt toast?

ACTOR:

She didn't know anything about sex. You wouldn't believe it, but she never heard of Kinsey let alone Masters and Johnson.

ACTRESS:

You never saw such a miser. How can you live with a man who spells love m-o-n-e-y?

NATIONAL CRIER:

Divorces Granted
Geraldine from Anthony
Edward Jones;
Donald Leroy and Mary
Ann Smith;
Betty Jean from Peter
H. Carson;
Stella from Marvin
Swift;
James J. and Corinna
Brito.

ACTRESS: *(to entire audience)*
It's great to be single again. The only problem is finding another man. You look and you look. Every good man is married. Only the louses pant after you. You end up watching the boob box at home alone. That's not a life. If anybody knows a good man for me, let me know will you?

(Overlapping, other members of the cast speak directly to individual members of the audience.)

ACTOR:

After my divorce, every morning when I woke up, there was no one to touch.

ACTRESS:

When you're divorced, get everything out of him you can I say. After all, you have to look out for yourself.

ACTOR:

I'll never get married again. From now on I'm just going to enjoy women.

III

ACTRESS:

After the divorce I could hardly remember him. But then he was nothing much to remember, that's for sure.

ACTOR:

It all seems like an end. I can't believe it. I never thought it would seem like an end.

NATIONAL CRIER:

Bankruptcy Petitions
Pablo Venceslous Garcia and Alma Garcia, student and housewife; debts, $3003; assets, $250; exemption, $250.
Dennis Porter Bengson, policeman, debts, $3657; assets $745; exemption, $745.

ACTOR: *(to entire audience)*

I got in over my head. They told me you've got to be deep in debt before you're really successful. I was so tied up in loans you wouldn't believe it. I wore out the carpets of bank offices. My credit rating was a beautiful thing of shadows. You know when I went bankrupt, I never really felt I was broke. I felt like a million bucks.

(Simultaneously, other members of cast speak directly to individual members of audience.)

ACTOR:

He never meant to pay me back. I trusted him. How can you ever trust anybody with money?

ACTRESS:

My parents always seemed to have plenty of money. Now they won't help me any more. How do you like that?

ACTOR:

You work so hard and suddenly everything caves in.

ACTRESS:

It's tough as a woman starting your own business. The banks wouldn't lend me enough money. That's why I went bankrupt.

NATIONAL CRIER:

We interrupt the time of National Crying for a message from the President.

(The PRESIDENT *appears in obvious television make-up.)*

THE PRESIDENT: *(in his most intimate, confidential manner)*

Friends and fellow citizens, I have asked for ten minutes of time from the national networks to tell you of an extraordinary journey I propose to make. At this moment, my assistant, Dr. Hans Messenger, is returning from a secret meeting with the few surviving medicine men of the old-time Indian pueblos. It is my intention to meet with these wise men some time before May 1972, and to discuss with them ways to bridge the gap that has unfortunately arisen between our cultures. I wish to announce now that they have invited me to descend into one of their sacred kivas and I am grateful to be the first president ever invited down there. Let me assure all of our other great minority groups in the United States of America that this meeting will not affect them. I make this journey in the cause of spiritual peace for all mankind. It is my intention to get back to the center of the earth.

(Along the inevitable course of the Official Pronouncements, the USHERS *have begun to doze or fall asleep.)*

NATIONAL CRIER: *(continuing without notice)*

Driving Charges

Max Alderson, 38 Saturday night at Fourth and Johnson NW; driving while intoxicated and reckless driving. Charlie Jamison, 23, Saturday night at Sixth and Central; drving while intoxicated and reckless driving. Isidore Chico Petrana, 25, Saturday night at Outer Drive; driving while under the influence of marijuana and reckless driving.

ACTOR:

That cop. How were we supposed to get home from the party? Walk?

ACTRESS:

Right, Saturday night is Saturday night. You have to relax sometime.

ACTOR:

That cop had no right to pick us up. We were only going 45.

ACTRESS:

You were driving perfectly safely.

ACTOR *(reacting)*

I wasn't driving. Don't you remember I asked you to drive?

(Simultaneously, individual voices speak to audience.)

ACTOR:

A car's no fun unless you can get in and go. How fast do you drive?

ACTRESS:

You know marijuana is not as dangerous as alcohol. I never drink when I'm driving.

ACTOR:

If they don't want me to drive fast, why do they keep putting all that power in those sporty cars?

ACTRESS:

I really did stop at that stop sign. But you can't make a full stop all the time. You'd never get anywhere.

NATIONAL CRIER:

District Court

Jay Colter asks for restraining order against Christine Mitchell;

Business Servants, Inc. asks $357 against Raymond Pearson, Pearson's Upholstery & Glass, alleged debt;

Curtis Earl Fleming granted name change to Earl Curtis Fleming;

American Savings & Loan Association vs. Glenn H. Barrett et al., dismissed;

Edward Allen Griggs vs. National Casualty Cort., dismissed with prejudice;

Barbara Gonzales asks $700 and $5000 punitive damages against Joe Gonzales.

ACTRESS: *(to actor as lawyer)*

You're my lawyer. Why can't you work this out faster? It's been six months already.

ACTOR:

You have to be patient. The court calendar is jammed.

ACTRESS:

I'm jammed too. What about me? I need that money. That son-of-a bitch owes it to me. Why don't they make him pay up?

ACTOR:

I know how you feel, but it takes time.

ACTRESS:

What do you mean, time? It's my money. He won't pay me back. All I want the judge to do is make him pay me back.

(Simultaneously, individual voices speak to audience.)

ACTOR:

Money, money, money, the lawyers get it all. That's why we've got mostly lawyers in politics.

ACTRESS:

Have you ever been in court? It's a scary feeling. I had to sit in court all morning before they called my case.

ACTOR:

I felt like a criminal I tell you in that courtroom. I'll never be a witness again. From now on, I'll just keep my mouth shut, no matter what happens.

ACTRESS:

What does *with prejudice* mean? I tell you I'll never understand legal language.

NATIONAL CRIER:

We interrupt the time of National Crying for a message from the astronauts of Apollo 17 on the moon.

OFFSTAGE ANNOUNCER'S VOICE:

There's Colonel Adams now trundling his rock cart back from the Sea of Tranquility. (COL. ADAMS *staggers into view trundling a cart*) Hello, Colonel, can you hear me? The whole world is watching you by satellite. It's another great triumph. I'll bet you've got some beautiful rocks in there for us, haven't you, Colonel? (COLONEL ADAMS *nods heavily and produces a golf club, an iron, from his cart.*) What have you got there, Colonel? A golf club. A seven iron? Ladies and gentlemen, we're about to see the first golf stroke on the moon!

(Laboriously, COLONEL ADAMS *drops a ball and hits the first historical golf shot on the moon.)*

NATIONAL CRIER: *(continuing without notice)*

Deaths and Funerals

Pinkerton—George W. Pinkerton, 73, died Tuesday in a local hospital; he is survived by his wife, Phyllis, of the family home. He was a member of the Methodist Church, Allegro Temple Shrine, Retired Officers Association, and the American Legion. Services are being handled by the Strongpewter Mortuary.

Rooston—Memorial Services for Perry R. Rooston will be held at 2 PM in the Fern Chapel of the Longlife Mortuary with Reverend I. A. Johnson officiating.

Sganzoni—Juan Sganzoni, 84, died, Wednesday at a local hospital

ACTOR:

You wouldn't believe what happened when I walked into that mortuary. They tried to sell me the fanciest coffin.

ACTRESS:

The fanciest coffin?

ACTOR:

They had 'em from plain to fancy. Of course the fancy ones cost the most. They wouldn't even show me the simple ones. They wanted me to buy the most expensive one.

ACTRESS:

What kind of people are those morticians? They just want to make money like everyone else.

ACTOR:

I tell you I could see her lying in

following a long illness. Sganzoni is survived by seven sons, Trinidad, Joe, Lawrence, Arthur, David Felipe, and Albert; 39 grandchildren, and 23 great-grandchildren. Rosary will be recited this evening at the Velasquez Mortuary Chapel.

that fancy coffin. I'd be dreaming about that.

(Simultaneously, actors address the audience.)

ACTOR:

Death isn't the end. I can't believe it's the end. Do you believe it's the end?

ACTRESS:

When I die, I want to go fast. All we do is sweep old age under the rug nowadays.

ACTOR:

I think a man should know how to die. I think it's very important to know how to die. All we do in this country is ignore death.

ACTRESS:

When your husband's killed, the phone or the doorbell rings and there's a telegram. Is that a way to tell you about death?

ACTOR:

I thought the old lady would live forever. She just hung on, she was afraid to die.

ACTRESS:

I don't believe in immortality, but I dream about it. Wouldn't you like to be immortal?

NATIONAL CRIER:

Arrivals and Departures

We take you now to Providence, R.I., where four Ushers are undergoing a strange journey through time. They have passed certain achievement tests and been awarded various certificates of membership. *(through the megaphone)* Hello, are you there? There seems to be some interference. Hello. Hello? *(The babble of voices rising in intensity makes it difficult for him to get through to the* USHERS.*)*

(Actors, all around the theatre through the audience, speak directly to individual members of the audience.)

ACTOR:

I like to get somewhere, but it's always hard for me to leave.

ACTRESS:

Every city I live in, I can't stand it. I'm going back to the country. How about you?

ACTOR:

Some day I'll just get in my car and drive away from it all. Do you feel that way?

ACTOR:

There's still hope if we can change things around, but we've got a long ways to go.

ACTRESS:

It's a funny thing about revolution in this country. We started there, but we don't want to go there any more.

ACTOR:

We don't know where we're going, but we're on the march. What I want to know is what do they mean by *march?*

ACTRESS:

At first I was scared to hitchhike, but it's pretty exciting. You meet a lot of interesting people. You're always going somewhere.

ACTOR:

All I want to do is earn enough money to buy a secondhand car. Then I'm off. I can sleep in the car or on the beach.

USHER 4:

Do you hear? Someone seems to be calling?

USHER 2:

Calling? I hear only a babble of voices.

USHER 3:

Just the usual background noise.

USHER 1:

Probably someone left the television on.

NATIONAL CRIER: (*shouting through his megaphone to the* USHERS)

You have learned to hear and ignore the Official Pronouncements.

(6) THE SEARCH FOR A STRUCTURE
WITH ANIMAL SPIRITS

(The BUILDING OFFICIAL *emerges briskly. He is an energetic business man in appearance, conservatively dressed, but with a flower in his buttonhole. With him comes an* INDIAN *in a blue-flowered shirt with white pants and moccasins who stands in the center of the playing area playing on a large belly drum throughout the scene.)*

BUILDING OFFICIAL:

Ladies and Gentlemen, we invite you to build your native American structures. The construction industry, with the help of loans from your government and your local banks, aims to please you by helping you build the structure you desire most. We want to help you design your ideal home, that private place where you can pursue your dream of American happiness.

USHER 4: *(to her husband)*

Oh J., I've always wanted my own home. Do you think we can afford it at last?

USHER 3:

Maybe it's time, Rose. Ushering is beginning to pay off.

USHER 4:

I hope our neighbors are nice.

USHER 3:

Don't worry, the real estate company promised us there won't be any troublemakers in the neighborhood.

*(*USHERS 1 & 2 *enter as the neighbors.)*

USHER 1: *(shaking hands)*

We heard you'd moved in. Glad you invited us over.

USHER 2: *(gushing)*

You have such a beautiful home and garden. It looks so much better than when the Jorgensons lived here. They were a little hippie you know.

USHER 3:

Can I get you a drink?

USHER 1:

I'll have a Very Dry Martini with a twist of lemon.

USHER 2:

I'll have a Bourbon and Ginger Ale, please,

USHER 3:

Have some hors-d'oeuvres.

USHER 4:

Cheese Tid-Bits with Bacon.

USHER 2:

They look delicious.

USHER 3: *(handing drinks around)*

Here you go. *(He raises his glass.)* Here's to Ushering.

> *(As they drink and converse, two* INDIANS *bring on a tall pole glistening with fresh, white paint.)*

INDIAN 1: *(to the pole)*

We have cut you down, Brother Pine Tree, but we know your life is as tall and proud as ours. We are all born from Mother Earth and Father Sun. We live in a world of natural wonder, where each of us has his place. As the river flows, as the magic lake speaks to us from its depths, each of us must give way to the other so that our life of unity may remain unbroken. Give consent then, of Brother Pine, to your death.

INDIAN 2: *(Bringing on a bloody deer-skin, he arranges it with the head toward the East and then sprinkles it with corn-meal and pollen.)*

Oh Brother Deer, we ask your assent for this sacrifice. May your proud spirit journey with us through the wilderness. I drop these drops of your blood, these bits of your flesh, on the ground in tribute to our Mother Earth. I sprinkle this meal and pollen in praise of our Father Sun. Grant us your assent, Brother Deer, to your sacrifice.

> *(Ceremonially, they fasten the deer-skin to the pole; another* INDIAN *brings squash and corn and an old flour sack full of freshly baked bread and groceries. All of these they lash to the pole.)*

USHER 3: *(as an actor playing a big dog enters on all fours and puts his big paw on* USHER 2*)*

Don't worry, he's very gentle. That's St. Julian, our St. Bernard.

USHER 2: *(trying to maintain her composure)*

He's awfully big. Are you sure he isn't dangerous?

USHER 4: *(sweetly)*
St. Julian? He's just a little baby. We've had him fixed.

(An actress as a cat enters meowing and jumps up in USHER 1*'s lap.)*

USHER 1: *(uncomfortably)*
My, she's friendly.

USHER 4: *(fondly)*
That's Geranium, our Siamese. She's very friendly unlike most cats.

USHER 1: *(uncomfortably)*
Don't you think she might . . . I'm a little allergic.

USHER 3:
You don't have to worry. She's fixed.

USHER 4:
We did want her to have a litter first, but she wouldn't stay home. You have to be careful with animals in the city.

USHER 3:
We were warned about the leash law you know. So many lawns being ruined.

(The INDIANS, *having lashed the bloody deer-skin, the vegetables, and the sack to the pole, begin to raise the pole. With a sudden yell, two* KOSHARES —the wise, older clown-spirits—rush in, prancing through the audience. They are naked except for breech clouts and moccasins. Their faces and bodies are striped with black and white clay. One* KOSHARE *has an alarm clock strapped to his wrist. They prance around mimicking the white tourists and scaring the children in fun. They paw at the purses of women in the audience and pat the men on the shoulder, mocking: "How much? Do you want to buy an Indian? For a drink of whiskey, we sell you cheap Indians. Give me a cigarette and I will give you magic beads. Do you have any candy and popcorn? How much? How much? I'll give you a bargain. You want a blanket or a ring? How about a beautiful necklace? I can get it for you cheap from a Trader . . . etc . . .)*

USHER 2:
It's so quiet and peaceful here.

USHER 1:
Here's to the cocktail hour. Can I have another drink?

USHER 3:
We're going to add another room soon.

USHER 4:

Just a little guest room with a bathroom. Then you can come and visit us.

USHER 1:

Are you going to make it Victorian too?

USHER 3:

Oh no, we want to try Modern this time.

USHER 4:

With an animal door.

USHER 2:

An animal door?

USHER 3:

So the animals can go in and out when they want to piss.

USHER 4:

It's for their convenience as well as ours of course.

USHER 2:

What fun to build your own home with every natural convenience.

USHER 4:

I've always had a dream of home. It should be a whole environment. You have to bring a little nature into the city, some plants, a few civilized animals. *(The animals nuzzle her affectionately and she feeds them a few Cheese Tid-Bits.)*

USHER 3:

Some day in the cities we'll have Magic Housing Machines. You'll be able to design any kind of fantastic house you want. You won't need any architect. A huge blow-pipe feeds into a reservoir of magic plastic. All you do is press a few buttons to change the air pressure and through the pipe you can blow all kinds of free forms.

USHER 4:

Think what that kind of technology will do.

USHER 3:

You just press the buttons and, bang, out pops your dream-building. It's on the drawing boards already. Just wait and see. Those kinds of forms will be as flexible as nature.

(The INDIANS *begin to dance around the pole. The mood of the* KO-SHARES *begins to change. They become serious and one of them, on all*

fours, picks up an animal scent. The DEER MOTHER *dances in. She is an extraordinary feminine animal figure, the graceful, hidden, mysterious fertility force. She is dressed in a white ceremonial buckskin gown and high white buckskin boots. On the back of her head are two eagle feathers and on top of her head a tuft of parrot feathers. On her cheeks are painted black spots and a black streak of paint runs around her jaw. They all approach her and draw back, approach her and draw back, as she dances gracefully, powerfully forward. As they draw back, they utter strange animal sounds of homage.)*

USHER 4:
It's so quiet. How about a little music?

USHER 2:
Great. I love music.

(USHER 3 *turns on some music. No music is heard except for the powerful beat of the Indian drummer.)*

USHER 2:
That's nice. I love rock.

USHER 4:
Isn't it too bad how the rock musicians are dying so young.

USHER 3:
It's the drugs. Everybody's popping pills. How would you folks like to dance? I feel like a little dancing after this drink.

USHER 4:
I'm not very good at the new dancing, but I do like it. Come on, J. *(She urges her reluctant husband up. They all begin to churn away, pseudo-rock style. The dog and the cat join in too. The Indian dance continues on its serene, fierce way as the scene ends.)*

(7) THE NATURAL DISASTERS

BUILDING OFFICIAL: *(calmly, dogmatically, as if reading from a pre-arranged Civil Defense routine for disaster)*
Stand by in your structures. There is momentary difficulty with the water system. Repeat—the water system is failing. Residents in structures above the twenty-fifth floor, please move to lower-level structures. Warning, repeat—the water level is falling. The water level is falling in the lower

structures. Do not be alarmed and move quietly. The water supply has been temporarily cut off.

(With a shake of his rattle gourd, the OGRE KACHINA *appears on a high platform. The* DEER MOTHER *enters and kneels below him. To mysterious, soft music, she begins to undress and go through a washing ritual as if in a sacred lake or river. The* OGRE KACHINA *has enormous bug-eyes, a long, bloodstained nose, and he carries a bundle of switching sticks in his hand. He is not a realistic Hopi kachina, but rather some fantastic, punishing image of the kachina that has been created in white imaginations after years of living with the extermination of the Indians. Occasionally, he utters weird cries. The* USHERS, *with their animals, pantomime alarmed response to the warning of the* BUILDING OFFICIAL. *There is no visible contact between the* OGRE KACHINA *and the* USHERS.)*

BUILDING OFFICIAL: *(continuing)*
Ground floor structures stand by to receive refugees. Conserve your water. The water failure is causing a power shortage in Public Utility stations. Do not vacate your structure if hit by a power failure. Conserve your water in any remaining receptacles.

(The lights go out on the USHERS. *The* OGRE KACHINA *shakes his rattle as the* BUILDING OFFICIAL *continues throughout the scene to speak his official, mechanical warnings, but he cannot be heard. The rest of the scene consists of the invisible, elegiac voice of the* INDIAN CHIEF *counterpointed against the ritual transformation of the* DEER MOTHER, *and the syllabic sound-poem utterances of the* USHERS *and their animals as they attempt frantically to rediscover the memories of objects and ideas they have suddenly lost.)*

INDIAN CHIEF: *(Only his powerful, elegiac, mournful voice is heard above the mocking presence of the* OGRE KACHINA *and the ritual washing of the* DEER MOTHER *as she disrobes. Part of the Indian Chief's words are based on the famous epitaph for the Indian race by Chief Seattle.)*
When the earth is despoiled, when the harvest fields no longer yield their plenty, when the rivers no longer flow purely to the thirsty soil, you will not be alone in the darkness.

(The OGRE KACHINA *starts to dance to the music as* DEER MOTHER *undresses and continues with her ritual washing. The music furnishes the essential rhythm of the scene to the counterpoint of the desperate, groping sound-poem words in their syllabic disintegration.)*

USHERS: *(echoing in their search for meaning)*
A—lone . . . a—looo—ne . . . aaaaa-loooooone . . .

INDIAN CHIEF:
When the last red man shall have become a myth among the white men, when your children's children think themselves alone in the field, in the store, upon the highway, or in the silence of their homes, they will not be alone. In all the earth there will be no place dedicated to solitude.

USHERS:
Sol-i-tuuude . . . soool-iiiiii-tuuuuude . . . soool-iiiiii-tuuuuude . . .

INDIAN CHIEF:
When all your time machines, your water machines, your air machines, fail and your earth-mother lies dead, you will not be alone.

USHERS AND ANIMALS: *(A syllabic sound-poem lament to music in which the animals, the dog and cat, also join. During this lament, the* OGRE KACHINA *punctuates each word and name with a lash of his bundle of switching sticks and his high-pitched cry. The* DEER MOTHER *completes her undressing and continues with her washing ritual.)*
Wa-ter . . . Waaaa-ter . . .
Hot water—*cold* water—*Hot* water—
                        cold water . . .
Re-frig-er-a-ted iiice . . .
Lawn sprink-ler . . . Spriiiink-ler . . .
Swiiiiim-ming Pooooollll . . .
Wa*shing* . . . Wa-*shing* . . . Wa-*shing* . . .
Wa-*shing* ma-*chine* . . . Wa-*shing* ma-*chine* . . .
                        Wa-*shing* ma-*chine* . . .

INDIAN CHIEF:
At night when the streets of your cities are silent and you prepare to depart for the rivers, the lakes, you have deserted, when you seek to regain the spirit of water you have destroyed, you will never be alone.

USHERS AND ANIMALS:
Naaa-ture . . . Con-ser-vaaa-tion . . . Com-mun-i-ty . . .
Con-ser-va-tion! . . . Com-muuu-ni-ty!

The DEER MOTHER *has thrown off her clothes and enters the river to continue her washing ritual)*

USHERS AND ANIMALS: *(as they observe the* DEER MOTHER *finally)*
Waaa-ter . . . Waaaa-ter Spiiiir-it . . .

(As they move towards her, she pulls from the water a serpent mask and turns into a hissing serpent as the OGRE KACHINA *lashes his bundle of switching sticks and utters his high-pitched cry. Falling into the water, she continues her snake-like motions as the* USHERS *and* ANIMALS *shrink back.)*

USHERS AND ANIMALS:
Des-sert . . . des-ert . . . de-sert-ed . . .
Vir-gin riiii-ver . . . smooog . . . smooooog . . .
Pol-lu-shuuun . . . Pol-luuuu-shuuuuunnnn . . .
Dead *lake* . . . *dead* lake . . . dead *lake* . . . *dead*
lake . . .

INDIAN CHIEF:
At night in the darkness of your cities when you prepare to flee in your time machines, the silent streets will throng with the returning hosts that once filled them and still love this beautiful land. The white man will never be alone.

USHERS AND ANIMALS:
Beau-ti-ful . . . a-lone . . .
beau-ti-ful . . . aaa-loooooone . . .

INDIAN CHIEF:
Let the white man be just and deal kindly with my people for the dead are not powerless. Dead? I say . . . There is no death. Only a change of worlds.

USHERS AND ANIMALS:
Death . . . change . . . deeea-th . . . chaaaaange . . .
DEEEEEA-TH . . .

(They blow out the candles and there is a long silence. Only a dim light is seen on the OGRE KACHINA *standing silent, immobile, above the transformed* SNAKE WOMAN, *his bundle of switching sticks held high.)*

(8) THE FREEWAY ESCAPE

(The USHERS *appear joyously coated and hatted in outfits of many radiant colors—transformed drivers ready for the freeway. Four cars, played by actors or, preferably, by dancers—a Mustang, Capri, Pinto, and Stag—await the* USHERS *in alert, eager, go positions.)*

USHER 1: *(eagerly)*
Away we go!

USHER 2: *(fervently)*
The Open Road!

USHER 4:
Thank god, we've escaped from that awful city.

USHER 3:
Hail to the Freeway!

USHER 1:
Salute to the Horizon! My Mustang.

(He throws himself ardently onto his car, The Mustang, and they wrestle around a little before USHER 1 asserts himself as the driver. As they wrestle, an invisible salesman's voice is heard.)

SALESMAN:
It's a personal thing. It's part of yourself, you know. The practicality of a beautifully organized instrument panel. The indulgence of deep-padded bucket seats.

USHER 2:
We who are about to travel salute my Pinto.

(She climbs onto her car, the Pinto, and they wrestle around a little before USHER 2 asserts herself as the driver. Again, an invisible salesman's voice is heard.)

SALESMAN:
A do-it-yourself car. Wide stance and silhouette with strong, beefy parts. You pick up a do-it-yourself manual and tool kit when you pick up this proud performer.

USHER 3:
My Capri.

(He hurls himself onto his car, the Capri, played by an actress or woman dancer, and they wrestle around before USHER 3 submits as the driver. Once more, an invisible salesman's voice is heard.)

SALESMAN:
What options does she offer? A brand new engine—a gutsy 2000 cc, 100 hp overhead cam four. We call it sexy.

USHER 4:
Come on, Stag, let's hit the road together!

(She climbs onto her car, the Stag, played naturally by an actor or male dancer, and they wrestle around before USHER 4 *asserts herself triumphantly as the driver. Another invisible salesman's voice is heard.)*

SALESMAN:
Your Stag has road-hugging, independent suspension. Solid, padded roll bar. A sports car which loves in return.

USHERS: *(excitedly, as they begin their journey)*
We're off! What's the freeway number? Follow 580 all the way. The speed limit is 70. That's just cruising along. Watch out for trucks. No problem, it's six lanes. What a ride! Smooth, huh? Like a featherbed.

USHER 1:
Where are we?

USHER 2:
Mountain country, I think. Look at the cuts.

USHER 3:
They've leveled everything. It must be Nebraska.

USHER 4:
It's corn country all right. Maybe it's Iowa.

USHER 3:
Look! It's the Great Salt Lake.

USHER 1:
When do we stop?

USHER 4:
We can't stop.

USHER 3:
There aren't any motels. Can't you read?

USHER 2: *(reading a sign)*
Next Service Area thirty miles.

USHER 1: *(reading a sign)*
Watch for Deer.

USHER 4:
Don't worry. They come out only at twilight.

USHER 1:
Yippee! It's Open Range country.

USHER 3:

Look! Another dead animal.

USHER 2: *(alarmed)*

Bugs battering against the windshield! I can't see.

USHER 4:

Look out! We're in a swarm of butterflies. They're smashing into blobs.

USHER 3:

Use the automatic wiper.

USHER 1:

I've got to stop. My car needs lubrication.

USHER 2:

A few hundred more miles won't hurt. Anyway, it's Sunday. The garages are closed.

USHER 1:

I'm tired. Can't we stop a little?

USHER 4: *(with relief)*

At last. A Rest Area.

USHER 2:

We'll have a picnic.

USHER 1:

About time. I need a rest.

> *(They drive into The Rest Area. The four cars collapse in a heap. The four* USHERS *picnic closely together. The two groups, Americans and machines, regard each other.)*

USHER 4:

It's a great place to picnic, but I wish there were some trees.

USHER 3:

Stinks of garbage. I wonder if they ever collect it.

USHER 1:

They'd have to drive a million miles to collect it out here.

USHER 2:

Look at those cars.

USHER 1: *(nervously)*

Maybe we've driven them too hard.

USHER 4:

Don't be silly. Good engines like to run *fast*.

USHER 3:

When we get where we're going, we'll have them serviced.

USHER 2:

What if there's no garage?

USHER 3:

There's always a service station.

USHER 1:

Where are we going?

USHER 4:

Mexico, I think. That's the way it looks on the map.

USHER 3:

South anyway. It's warmer there.

USHER 2:

We can sleep on the beach if necessary.

USHER 3:

No, the cars might not like that. We can sleep in the cars.

USHER 1: *(nervously, looking at the cars)*

I don't like the condition of those cars.

USHER 4:

Don't get uptight. Machines get touchy if you don't trust them.

USHER 2:

They can always be replaced.

USHER 4:

Out here?

USHER 1:

Look! They're starting.

USHER 3:

It's time to go.

USHER 2: *(as the cars approach)*

I don't want to go yet. I haven't finished my sandwich and hardboiled egg.

USHER 4:

There's a little beer left. I'm still thirsty.

USHER 2:

But they want to go.

USHER 3:

Take the keys out. We've been too permissive with them.

USHER 2: *(alarmed)*

They're starting up.

USHER 1:

What if they leave us behind?

USHER 3:

Don't be stupid. We're the drivers.

USHER 4:

They can't leave us behind. We have to go.

USHER 2:

Where?

USHER 3:

The cars will tell us.

USHER 4:

The cars will find the Freeway.

(They start off again with a venomous roar.)

USHER 1:

Whew. It's great to be traveling again.

USHER 2: *(happily)*

Under the stars.

USHER 3:

Look at that full moon.

USHER 4:

Is there anybody up there now?

USHER 3:

They've got a lot of machines traveling around.

USHER 2:

It's so exciting to travel. I feel like the Flying Dutchman!

USHER 1:

Or the Wandering Jew.

USHER 4:

The Traveling American.

USHER 1:

We'll never stop again.

USHER 2:

Where are we?

USHER 4:

Traveling on the Freeway.

USHER 3:

Look! We're arriving.

(A sign in blinking neon lights, says TWENTY-FOUR HOUR WEDDING CHAPEL*)*

USHER 1:

The Twenty-Four Hour Wedding Chapel. We must be in Nevada.

USHER 3:

Or Tijuana. Who's getting married?

USHER 2:

Let's go on. There must be a service station somewhere.

(The MARRYING MECHANIC *appears in a greasy, gaudy uniform.)*

MARRYING MECHANIC:

Glad to see you, ladies and gents. It's kinda late, but we're glad to do business with you any time. Devoted, tasty service is our motto. Twenty-four hours a day or night. We never fail to please. Just let me copy down your license plate numbers. Just fill in the forms. Engine number. What kinda car your driving. Credit card data. If you want the special service that's ten dollars extra.

USHER 1:

Wait a minute. What's going on?

USHER 2:

We don't want to get married.

USHER 3:

You don't look like a Justice of the Peace.

MARRYING MECHANIC:

Justice of the Peace? Ha, ha, I'm a Marrying Mechanic. Don't worry, everyone who turns off the Freeway needs things welded together. I put back your missing hearts. I power up your batteries. I transplant your fuel filter. I marry you to the Freeway.

USHER 4:

Thank god, we've found a mechanic.

USHER 2:

We're safe now.

USHER 3:

We can go on.

MARRYING MECHANIC:

That Mustang looks pretty tuckered. You've been driving 'em hard. No matter, that's what they're for. Get up and go, right? *Zoom*—down that white lane, everything vanishes to left and right. Driving free. Don't you worry. I'll hitch everything up. *(with increasing ecstasy to the end)* Marry man to machine. I'll merge your blood and metal. I'll give you the final fusion process. Marry you to the road. You'll see the landscape whirl by with new tinted vision. Any mechanical flesh you want I guarantee. When I get through with you, you'll zoom off like newlyweds. Glasses and windshield, I'll polish you up. You'll run so smooth, you won't hear your hearts ticking. Float like a feather. Stop on a dime. Accelerate in a minute to the land of plenty. I'll give you spectacular performance. It's a world of cars and I'm your Marrying Mechanic. Say, *I do.*

USHERS: *(slowly, fearfully, to cars)*
I do.

MARRYING MECHANIC:

Say, *I DO!*

USHERS:

I DO!

(9) MONTEZUMA'S REVENGE

(There is a certain inexorable, driving rhythm to this scene, the rhythm of American tourists who must see everything—however briefly—and then speed on to the next place.)

132

USHERS AND CAST: *(together)*
Tourists, infiltrate!

USHER 1:
Hats.

USHER 2:
Raincoats, dark glasses.

USHER 3:
Travelers checks.

USHER 4:
Credit cards.

USHER 1:
Cameras, cameras. Pose!

USHER 2:
Ancient ruins.

USHER 3.
Snapshots.

USHER 4: *(as they pause briefly)*
The Pause That Refreshes.

USHERS AND CAST: *(together, as they're off to a new place)*
Tourists, assemble!

MEXICAN GUIDE: *(appearing)*
I am your guide, Señor.

USHER 1:
How much?

MEXICAN GUIDE:
The banks give you 12.49 pesos to your U.S. dollar.

USHER 4: *(worried)*
Do the banks speak English?

MEXICAN GUIDE:
Don't worry, Señora. Most banks have English-speaking dollars.

USHERS AND CAST: *(together)*
Tourists, unite!

PASSING TOURIST: *(cautioning)*
Remember, don't buy milk in bottles.

USHER 2:
What'll we do? What's the best and safest brand of milk?

PASSING TOURIST:
Leche Preferente. Buy it at Sumesa Supermarkets.

USHER 3:
They got Supermarkets?

PASSING TOURIST: *(as he shoots off)*
With Super-Tourists, you've gotta have Supermarkets.

USHERS AND CAST: *(together)*
Tourists, get your taxi!

USHER 1:
Hey, taxi! I'll be damned. That cab is painted with white teeth.

MEXICAN GUIDE:
That's a cocodrilos, Señor.

USHER 2:
Coco-what?

MEXICAN GUIDE:
Cocodrilos. 3000 green taxis are painted with white teeth.

USHER 3:
White teeth. Hey, that's a neat idea.

USHER 4:
What's it mean—coco-drill-us—or whatever it is.

MEXICAN GUIDE:
Cocodrilos means crocodiles, Señor.

USHER 1: *(laughing uneasily)*
Who's the crocs? Them or us?

(The Guide plays a quick, little Game of Crocodiles with the tourists)

USHERS AND CAST: *(together)*
Tourists, tip!

USHER 1:

It says here in the guidebook that, like most countries, the tip is 10 to 15% of the bill.

MEXICAN GUIDE: *(as two car-parking helpers in grey coveralls enter)*

Official car-parking helpers in grey uniforms will help you to park your car, Señor. They'll watch it for you.

USHER 4:

What if I don't want my car watched?

MEXICAN GUIDE:

Do you want it eaten, Señor?

USHER 3: *(laughing)*

Oh, go on, they don't eat cars here.

MEXICAN GUIDE: *(shrugging)*

I would give him a peso, or he'll eat your car.

USHER 1:

That's crazy.

MEXICAN GUIDE:

They're eating.

(The Car-Parking Helpers perform a quick Car-Devouring Ceremony as the tourists gape.)

USHERS AND CAST: *(together)*

Tourists, signal!

USHER 2: *(frantically)*

What kind of signal?

MEXICAN GUIDE:

Don' you know your signals?

USHER 4:

It says here in the book.

USHER 3:

What signals?

MEXICAN GUIDE:

You'd better learn your signals, Señor. Look out! They're coming!

(Several eager vendors accost the tourists and wander through the audience, selling fervently their incredible variety of wares.)

USHERS 2 & 4: *(desperate)*
What's the signal? What's the signal? Teach us, please.

MEXICAN GUIDE:
Wag your finger.

USHER 1:
Wag my finger?

MEXICAN GUIDE:
That's all, Señor. Wag your finger.

USHER 1:
Wag my finger? What the hell good is that?

USHER 3: *(trying)*
You can't chase a dog away just wagging your finger.

MEXICAN GUIDE:
Wag your finger severely, Señor, like this. *(He illustrates.)* Remember, severe finger-wagging!

(Severe finger-wagging taken up by everyone finally succeeds in chasing the Vendors away.)

USHERS AND CAST: *(together)*
Tourists, collapse.

USHER 4: *(moaning)*
That's enough sight-seeing. My feet ache.

USHER 3:
I'm thirsty

USHER 2:
I'm starved.

USHER 3:
I'm thirsty. I want a cold beer.

USHER 1:
Out here? Are you crazy? There's no beer.

USHER 3: *(grimly determined)*
I'm going to drink the water.

USHER 1:

Out of the tap? Are you crazy? Do you want to get Montezuma's Revenge?

USHERS 3: *(taking out pills confidently)*

Don't worry. I've got my own purification system. *(He reads the label.)* One tablet per pint of water.

USHER 2:

Oh, I am thirsty. Do you think it'll work?

USHER 3:

Of course it'll work. Guaranteed by the pharmaceutical company. Let's see. About ten pints of water. Ten pills ought to be enough for everybody.

(He mixes and they all drink, some confidently, some with anxiety.)

MEXICAN GUIDE AND OTHER CAST MEMBERS: *(calling impatiently)*

Tourists, sightsee!

USHER 2: *(with renewed enthusiasm)*

We must go to the Floating Gardens.

USHER 4:

Oh yes, I want to see them.

MEXICAN GUIDE:

Red canoes cost 20 pesos. Black canoes cost 25. Green canoes cost 30.

USHER 4: *(giggling)*

I want an Aztec raft, I don't want a canoe.

USHER 3: *(staring suddenly offstage)*

What's that?

MEXICAN GUIDE:

You have your wish, Señora. Your Aztec raft.

(The raft floats in. MONTEZUMA is aboard in full regalia.)

USHER 1: *(gaping)*

Who's that on the raft?

USHER 2:

Must be some guy they dress up that way.

USHER 4:

Maybe some Aztec.

USHER 3:

They don't have Aztecs any more.

USHER 4: *(doggedly)*

Well, they have some Indians left.

MEXICAN GUIDE: *(frightened)*

You have your wish, Señores. It's Montezuma! *(He runs away.)*

USHER 1:

You can't trust these guides. Now what are we going to do?

USHER 3:

God, these canals are polluted. I can't stand the stench.

USHER 4:

The Aztecs used to build gardens on rafts and set them afloat. Look, he's riding on a raft of flowers!

USHER 3:

Yeah, through the crap in the water.

MONTEZUMA:

Tourists! I summon you to Montezuma's Revenge!

USHER 4:

What's up? What's he mean?

USHER 3:

Don't worry; he's joking.

MONTEZUMA:

Clutch your asses. Grab your intestines. I am the God of Scattering.

(All of the tourists begin to writhe.)

USHER 1:

What the hell's he saying? I can't understand a word.

USHER 3:

Speak English. We can't understand you.

(The tourists begin to clutch their asses, intestines, etc.)

MONTEZUMA:

The God of Scattering can never die. His sins have committed him to the winds of time. Unable to sleep, he weaves his scattering through the Star-Gods of Night and the Sun-God of Day. My people scattered my desire forever through their floating flowers, as the Spaniards scattered my gold in their lust for power. Reborn, the God of Scattering lives forever. Through your blood, he scatters the pain of his conquerors! Through your bowels, he scatters the ache of his bondage! Invisible, blowing through your flesh, he scatters you!

(He scatters flowers over them as the tourists writhe in agony.)

USHER 1: *(writhing)*
It must have been the water. We should have drunk bottled water.

USHER 3:
No, it was those refried beans. How can you re-fry beans?

USHER 4: *(moaning)*
That damn lunch. It must have been the green mole sauce. I never could stand green sauce.

USHER 2:
We should have stuck to American food.

MONTEZUMA:
Remember the lost God of Scattering. Wherever you go, recall my scattering power. Montezuma's Revenge!

(He holds up his arms and cries out savagely and mournfully several times, "Montezuma's Revenge!" as the tourists continue to writhe.)

(10) CLOSE WAR, DISTANT WAR

(Man's "progress" in war, with emphasis on American variations. The entire cast plays this piece and divides up the sound poems. The USHERS should usher, watch, and play prominent parts. Rhythmically, this piece is dependent on music. Shock cords can be used to simulate weapons at various points. The effect of the scene should be a kind of miniature history of war from naked early man to grotesquely uniformed modern man. The scene moves from an intimate, growling animal warfare to remote, distant technological warfare. As the scene begins, two almost naked, animal-looking tribesmen hop about a pile of stones. As they hop, they utter weird sounds of recognition.)

TRIBESMEN:
Sto-oh . . .
ohh . . .
stooo . . .

on . . . onnn . . . *(They sit on stones as if on eggs.)*

sto . . . sto . . .

oh . . . sto . . . ohhh . . .

stones . . . stones . . . stones!

(They get into a fight, throwing stones at each other, and run away. High up on a perch, a hunter appears. He is a little more clothed, although still semi-naked. The tribesmen threaten him from below, throwing their stones.)

HUNTER: *(muttering, as he improvises a desperate, defensive weapon)*

Sli . . . ing . . .

Sli . . . ing . . .

Sliiiinggg . . .

Sho . . . shoooo . . .

Show!

Sliing-shooow . . .

Sliing-shooooow . . .

Sliiing-shoot . . .

Sliiing-shooot . . .

Sliiing-shot! . . .

(In ecstasy, firing stones with his slingshot, he chases the tribesmen away.)

(A Wild Beast played by two actors appears and attacks the Hunter whose sling shot is totally ineffective against the Beast. The Beast conquers and is dragging the Hunter off when another, more sophisticated [and just a little more clothed] Hunter appears high up.)

HUNTER II: *(improvising a bow and arrow)*

B . . . b . . . b . . .

ow . . . ow . . . ow . . .

B . . . bb . . . bow . . .

Bow . . . bow . . . bow

air . . . air . . . air . . .

oh . . . oh . . . oh . . .

air—oh! . . . air—oh! (with delight)

Bow—air—oh! . . . Bow—Arrow!

(He shoots and the Beast falls. Now two groups of tribesmen appear. The High Tribesmen are up high crawling around as if in trees and foliage. They improvise blowguns and throwing spears against the Low Tribesmen. Dancing around in a circle, the Low Tribesmen improvise Boomerangs. Then as the Boomerangs prove ineffective, they improvise Guerrilla Warfare with Darts and Javelins.)

HIGH TRIBESMEN:
Blooow . . . Blooow . . . Wiind . . .
Blooow-Wiiind . . .
Blooow-Suuun . . .
Blooow-Guuun! . . .

OTHER HIGH TRIBESMEN: *(improvising spears)*
spiii . . . spiii . . .
peeer . . . peeer . . .
speeer . . . speeer . . .
throoowing-speeear . . .

(They hurl their spears and blow their guns.)

LOW TRIBESMEN: *(chanting in their circle)*
ang-ry . . . ang-ry . . . ang-ry . . .
boom, boom, angry, angry,
boom, boom
boom-er-angry
boom-er-angry
boom-er-ang!

(They hurl their boomerangs unsuccessfully and are forced to scatter. They crawl around like apes for shelter.)

grrr . . . gorrr-ill-a . . .
gorr-ill-a . . .
war-war-WAR! . . .
Guerrilla War!

LOW GROUP 1:	LOW GROUP 2:
Dare . . . dare . . . dare . . .	Jab . . . jav . . . jab . . .
dar . . . dar . . . dart!	Jabber them . . . jabber
	them . . .
	Jav-e-lin . . . Jav-e-lin!

(They throw their darts and hurl their javelins from guerrilla warfare positions and scatter the High Tribesmen. Two Catholic soldiers ride on, one with a sword, one with a lance. They ride imaginary horses.)

SOLDIER 1: *(improvising as he fights)*
Sooore . . . Sooore . . .
Orrrder . . . Orrrder . . .
Soooreder . . . Soooreder . . .
Soord . . . Swoord . . .

SOLDIER 2:

Chaance . . . chaaance . . .
Laaash . . . laaaash . . .
Laaance . . . Laaance! . . .

(The soldier with the lance is the victor and rides off in triumph. A Chinese gentleman in ninth-century China is seen mixing and improvising gunpowder.)

CHINESE GENTLEMAN:

pow . . . poow . . . pooow-der . . .
po-tass-i-um—niiight . . .
po-tass-i-um ni-trate—seventy-five
                        per cent
sell . . . selll . . . selll . . .
sell-for . . . sell-for . . .
sul-fur . . . sul-fur . . . sul-fur . . . ten per
                        cent
core . . . core . . . core . . .
car-bon . . . car-bon . . . car-bon . . . fifteen
                        per cent

(He lights it with delight and disappears in the explosive smoke.)

(The Lower and Higher Tribesmen come back now more fully dressed in pieces of 17th- and 18-century battledress. The rhythm of the music is faster and increasingly jagged.)

LOWER TRIBESMEN: *(with pistols as they crawl towards the Higher Tribesmen)*
pisss . . . pisss . . .
telll . . . tellll . . .
pisss-tol . . . pisss-tolll . . .

re-volve . . . re-volve . . .
re-volve-er
re-volve-er . . .

HIGHER TRIBESMEN: *(improvising rifles)*
ri-hit . . . ri-hit . . .
tri-fle . . . tri-fle . . .
ri-fle . . . ri-fle . . .

LOWER TRIBESMEN: *(Seeing that they're losing, they improvise machine guns.)*
smash . . . smash . . . smash . . .
mash-een . . . mash-een . . .

smash-een guns
smash-een guns . . .

HIGHER TRIBESMEN: *(In danger of rout, they return fire with bombs.)*
High-er, high-er!
Boom, boom, boom . . .
ohm, ohm, ohm . . .
Bomb . . . boomb . . . bomb!

LOWER TRIBESMEN: *(In danger of defeat, they take to naval power.)*
Low-er . . . low-er . . .
Take to sea . . .
Booat . . . boooat . . . booat . . .
Gun-booat . . . Gun-boooat . . .
Des-troy . . . des-troy . . . des-troy . . .
Des-troy-er . . . des-troy-er . . .
Battle, battle, battle!
Battle-ship! Battle-ship! Battle-ship!

(They tow small ship-models across the stage.)

HIGHER TRIBESMEN: *(suffering from naval warfare)*
Higher! Higher! Higher!

(The higher and lower distances between the Tribesmen are more and more emphasized. The Higher Tribesmen begin to hurl model airplanes at the Lower Tribesmen. Most of the planes can be paper, but it would be visually effective to have a few more threatening wooden or metal models—or even wild-sculptured, abstract plane shapes—to hurl down. The Higher Tribesmen improvise names of planes from World War I to World War II.)
Puuup . . . Pup!
Caaam-el . . . Camel . . .
Salamander . . .
Dolphin . . .
Sniiipe . . .
Spad . . .
Albatross . . .
Fokker Tri-plane
Red Barrron . . .

Wild-cat,
    Bear-cat,
        Double Wasp,
            Sky-raider,

Messy-schmitt ty-phooon,
Yak, Yak! Yak!
Flying Fortress
(Little Friends, Little Friends!)
Spit-fire, Spit-fire, Spit-fire,
Mustang, Mustang,
Sabre-jet, Sabre-jet, Sabre-jet!

LOWER TRIBESMEN: *(responding to the threat)*
Periscope . . .
Submarine . . .
Torpedo . . .
Polaris missile!

(A missile soars out of the floor towards the Higher Tribesmen.)

OFFSTAGE VOICE: *(very metallic and loud and impersonal)*
Trinity!

(The Tribesmen are all dead, frozen in position)

OFFSTAGE VOICE:
A - Bomb . . .
H - Bomb . . .
Anti-Personnel Bomb . . .
Automated Battlefield . . .

(After the word, Trinity, *the lights go out.* A-Bomb, H-Bomb, *and* Anti-Personnel Bomb *are spoken very slowly and impersonally in total darkness. There is a long pause after* Anti-Personnel Bomb *and a series of tiny lights like an illuminated computer glow and flicker rapidly in the dark. After the words,* Automated Battlefield, *the music stops, while the tiny lights continue to blink around the theatre. The scene ends with a sound poem performed by the entire cast based on the word* Vietnamization *and uttered as a curse and exorcism.)*

CAST:
MIRV War-heads . . .MIRV War-heads . . .
Viet Name—Atten-tion . . .
Viet . . .
Vie—et . . .
WE ET . . .
WE ET
WE ET NAME

WE ATE NAME OF NA-TION
VE-ET-real . . . *real* . . . *real* . . .
VI-ET-REEL-IS-A-TION
VI-ET TV REEL-IS-A-TION . . .
VI-ET NAME IS OUR NATION . . .
VI-ET NAME IS OUR MISS-SION . . .
VI-ET NUUUUMB . . .
VI-ET NUUUMMMB . . .
VI-ET DAAAMMMNAAA-TION . . .
WE-ET NAME-OF-NATION . . .
WE-ET-NAME-OF-NAA-SSHUUNN . . .
VIET-NAM-IZ-A-TION . . .

(Slowly, the lights blink out as the actors go off.)

(11) THE REVOLUTIONARY FIGUREHEAD

USHER 1: *(looking around slowly)*
All those dead people.

USHER 3:
They just look dead. We only saw them, we only ushered them on tele-vision. It's just a television death.

USHER 2:
You mean we never really saw them killed from the air?

USHER 4:
Of course not. They're too far away to die. We just ushered them.

USHER 3:
Don't be stupid. Don't put it that way. We didn't *just* usher them. We survived didn't we? We've made the longest journey ushers have ever made.

USHER 4:
Really? The longest journey?

USHER 3:
An usher learns how to travel. We're the survivors.

USHER 1: *(pointing to the grimy, bloody figure of the* REVOLUTIONARY FIGUREHEAD)
What's that? Isn't that a survivor?

USHER 3:
Don't you know what that is? It's not alive really.

USHER 2: *(frightened)*
But it's moving!

USHER 1: *(pointing)*
Look! It's opening its mouth!

USHER 3:
Nothing. It's only a Revolutionary Figurehead.

USHER 4:
Do we have to usher *it* again?

USHER 1:
You mean you've ushered it before?

USHER 3:
Over and over.

USHER 4:
It endures.

USHER 2:
Look at the insignia.

USHER 1: *(alarmed)*
Is that color war paint?

USHER 2:
Is it Indian?

USHER 3: *(examining the* FIGUREHEAD *cautiously)*
It's covered with illegible inscriptions. Look.

USHER 4: *(trying to decipher an inscription)*
Make . . . War . . . Not Peace . . .

USHER 3:
Stupid! It's the other way round.

USHER 1: *(examining)*
I can make this out vaguely . . . 17 . . . 76 . . .'

USHER 2:
Looks like it. But we can't be sure.

USHER 3:

We hold these truths . . . to be self . . . I can't make out the rest.

(Slowly, the REVOLUTIONARY FIGUREHEAD *has come to life. Now, it breaks away suddenly from the* USHERS *in terror and begins to dig frantically.)*

USHER 4:

What is it doing?

USHER 3:

Can't you see? Digging.

USHER 2:

Digging? For what?

USHER 4:

Revolutionary survivors. Companions.

(The REVOLUTIONARY FIGUREHEAD *throws down the shovel and plunges his hands in the earth.)*

USHER 1:

How lovely the earth is.

USHER 3:

The black earth.

USHER 2:

The dying leaves.

USHER 4:

The seed.

USHER 2: *(pointing to the Figurehead)*

It's *enjoying* the earth.

USHER 3:

No, it's committing a funeral.

USHER 4:

Committing a funeral? Do we usher that?

USHER 1:

It can't speak.

(The REVOLUTIONARY FIGUREHEAD *begins to mumble wildly.)*

USHER 4:

Listen . . .

REVOLUTIONARY FIGUREHEAD: *(digging and speaking wildly)*

I bury myself. I bury myself. I bury myself. *(looking around suspiciously)* Who's watching. No one. Good, I bury myself. As the Voice of Revolution, I am forgotten. I bury myself in every store, on every highway. In banks, in real estate offices, I bury myself in coins, in cash, in mortgages. Look for me in your automobile graveyards. Watch me freeze in your all-night, air-conditioned supermarkets. Listen for my burial as your television antennae pierce the night with selling messages. In the hustling wind you'll hear my buried signal from the past. In Pioneer Museums, Veterans Hospitals, Daughters of the Revolution, Sons of Foreign Wars, Old People's Rest Homes, I bury myself.

USHER 4:

Old. It's so old.

REVOLUTIONARY FIGUREHEAD: *(looking around frantically)*

Only once a year I revive. I resurrect! Once a year I am liberated. Once a year I walk through my lost country in freedom, independence.

USHER 2:

Once a year?

USHER 4:

That's when it comes out.

USHER 1:

Out of what?

USHER 3: *(pointing)*

Out of its grave.

USHER 2:

It's unfair. We have to usher that too.

USHER 1:

It's only a Figurehead.

USHER 3:

Once a year it's liberated.

USHER 4: *(protesting)*

We don't know when it is.

USHER 2:

If we pretend to help it bury itself, maybe it'll tell us the date.

USHER 1:

What difference does the date make?

USHER 3:

It's the date of liberation. Even you should know what liberation means.

USHER 4:

Let's try. *(They help the* FIGUREHEAD *dig. After a moment the* FIGURE-HEAD *thrusts them away.)*

REVOLUTIONARY FIGUREHEAD:

You can't trick me. You're trying to bury me. I bury myself!

USHER 3:

We want to help you. It's our duty to usher you.

REVOLUTIONARY FIGUREHEAD:

No, I bury myself. *(digging frantically)* Look, here, I buried it. I've found it.

USHER 4:

What?

REVOLUTIONARY FIGUREHEAD: *(showing objects)*

My firecrackers, my sparklers, my mementos.

(The FIGUREHEAD *lights a sparkler.)*

USHER 3: *(slowly)*

It thinks it's July 4.

USHER 4:

The date of liberation.

USHER 2:

That's when we usher it.

USHER 1:

To independence. To 1776.

USHER 3:

We can't go backward. We lead the parade.

USHER 2:

Where do we lead it?

USHER 3:

Remember we are ushers. It is enough to lead.

USHER 4: (echoing)

We merely usher. We attend to things. We watch. We celebrate the Revolutionary Figurehead.

REVOLUTIONARY FIGUREHEAD: (setting off a firecracker and waving a sparkler as they approach to escort him.)

Take me! Take me! I will show you the way to Freedom. The way to liberation!

(They usher and parade the REVOLUTIONARY FIGUREHEAD around to brassy music and fireworks. Finally, they arrive at the STATUE OF LIBERTY.)

(12) THE AMERICAN ORACLE

(The parade ends inevitably before the STATUE OF LIBERTY. The fierce, mask-like face of the STATUE that has been carried in during the opening processional is still on the floor. At the foot of the Statue is a cave-like opening. Two Contemporary Prophets wait here to write out the Oracles which they pass up to the invisible STATUE-GODDESS to speak.)

STAGEHANDS:

Give us a hand. This damn face gets heavier every time. You lousy ushers are always early.

(The USHERS help the stagehands lift the face of the STATUE into place.)

PROPHET 1:

Joe, you've got to write today. I've got a hangover. Those aspirin didn't help.

PROPHET 2:

What's the Oracle scheduled for today?

PROPHET 1:

Who knows what they brought this time. Some small hick town parade.

PROPHET 2:

Looks like an old figurehead. They probably picked it up in some weird antique shop.

PROPHET 1:

What the hell good does it do to prophesy the past? That's what they always want. This is really a future business. *(They continue discussing and arguing.)*

USHER 1: *(as the* USHERS *struggle with the face)*
Her face is so big.

USHER 2:
She looks fierce.

USHER 4:
She's got an eagle face.

USHER 3:
So she can see a long distance.

STATUE OF LIBERTY: *(Her invisible voice is heard.)*
All right, let's get going. I don't have all day.

(They swing the face-mask into place. Behind the face-mask, the Oracle's voice is heard over the loudspeaker system.)

STATUE OF LIBERTY:
Testing . . . 1 . . . 2 . . . 3 . . . 4 . . . All right, Ushers . . . Are you ready?

(Through the usual bureaucratic confusion, with the Prophets showing increasing irritation, a sheaf of enigmas is handed out to USHER 1*)*

USHER 3: *(trying desperately to assert order)*
We're ready, Goddess.

STATUE OF LIBERTY:
Let the usher approach.

USHER 1: *(approaching, mounting a stand or pulpit)*
Oh Goddess of Liberty, we bring you the enigma of a lost figurehead wandering in time who cannot rest, a figurehead who needs the peace of your sacred prophecy.

(Some of the USHERS *circulate through the audience with paper and pencil asking members of the audience if they wish to submit an enigma for prophecy.* USHER 1 *reads from an old list of enigmas.)*

USHER 1:
What crawls on four legs at dawn, walks on two legs at noon, and sports three legs in the evening?

STATUE OF LIBERTY:

You are reading archaic enigmas. Where is the clerk? Can't you ever get the agenda straight?

USHER 1: *(After a flurry of activity beneath the* STATUE, *more recent clipboard enigmas are handed up to* USHER 1.)

"Give me your homeless . . . yearning to be free . . . Who will fly in freedom, oh Goddess? Where will the homeless fly to find homes?

STATUE OF LIBERTY: *(in her oracular voice)*

For those people who can fly, I see a desert lake opening in the wasteland, a desert lake created by a miraculous dam. Over that lake in the desert soars the transplanted cultural landmark of the London Bridge. On an island in that desert lake, guarded by new electronic warning system, live the freedom-seekers. *(a roll of drums)* Next enigma.

USHER 1: *(reading)*

What balm will flow to heal the Generation Gap of old experience and young energy?

STATUE OF LIBERTY:

The balm of youth, of vigorous action. There will be no death. All veins of metal and blood will flow freely. Everyone will be eternally young. *(a roll of drums)* Next enigma.

USHER 1: *(reading)*

"Gemini has soared into space. How will Gemini affect the American system of checks and balances?"

STATUE OF LIBERTY:

Gemini will rule. The President and Vice-President shall be interchangeable twins. Political faces will be as sensitive as masks. Neither twin shall be more powerful than the other although both twins shall masquerade for each other.

(By this time the USHERS *have collected questions from the audience.* USHER 1 *reads the questions, or each usher can read them in turn. Certain answers are improvised on the spot by the Contemporary Prophets to meet local situations and needs depending on where the play is being performed. Other answers are selected by the Prophets from their Book of All Possible Answers. The latter include:*

1) "I Hear America Singing," cried our Great, Grey Poet. Join the Song Festival. If you can't sing, have your American hearing checked. The new American hearing aids are excellent.

2) Don't worry about Death. There is no death. There is only American Youth. Worry about your American Resurrection.

3) Liberty believes in Freedom of the Press. Everyone is free to sell as many newspapers as possible. Pleasure is freedom.

4) Love is the end to all problems. Give yourself to love. Don't forget to take a little too. Taking is perfectly American.

5) "Self-Reliance" is the American motto. Rely on yourself and forget about others.

6) There is no Greening of America. America is Red, White and Blue. Pursue your American stars.

7) America is the most religious country in the world. We have more churches, more religions, than any other country. If the world needs a better religion, we'll make it.

8) Take advantage of the new moon status. Visit the American moon for sanctuary. Use the American moon for lost magic.

9) Someone is ready to pay for your ideas. Approach with caution. Acquiesce only if the price is right. Modesty is not an American virtue.

10) Good household buys are available. Team up with personable individuals to raid the stores. The time is now to add to your personal possessions.

11) American Power is constitutional. Make certain that your American Power is stronger than your opponent's power.

12) Practice your vacations. Get out on the highway and go. American practice makes perfect.

13) Believe in your President because he has more information. Remember you have no hot-line telephones. The President is informed by telephones and computers.

(The number and rhythm of the answers depend of course on the immediate performing situation. At the appropriate moment, the enigmas from the audience are cut off and USHER 3 *approaches the* STATUE OF LIBERTY.*)*

USHER 3:
Oh Goddess, we Ushers request permission to add the enigma mentioned earlier by my colleagues to the agenda.

STATUE OF LIBERTY:
Oh yes, that figurehead. What time is it?

USHER 4:

July 4.

STATUE OF LIBERTY:

In that case, just one more enigma. But make it short.

REVOLUTIONARY FIGUREHEAD: *(approaching, pushing* USHERS *aside)*

This is my enigma. Mine. I'll present it myself. Get out of the way.

USHERS: *(protesting)*

We're the Ushers. You can't present your own enigma. That's out of order. Against the rules.

STATUE OF LIBERTY:

Stop wasting time, Let him present his enigma.

REVOLUTIONARY FIGUREHEAD:

My enigma has few words. It speaks to the winds of time. You are a Statue. Can you answer it?

STATUE OF LIBERTY:

I can answer anything.

REVOLUTIONARY FIGUREHEAD:

What is the future of the American Revolution?

STATUS OF LIBERTY:

What's that? Repeat, please.

REVOLUTIONARY FIGUREHEAD:

What is the future of the American Revolution?

STATUE OF LIBERTY:

That's what I thought you asked. *(with a loud whisper)* Hurry up with the prophecy, you dolts. *(after a rustling of papers, she pronounces:)* "The future of the American revolution lies in the past. When the past is accepted and tamed, when the rough is made smooth and the land lies pacified, blessed by the wires and machines of plenty, then the future of law and order, the destiny, the victory of Revolution, shall be secure.

REVOLUTIONARY FIGUREHEAD:

I do not accept your prophecy.

USHER 1:

Wait a minute, you can't do that.

USHER 2:

You have to be buried.

USHER 3:

Just lie down here quietly.

USHER 4:

We'll usher you.

STATUE OF LIBERTY:

What's going on down there? I can't hear myself speak. What the hell's the noise about?

USHER 1:

This figurehead refuses to accept your prophecy.

STATUE OF LIBERTY:

One of those, huh? A resister. Don't you know it's almost impossible to change a prophecy? It takes a two-thirds majority. So you don't want to accept my prophecy. Who do you think you are?

REVOLUTIONARY FIGUREHEAD:

I will not accept your prophecy.

STATUE OF LIBERTY:

There you go again. *(to the* USHERS*)* All right, usher him up here.

USHER 1:

You want him in the Statue?

STATUE OF LIBERTY:

Never mind where I want him. What business is it of yours. Stick to your god damn ushering and bring him up here. We'll see what happens. I could use a substitute for some of those stupid prophets.

(As the REVOLUTIONARY FIGUREHEAD *is ushered warily up to the head of the* STATUE OF LIBERTY, *several veterans in ragged, worn uniforms appear around the* STATUE. *In passionate, crazy fury, while the veterans watch impassively, the* REVOLUTIONARY FIGUREHEAD *addresses the* STATUE *and the audience.)*

REVOLUTIONARY FIGUREHEAD:

Have you sold Santa Claus on July 4? Have you masqueraded in your revolutionary costumes? I hear America singing, but why are your songs so sad? Why are your movies X-rated? If there's a revolution here, I'm for it. Find your color. Find your humanity. Break out of your secret status quo.

155

One shout of laughter by land. Two shouts of freedom by sea. Why is freedom a plastic in your breakfast food? Shall we save ourselves by killing foreigners? Have you checked your color in the mirror? All power to the people who are people.

(*Silence as the veterans close in around the* REVOLUTIONARY FIGUREHEAD *facing the audience. Through the silence, the voice of the* STATUE OF LIBERTY *is heard.*)

STATUE OF LIBERTY:
Wait!

USHER 3: (*calling to the Statue*)
This Figurehead is taking over. What'll we do with him? Shall we usher him out?

USHER 1:
Leave him alone.

USHER 3:
I'll call the police. They'll take care of him.

USHER 4:
No, call a doctor. He's insane. He must be committed.

USHER 2:
You can't do that. Let him talk.

USHER 3:
Don't be stupid. He's crazy. It's our job to usher him out.

USHER 1:
If you call the police you'll start a riot.

USHER 2: (*from the audience*)
They're nervous back here.

(*They quarrel amongst themselves until the* STATUE OF LIBERTY *cuts them off impatiently.*)

STATUE OF LIBERTY:
Stop your quarreling. Get back to ushering.

USHER 3:
Wait a minute. How do we usher them?

STATUE OF LIBERTY:
Serenade me. Praise me. Entertain them. Take their minds off things.

156

Give them a final song, a little fancy footwork. Then usher them out
politely so they don't watch any more. Usher them with proper ceremony.

*(The entire cast join in the exit ceremonies. They turn facing the audience
and sing the final hymn of the Ushers:)*

HYMN OF THE USHERS:
Oh Goddess of Liberty
We sing you to sleep—
When the morning comes,
Will you smile or weep?

Save us, oh Goddess
On our journey through time,
As Ushers we travel
Through cities, through crime. . .

As Ushers we walk,
We laugh and we fly
Away from our homes—
We seek till we die . . .

Oh Goddess of Liberty
We sing you to sleep . . .
When the morning comes,
Will you smile or weep?

(As the cast continues singing, the USHERS *begin to usher the audience out.
The ragged, anonymous veterans stand watching silently as the audience is
ushered out. At a given moment, the cast suddenly stops singing. They
stand, watchers in time, as the* USHERS *continue their polite, ceremonial
ushering.)*

THE END

NOTE

In 1970, Brown University, where I was teaching, was shut down by a strike, like
many other universities, because of the invasion of Cambodia that expanded the Viet
Nam War. In Providence, and in Washington where I was sent as a member of a university delegation to protest the invasion to government officials, I witnessed many
of the events that I transformed into *The Ushers*. It seemed to me the country was
drifting dangerously, being *ushered* along without any real debate of ideas. *The*

Ushers was written as the second play of a trilogy about "The Fantasies of Power" emerging out of the 1960s around the world. This trilogy includes *Lovecraft's Follies, The Ushers,* and *Cathedral of Ice,* which was printed first by Peter Kaplan's Pour-Boire Press, and re-printed in 1987 by Theatre Communications Group, Inc., in the anthology, *Plays of the Holocaust,* edited by Elinor Fuchs.

In *The Ushers,* too, I was interested in experimenting with the possibilities of environmental theatre which was becoming prominent in the 1960s. Later, in 1973, I wrote and edited a book called *Breakout! In Search of New Theatrical Environments* that was published by The Swallow Press. *The Ushers* was written for the Brown University Theatre. The occasion was a special environmental production in Andrews Hall, a large dining hall in which we utilized many different spaces. The play was staged as part of the Brown Festival of the Arts in November, 1971.

The Ushers was directed by James O. Barnhill, chairman of the Brown University Theatre Department; Julie Strandberg was the choreographer; John Lucas the designer; and Gerald Shapiro composed the music. The cast included actors from the community as well as students from Brown University: Gordon M. Stanley, Anne Winter, Jane Schickler, John Edinburg, Kate Phelps, Andrew Roth, Marilyn Meardon, Marc W. Kohler, Steven G. Judd, David Welch, Joel Leffert, Linda Reif, William Fritzmeier, Barton St. Armand, Keith Waldrop, Rob Anderson, Nancy A. Chrestos, Melissa C. Bradford, Jenny Sachs, Amanda Hansen, Judy Dashevsky, Sherifa Zuhur, Margot Schevill, Kathy Spiegelman, Michael Tobin, Guy Tuttle, Ancelin Lynch, and Cushing Pagan. Frank Baranowski and Larry Dilea helped John Lucas with the technical side of the production.

MOTHER
MOTHER O
O

or the last American Mother

To Judith Swift and Charles Caffone

"The Mother is a matchless beast."

Spanish proverb

"If a woman grows weary and at last dies from childbearing, it matters not. Let her only die from bearing; she is there to do it."

Martin Luther

"Let France have good mothers and she will have good sons."

Napoleon

"My mother's birthday is my most holy holiday."

Harry Houdini

CAST

——

MOTHER O, Miriam Abendstern, the Last American Mother, a striking fifty-two-year-old powerhouse with a craze for Cole Porter's music and Martha Graham's dances.

THE SON, Henry Abend, a thirty-year-old schizophrenic linguistic genius.

THE GHOST FATHER, Rudy Abendstern, some fifty-five ghost-like years, mathematician and computer specialist, a haunting presence.

THE PIANIST, He does not speak, but he interacts with Mother O as her alter ego. He is an integral part of the production, sitting at an upright piano upstage on the edge of Mother O's room, playing Mother O's inimitable music in the vein of Cole Porter. His effect should be film-like, as in the old days of a pianist accompanying a silent film.

SETTING

The single setting shows the Son's room at stage left, Mother O's room at stage right, and part of a kitchen in between. More expressionistic than naturalistic, the rooms have been altered to express the personalities of the occupants. At the beginning, the kitchen is filled with a variety of canned goods, with most of the labels torn off or written over with huge images and letters. Mother O's room is neat and strictly arranged for artistic escape. A conspicuous, large portrait of Cole Porter, painted by Mother O, is on the wall. On a desk is a smaller photograph of her Ghost Husband. The Son's room is incredibly littered with books, pamphlets, magazines, newspapers in foreign languages, dictionaries. A rickety writing desk holds an ancient, battered office typewriter. On the walls are strange, colorful, concrete linguistic poems, one very sexual. On one wall is painted in large letters, Joyce's famous line, "SILENCE, CUNNING, EXILE . . ." The play takes place today.

PROLOGUE

(At stage right, the SON *is asleep, dreaming, tossing and turning on his cot in his littered room. At stage left,* MOTHER O *and the* GHOST FATHER *toss in their bed. The lights come up mysteriously on the potted palm by Mother O's piano, where the* PIANIST *is playing her inimitable music in the style of Cole Porter. In the Son's dream, it is as if the scene were transformed into the Garden of Eden. Startled awake by the Son's screaming, "Mother O!", the* GHOST FATHER *rushes over and pushes the* SON *back in his bed. A male voice is heard on tape echoed by a woman's voice in Hebrew:)*

MALE VOICE ON TAPE:
"And the Lord God planted a garden eastward in Eden . . ."

SON:
Father! You look like a ghost!

GHOST FATHER:
You need to escape from Mother O! You know how she was born?

MALE VOICE ON TAPE:
"And the Lord God caused a deep sleep to fall upon Adam . . ."

SON *(still in his nightmare):*
I'm not Adam!

MALE VOICE ON TAPE:
"And the Lord took one of Adam's ribs . . ."

SON:
Not my rib! God, I'm dreaming!

MALE VOICE ON TAPE:
"And out of the rib, which the Lord God had taken from man, made he a woman and brought her unto the man . . ."

(MOTHER O *rises up from her bed.)*

SON *(crying out):*
He brought me Mother O!

MOTHER O *(to the Ghost Father):*
What are you doing to my boy?

163

GHOST FATHER:

Trying to teach him independence . . . *(With a great gesture, he produces a rib, as if out of the son's body.)* You see that?

SON:

What is it?

GHOST FATHER *(flourishing the rib):*

A man's rib! *"And Adam said she shall be called Woman because she was taken out of man!"* . . . That's all Mother O is, a man's rib!

SON:

You're crazy!

MOTHER O:

It won't work, Rudy. He doesn't get it.

GHOST FATHER *(doggedly):*

Look, son, God took the rib out of Adam and transformed the pronoun it into she. That's in the Old Testament. A male rib becomes a woman. That means woman is subordinate to man, and you don't have to hide in bed anymore from your mother.

SON *(wildly):*

Maybe God got it wrong! There she is, Mother O! Maybe I was formed out of *her* rib!

MOTHER O:

You're striking out, Rudy.

GHOST FATHER:

Son, she's just your mother. You don't have to worship her. You were born out of her womb . . .

SON:

If I was born out of her womb, how come ribs are so important?

MOTHER O:

He'll never get past the rib stage, Rudy.

GHOST FATHER:

He calls you Mother O because he loves you. I'll make him think of you as Ma Barker. That'll cure him!

SON *(alarmed):*

What are you up to? Who's Ma Barker?

(The GHOST FATHER *puts on a hat and transforms into J. Edgar Hoover, pulling a toy machine gun out from under the Son's bed.)*

GHOST FATHER *(as if hypnotizing the* SON *in the dream):*
Look at me . . . I'm J. Edgar Hoover, the most famous law man in American history, the head of the F.B.I. I'm a bachelor who lives with my mother in Washington, D.C. until she dies at the age of eighty . . .

SON *(shouting):*
I've got a long time! Mother O has a long way to go until eighty!

GHOST FATHER *(impatiently):*
No, no, watch! . . . J. Edgar's foremost enemy is a woman, the great criminal gangleader, Ma Barker . . . Ma Barker is adept at disguises . . . One of her disguises is . . . *(Holding a toy machine gun,* MOTHER O *transforms into Ma Barker.)*

MOTHER O:
I'm Ma Barker, J. Edgar! . . . You'll never take me alive!

(They fire at each other with a shrill "Rat-atat-tat! Rat-atat-tat! as the SON *scrambles for cover.)*

GHOST FATHER:
At Ma Barker's knee, her sons become the most vicious, cold-blooded crew of murderers and kidnappers we at the F.B.I. have ever known!

SON *(shouting from behind the bed):*
You can't say that about Mother!

GHOST FATHER *(angrily):*
Open your eyes! In the case of the Ma Barker gang, the major criminal factors were home and mother!

(As Hoover, he and Ma Barker shoot it out, and Ma Barker falls, with her toy machine gun "clutched to her breast." The Ghost Father, his gun drawn as Hoover, approaches her body cautiously.)

Ma Barker was killed in a shoot-out with my F.B.I. agents in Florida in 1935, her machine gun, still hot, clutched to her breast . . .

SON *(accusingly):*
You killed Mother!

MOTHER O *(lifting herself up):*
You draw another blank, Rudy. How are you going to get out of this?

GHOST FATHER *(to the Son consolingly):*
> Don't worry, son, I made amends . . . After we killed Ma Barker, I paid
> a special Thanksgiving tribute to my mother. I gave Mama a canary that I
> bought from our famous federal prisoner, the Birdman of Alcatraz . . .

SON *(in anguish):*
> If J. Edgar Hoover, the Master of American Power, was tied to his mother,
> how can I ever escape from Mother O?

MOTHER O:
> All right, stupid family! Let's admit it. Mother O is supreme! . . . Walt
> Whitman celebrates "the delicious singing of the *mother* . . ."

SON:
> Oh God, another song . . .

MOTHER O *(breaking into song):*
> We mothers sing deliciously,
> So don't accuse us viciously
> Of loving children till they're weak
> With creepy passions Freud called Greek—
> When all we do is sing deliciously . . .

SON *(shouting):*
> I can't stand it, Mother O!

> *(He starts translating her song, scribbling on a pad.)*

> I can't stand your fake English Cole Porter songs! I've got to translate
> them!

GHOST FATHER *(despairing):*
> We're not getting anywhere, Miriam! He's translating you into Russian
> again!

MOTHER O:
> If he wants a showdown song, he gets it! . . . *(She sings defiantly.)*

> I'm just your oldtime Mother O,
> The mistress of the Oedipus show:
> A true-blue mother of the family flag,
> Singing like any delicious old bag.

> Watch out, you men! The times have changed!
> We mothers are about to roam.
> You can't confine me in this house.
> I've had it with this jail called home!

166

(She steps forward and speaks to the audience.)

We present to you the mystery
And fate of our real family history—
How the last American mother came to be—
How Mother O revolted to be free!

SON:

It's only a dream! You'll never get rid of me, Mother O!

(Blackout.)

(1)

(The lights come up to show MOTHER O *standing by the* PIANIST *and singing through the wall to her* SON *in his room. She is changing out of her pajamas, getting dressed, as she sings her passionate musical message, ''Get Out,'' influenced strongly by Cole Porter's ''Get Out Of Town.'')*

MOTHER *(singing):*
The farce is ended . . .
Our family drama of the home
Is ended, it's time to hit the road . . .

(Trying desperately to avoid listening, the SON *stuffs his fingers in his ears.)*

SON *(moaning):*
Oh god, there she goes again! "Hit the road!" Who does she think I am, Jack Kerouac?

MOTHER O *(continuing to sing loudly):*
You're like a hermit in this house.
I'm through with being Mother O! . . .

(The SON *is searching frantically through his littered papers for his earplugs, which he discovers finally with relief.)*

SON:

Hell will freeze over before she's through with being Mother O!

MOTHER O *(continuing):*
It's time for you to grow
Up! Hear this from Mother O!

SON *(mockingly):*
Hear this! Commander of the Mother O Navy!

MOTHER O *(shouting through the wall)*
Did you find your silly ear-plugs, darling?

SON *(inserting the ear-plugs):*
I can't hear you, Mother O!

MOTHER O:
You can't hide from Mother O!

(She begins to sing the pulverizing refrain loudly and clearly.)

Get out! Leave home!
Before it's too late, Genius Son!
Go find your fame!
The thrill when you came
Is gone, Genius Son.
Get lost! Leave home!
Burn in hot Madagaska!
Go be contented in Nome,
In icy Alaska!
Go to Rome,
Drown in the Mediterranean,
Become a Subterranean! . . .

SON *(shouting):*
I can't stand your stupid Cole Porter rhymes!

MOTHER O *(continuing implacably as she interacts with the Pianist, sliding over him in a sensuous dance):*
You're in this house much too much
And when I'm with you I clutch too much,
So on your mark! Get set, leave home!

(Frustrated, the SON *hurls away the ear-plugs.)*

SON *(disgusted):*
Why did I buy ear-plugs from the Salvation Army?

MOTHER O:
How do you like my new song?

SON:
The same old Cole Porter and Mother O mix!

(He begins to scribble frantically at his desk.)

MOTHER O:
What weird language are you translating me into now?

SON *(scribbling away):*
None of your business!

(MOTHER O *motions to the* PIANIST *to play and prepares to sing again.*)

MOTHER O:
You're schizo, dear. I'll cure your soul with Cole.

(She sings.)

Get lost! Leave home!
Go to Rome,
Drown in the Mediterranean,
Become a Subterranean . . .

SON *(translating feverishly):*
I'm improving your terrible lyrics in Russian!

MOTHER O:
You're born American. I'm tired of you lying around, dreaming your crazy languages.

SON:
I hate your bastard American language. I love foreign languages!

MOTHER O:
Your psychosis bores me, darling. *(She begins to sing again.)*

Just disappear, you're in this house
Much too much, and when you are near,
Close to me, dear, I clutch too much,
So, on your mark! Get set!
Get out! Leave home!

SON *(In despair, he rips up the paper and throws it away):*
I can't translate your damn rhymes into Russian!

(He covers his ears with his hands.)

MOTHER O:
If you don't cure yourself, Henry, I may have to put you away, dear. I can't handle you anymore.

SON:

Never again! That god damn institution has only stupid English dictionaries.

MOTHER O:

Do you know, termite son, when Cole played his beautiful songs to that
tough Hollywood tycoon, Louis B. Mayer, the tycoon burst into tears!

SON *(muttering bitterly):*
Ars gratia artis . . . You're crazy, Mother O!

MOTHER O:
Not me. You're the schizo!

SON *(pleading):*
Why can't you understand? I know my problem. It's just *English* that
makes me ill.

MOTHER O:
You hide in your foreign languages. It's as bad as masturbating.

SON *(shouting):*
Masturbation is not bad! In some ways you're so damn old-fashioned,
Mother O! You castrated my father!

MOTHER O:
What nonsense! I assure you your Ghost Father's balls are perfectly
intact!

SON:
Then why does he live like a ghost?

MOTHER O:
He got tired of the crossfire. You and I were too much for him. Now it's
the end and you've gotta say goodbye to Mama Nurse and Mama Cook
and Mama . . .

SON *(bitterly):*
You haven't cooked for me for ten years.

MOTHER O:
I used to cook great meals for you but you kept translating every dish and
gagging on every bite of food . . .

SON *(gagging on the memory):*
Can I help it if English makes me vomit?

MOTHER O *(starting to sing again):*
I'll sing your brains out till you start talking English like any good American son! *(She sings.)*

Just disappear!
You're in this house much too much
And when you appear
I clutch too much . . .

SON *(writing frantically):*
I can rhyme you in French!

MOTHER O:
You'll never make it in French, darling. I'll sing you right out of this house!

SON:
I told you that the only way to survive my schizophrenia is to become the greatest translator in the world!

MOTHER O:
Mother O is a survivor too, darling! *(She finishes the song.)* So, on your mark! Get set! Get out! Leave home!

(As she sings these two final lines again, the SON *jumps desperately into bed and pulls the covers and pillows over his head to block out her song.)*

SCENE 2

(The lights come up on the SON *working away feverishly in his room. He is creating a large Concrete Poem sculpture based on his maternal obsessions. Into the sculpture, he is fitting different foreign language words for mother, trying to understand the difference in tone.)*

SON:
Mère . . . In French, mother sounds like the sea, the eternal sea of being . . . *MÈRE* . . . (He fits the word prominently into the sculpture.) *Mutter* . . . In German, it's a soft sentimental butter-spread . . . *Mutter-Butter!* . . . Not Mother O! *(shouting)* You were never butter-soft! Stupid Cole Porter! You worship him because he was a fancy society boy, and that's where you'd like to be! *(He hurls a thick dictionary in the direction of her bedroom.)* I'll build a Mother Totem to end all mothers!
Madre . . . Spanish sounds like a southern shimmer of light . . . *Madre,* too soft and reverent as if you were touching silk . . . *(He throws the*

word away.) Mae . . . Portuguese is better . . . *Maeeee* . . . A little more urgent—like a cat meowing for attention! *(He fastens it into the sculpture, then shouts defiantly in the direction of Mother O's room.)* This is my language laboratory, *puta!* My international world, not your crappy neighborhood! You can't throw me out of my home! . . . *Moeder* . . . Dutch sounds like cooking instructions, but there's no more cook . . . *Moeder—I'm stuttering on that word! (shouting in the direction of Mother O again)* Mother O, do you know it's a scientific fact that anyone who stutters has trouble saying the word, *mother?* In whatever language they speak, stutterers can't say *mother!* Isn't that amazing? They can't get beyond the first syllable without stuttering!

(Then, as if praying) God, give me some peace, if there is a God . . . *Gott strafe meine Mutter!* Please, God, help me to murder Mother O . . . The problem is, to murder Mother O I need more energy and will than she has . . . How did she get the energy, when I got the brains? . . . *Nana, Mitera,* Numero Uno Amazon mother . . . *(He attaches the words savagely.)* Damn you, Mother O! You toilet trained me into submission! Every time on the can, I hear you say, "Keep trying! Get it all out!" *Nana!* Albanian catches your quality . . . Nanny goat! *Nana!* . . . *(He slaps the word into place, and turns again in the direction of her room.)* You'll never get rid of me, *Merde Mama! (He picks up several words and goes into a chant.) Ema* . . . *Mate* . . . *Ema* . . . *Mate—El-Oum* . . . *El-Oum* . . . *El-Oum!* . . . How do you like your name in Arabic, Mother O, you old Oedipus Momma? Mother, mother, mother . . . *(He pounds on the statue and embraces it, weeping.)*

SCENE 3

(Lights up in Mother O's room. MOTHER O *is standing at the wall facing the Son's room. Behind* MOTHER O, *the* GHOST FATHER *is sitting, reading a newspaper. In his room, the* SON *is lying on his bed, the blanket pulled over his head.*

MOTHER O *(shouting through the wall):*
Don't try to give me the old silence treatment! Silence is a wet blanket!
(turning to snap at the Ghost Father, who goes on reading) Rudy, why are you always reading when I'm in trouble? When we got married, we made a deal to talk at least once a day.

GHOST FATHER *(continuing to read):*
Brown University is spending forty million dollars to become a major computer university . . .

MOTHER O *(snapping):*
How am I supposed to measure millions of dollars? Before our marriage, you never told me you got nothing but numbers in your head and an eager cock.

GHOST FATHER:
A mathematics professor is making films about the Fourth Dimension . . .

MOTHER O:
How come one or two dimensions aren't enough for you? You want to escape into the Fourth Dimension?

GHOST FATHER *(calmly):*
The Fourth Dimension is mainly invisible . . .

MOTHER O *(irritated):*
You talk invisible Fourth Dimensions and I gotta worry about a son you drilled numbers into and they came out foreign words! *(She moves to the painting of Cole Porter on the wall.)* How come you can't be more like Cole? He's the only one around here who makes me want to sing and dance. *(She addresses the portrait.)* Cole, you know how tough it is with a Ghost Daddy and a schizo genius son . . .

GHOST FATHER *(continuing to read):*
The Mayan civilization invented the concept of zero . . .

MOTHER O:
The hell they did! We invented zero right here in this house. I grew up in the country with lilacs, daffodils, tulips big as teacups. Flowers and trees in this god damn city are for dogs to piss on, and then you have to pick up the shit with a pooper-scooper. What kind of life is that?

GHOST FATHER:
You don't understand, Mother O. Zero is the beginning of everything.

MOTHER O:
Rudy, how did Zero and Mother O conceive a schizo genius son? One day we were blind, happy, dancing on a level floor. Next day the floor tilts, we're walking the edge . . .

SCENE 4

(As the lights change, the SON *is lying on the floor in Mother O's bedroom, playing himself as a young baby beginning to wriggle around the floor. Suddenly the* GHOST FATHER *is startled as he hears his baby son mumble a few words.)*

MOTHER O:
Isn't he a little beauty, Rudy? Listen! He's trying to speak!

GHOST FATHER *(agitated):*
I can't believe it! He's beginning to speak!

MOTHER O *(staring with pride):*
He's a bright kid, Rudy!

(The Son says clearly in French, "Je t'aime.")

GHOST FATHER:
My god, he's speaking his first words!

MOTHER O:
No, he's just babbling, but he's gonna be a smart boy!

(The Son repeats directly to MOTHER O *this time, "Je t'aime."*

GHOST FATHER:
Jesus Christ, he's talking French!

MOTHER O:
Forget it, he hasn't said a word in English yet.

(The SON *says "Je t'aime" precisely and lovingly again.)*

GHOST FATHER:
You hear? *Je t'aime,* I love you.

MOTHER O *(aghast, unbelieving):*
To me he says "I love you" in French?

GHOST FATHER:
That's what he said!

MOTHER O:
I don't speak French. You speak numbers!

GHOST FATHER:
I've got some French books on computer techniques. Maybe he heard me reading from them . . .

MOTHER O (*sarcastically*):
Do computers say "I love you"?

GHOST FATHER:
They say it in binary numbers.

(*The* SON *says, "Ich liebe dich."*)

MOTHER O:
What's he babbling now?

GHOST FATHER:
This is serious. It sounds like German.

MOTHER O:
You're full of crap.

(*The* SON *repeats, "Ich liebe dich."*)

GHOST FATHER:
He said "I love you" in German! (*trying to joke*) At least he likes his mother.

MOTHER O (*more and more worried*):
How come he can't say it in English like every son?

(*The* SON *says, "Te amo."*)
What's he saying now, Rudy?
(*The* SON *repeats "Te amo" lovingly.*)

GHOST FATHER:
It's a miracle! He's talking Spanish!

MOTHER O:
Same message?

GHOST FATHER:
He's programmed!

MOTHER O:
Rudy, if this is from your foreign language computer books . . .

GHOST FATHER:
I think we've got a genius on our hands.

MOTHER O (*anxiously*):
What are we going to do? He can't talk English. We've got to throw out your crazy books . . .

GHOST FATHER:

Over my dead body. *(As their argument is about to erupt, the* SON *pronounces clearly and happily in sequence,* "Je t'aime," "Ich liebe dich," "Te amo.")

MOTHER O *(bursting into tears):*

How am I going to talk to him if he can't speak English?

GHOST FATHER *(trying to console her):*

Don't worry, you've born a genius son. He just wants to love his Mother O. You're a magical Mother Oedipus.

MOTHER O:

You promise, you *promise* he'll be ok?

GHOST FATHER:

I promise. *(The* SON *continues babbling* "Je t'aime," "Ich liebe dich," "Te amo," *as the parents' expressions suddenly turn anxious and worried.)*

SCENE 5

(As the lights change, the GHOST FATHER *assumes the role of an American teacher in a special private school confronting* MOTHER O. MOTHER O *begins the scene speaking to the audience.)*

MOTHER O:

A promise is something you shout into the wind and it blows away. Who wants a genius son if he won't leave home and turns your house into a defensive fortress. Rudy is a retired engineer who spends all his time with computer books, his new obsession. It's easy for him to escape. He advises me to get genius son Henry tutored privately. He says a Frenchman or Spaniard can slip English in through the back door! I run this house through the front door! You know when Rudy nicknamed me Mother O for magical Oedipus mother? Pretty soon genius son calls me Mother O. I like it! The truth is I'm proud of my son saying he loves me in all those foreign languages. Maybe I shouldn't have let the nickname Mother O stick. My son loves me, but Rudy's turning into a Ghost Father, and I'm worried about the family's future. So I look for a teacher, an American teacher . . .

GHOST FATHER *(as the American teacher):*

Madam, I'm sorry to say that your son is impossible to teach.

MOTHER O:

What kind of school is this; you can't teach a genius?

TEACHER *(stiffly)*:

Your son has a total block about English. We've tried everything possible. We've even tried teaching him English as a foreign language . . .

MOTHER O:

English as a foreign language? What kind of nonsense is this? He's no foreign kid!

TEACHER *(trying to control himself)*:

Whatever he is, Madam, he refuses to speak a word of English! He is a complete rebel. No one can communicate with him. He turns every class into a foreign language Tower of Babel!

MOTHER O:

You call yourself a teacher and you can't even handle a Tower of Babel?

TEACHER *(icily)*:

Your son cannot stay here.

MOTHER O *(wailing)*:

What am I going to do with him? *(then proudly)* You got any other kids with so much talent in languages?

TEACHER:

Thank god, no. I suggest you try a psychiatrist. Your son needs special help. I have a recommended list for you . . .

SCENE 6

MOTHER O:

So I take genius son to a shrink . . . *(The* GHOST FATHER *assumes the role of the psychiatrist, playing him with a hint of Groucho Marx's television show.)*

GHOST FATHER AS PSYCHIATRIST:

Mrs. Abendstern, I'm sorry to say there is an unusual split in your son's mind . . .

MOTHER O:

You mean he's crazy?

PSYCHIATRIST:

Usually, schizophrenics are so split apart in their personalities that they need special clinical care. They are unable to function because they don't understand their situation. Your son is a rare case because he knows his problem. His brain functions on the genius level. His ability to translate

177

the most unusual English idioms into difficult foreign languages is unique. He knows that his deep-rooted hatred of English is the shadow that splits his mind . . . I hypnotized him to discover the cause of this hatred . . .

(The SON *appears nervously through a door, as the Psychiatrist questions him as if on a television show.* MOTHER O *retreats to the piano, waiting, humming her commentary.)*

PSYCHIATRIST:
Relax . . . You're safe now, perfectly at ease . . . Don't stiffen up . . . Relax . . . Tell me how you first began to hate English . . .

SON *(bursting out):*
I couldn't escape! I was in the womb!

PSYCHIATRIST:
How can you be certain it happened to you in the womb? *(In the background Mother O is singing now.)*

SON:
Mother O told me she played and sang her dumb Cole Porter songs all the time when I was in the womb! And she kept it up after I was born!

PSYCHIATRIST *(slowly):*
Let me get this straight . . . She played her version of Cole Porter songs to you in the womb and kept on playing them after you were born . . .

SON:
Yes, she never stopped, and I discovered I could escape into foreign languages . . .

PSYCHIATRIST:
Wasn't her singing just a kind of entertainment?

SON *(agitated):*
The root meaning of entertainment is from the Latin *enter into* . . . In the womb it's like a succubus that devours you! We're not talking movies or television. It was like a giant maternal worm devouring me with sadistic songs!

PSYCHIATRIST:
I see . . . How fascinating! . . . A giant maternal Oedipus worm . . . Do you know that recent psychological studies show that newborns tend to pay more attention to female than to male voices?

SON:
I don't need studies to know that!

178

PSYCHIATRIST:

Why didn't you just ask her to stop?

SON:

I was in the womb!

PSYCHIATRIST:

I mean after you were born.

SON:

You don't understand. She loves Cole Porter. She's not going to stop. She never stops anything. She wants to be a liberated woman.

PSYCHIATRIST:

That's perfectly natural.

SON:

Not for mothers! They're supposed to take care of their children, not torture them. So I grew up on the defensive. I discovered foreign languages are a very good defense . . .

PSYCHIATRIST:

But you're an American boy growing up . . . You can't play defense forever.

SON:

Why not? I speak English only as if I were encased in armor. Inside, I begin to translate everything into foreign languages.

PSYCHIATRIST:

Don't people look at you rather strangely when you translate them inside your mind into foreign languages?

SON:

They don't know I'm doing it.

PSYCHIATRIST:

Do you?

SON:

They don't know what to do with me in school. I have a hard time communicating with girls . . .

PSYCHIATRIST:

You're afraid of girls?

SON:

I hate American-speaking girls! They chew gum all the time!

179

PSYCHIATRIST:

Really? You hate even good-looking American girls?

SON:

I love foreign-speaking girls!

PSYCHIATRIST:

Maybe you should go to a school with a lot of foreign refugees.

SON:

I've tried that! I created a lot of foreign language speaking clubs in the schools. Pretty soon the schools have so many language clubs they clamp down on me!

PSYCHIATRIST:

They clamp down on you?

SON:

They want foreigners to learn English and they say I'm holding them back on the test scores. They claim I'm not patriotic and throw me out of school! I become a recluse at home and create my own language laboratory. But there's no insulation. I have to listen to Mother O play her fake Cole Porter songs through the wall!

PSYCHIATRIST:

And you can't reason with her . . . You can't get your father to reason with her . . .

SON:

Mother O is the only reason in the house! So I have to defend myself by becoming the greatest translator in the world!

PSYCHIATRIST:

I see . . . Translation as defense . . . *(He gets up and crosses to speak to* MOTHER O *as she returns to consult him.)* What a fascinating case . . . It proves my theories of in-utero memories . . . I've never had such a fascinating case . . . *(to* MOTHER O*)* I'm sorry, Madam, we cannot cure him . . .

MOTHER O:

So you're sending him home . . .

PSYCHIATRIST *(cautiously):*

I think you need a special halfway house . . .

MOTHER O:

How do you get a halfway house for English haters?

PSYCHIATRIST:

I'm sorry, Mrs. Abendstern. He needs special care outside of the home.

MOTHER O:

I agree with you there, but institutions cost a lot of money.

PSYCHIATRIST:

Might I suggest you study foreign languages to improve your basic relationship, and stop singing to him.

MOTHER O:

Me stop singing? Me and foreign languages? Basic American is all I got in my bones . . .

SCENE 7

(MOTHER O *in her room. The* GHOST FATHER *and the* SON *are in the Son's room, conferring together about computer problems in the Ghost Father's foreign language computer books.*)

MOTHER O:

They're in there again, hiding from me. Rudy's got genius son on an escape route, teaching him French out of his foreign language computer books. I tried to study French, son, like sticking a clothespin over my nose! (*Accompanied by the* PIANIST, *she sings a few bars in French from Cole Porter's "Night and Day—"Nuit et Jour . . ."*) I can't help it, male animals! My ear is for Cole's singing and dancing music, not your nasal French. (*angrily*) They're in there Night and Day together! (*Angrily, she sings a few more bars of "Night and Day" in her grotesque French.*) I'm alone in my own house! But there's one thing I do learn studying French. I learn about the Statue of Liberty! (*She climbs on the piano and strikes a pose like the Statue of Liberty.*) Hey, family, remember this lady? (The GHOST FATHER *and* SON *approach her, amazed.*)

SON:

How come Momma's standing like that?

GHOST FATHER:

It's trouble, son. She's changing. That's the Statue of Liberty.

SON:

What's the Statue of Liberty?

GHOST FATHER:

You never read about it in the French books I gave you?

SON:

I skipped over it. I thought it was American.

GHOST FATHER:

A French sculptor created her to idealize his mother. The first thing you see when you sail into New York is a giant French mother.

SON *(awed by this image):*

A giant mother holding up the torch of freedom . . . Are you sure she's *French?*

GHOST FATHER:

She's French all right.

SON *(staring at* MOTHER O):

I wish I had a French mother . . .

MOTHER O *(holding the pose):*

Take a good look, family machos . . . Freedom for mothers is the message! The Statue of Liberty was inspired by Delacroix's bare breasted Mother Liberty leading the French Revolution!

SON:

Bare breasted?

GHOST FATHER:

In Delacroix's famous painting, son. A revolutionary interpretation of liberty . . .

SON *(troubled):*

What does she mean, freedom for mothers?

MOTHER O:

Go back to your cave, son. I want to talk to your Daddy. It's New Year's Day!

SON:

It's not New Year's Day!

GHOST FATHER:

You'd better go, son. *(looking at* MOTHER O's *determined stance.)* She's got something big in mind. She's going to drop the Big Change on me . . .

SON:

What Big Change?

GHOST FATHER:

I don't know, but I can feel it coming . . .

SON:

Call me if you need help.

GHOST FATHER:

Thanks . . .(*The Son withdraws, but listens through the door as* MOTHER O *drops her stance and the confrontation between* MOTHER O *and the* GHOST FATHER *erupts.*)

MOTHER O:

I want you out of this house, Rudy! I want you to take your foreign language computer books with you. No more ganging up on me!

GHOST FATHER (*clutching his computer book tightly in his hand*):
Out is an impossible word.

MOTHER O:

It's a New Year. We gotta change things around.

GHOST FATHER:

Change is possible. *Out* I don't understand.

MOTHER O:

Open your eyes, Rudy. We don't have a home anymore. This is some kind of crazy hide-out. Our son is becoming an invisible person who doesn't recognize the outside world. And you're taking his side.

GHOST FATHER:

I'm just trying to keep the peace and quiet. Whenever you want, I'm at your side. I'm your husband.

MOTHER O:

You come for my cooking and bed, that's all. We don't even go out to the movies anymore.

GHOST FATHER:

I bring in Chinese food. I listen to Cole Porter . . .

MOTHER O:

You're a retired engineer. You don't go to work anymore. You're haunting this house too much. You're turning into a Ghost Father. We've got to make a new arrangement.

GHOST FATHER:

How do you arrange *out?*

MOTHER O:

You can change from husband to frequent visitor. That way we leave only the loving essentials.

GHOST FATHER:

You think of the loving essentials as a *visit?*

MOTHER O:

Why not? We get rid of the heavy duty obsessions. After genius son sees you leave, maybe he'll leave. *(Listening from his room, the SON reacts negatively.)*

GHOST FATHER:

It'll never work, Miriam. The heavy duty obsessions are what marriage is supposed to be.

MOTHER O:

Rudy, you macho men wrote the book of marriage to make woman a servant. Even the Moslems have a better system. They've got harems with a lot of women to serve men.

GHOST FATHER:

I believe in a liberal marriage. I want you to be free to do what you want to do.

MOTHER O:

You're a pink-kneed liberal, Rudy. You think one way and act wishy-washy. Take your foreign language computer books out of my house so my son can speak English!

GHOST FATHER:

You really mean *out?*

MOTHER O:

Rent a room nearby and install your library!

GHOST FATHER *(angrily):*

Install my books in a rented room?

MOTHER O:

Safe and sound. From there you can visit. I like you around when you're not just a ghost. You can visit any time you like. Our son can visit you. That'll help him to get out of this house. *(Again the SON shakes his head vehemently.)*

GHOST FATHER:

You can't do this, Miriam. You're ruining the family.

184

MOTHER O:

I don't believe in ruins, but I'm not a dummy servant for you men either. The Statue of Liberty is for women too! *(Defiantly, she strikes her Statue of Liberty pose as the scene ends, and the* PIANO PLAYER *plays his encouragement.)*

SCENE 8

(Lights up in the kitchen area. Hungry, the SON *enters to steal some food, thinking* MOTHER O *is asleep. In her room,* MOTHER O *is seen dimly, nodding, half-asleep in her chair. A mysterious large box is beside her.)*

SON *(as if whispering encouragement to himself):*

All quiet on the Mother Front? . . . God, I'm hungry! *(looking furtively around the kitchen) Küche als Mutterrecht*—Mother O's Kingdom that she abdicated . . . *(He begins to poke around on a shelf, pulling down some breakfast cereals.)* Damn English labels on every box . . . *(He mocks the names, drawing out the syllables like a sound poem.) Wheeee-teeeeese* . . . *Shreeeed-deeaad Wheeeeat* . . . Mother O's plot to starve me out of the house! . . . *(He mounts a chair to peer at a higher shelf. The sound arouses Mother O and she sits up, listening.)* Goethe knew, *Über allen Wipfeln ist Ruh,* you've got to climb into the highest branches to find peace . . . *(He finds a can.)* What's this? . . . *Merde,* it's all cat food . . . She feeds that bastard cat more than she does me . . . *(He takes down another can.) Au-ber-gine* . . . How lovely in French, pure vowels singing to be eaten . . . *Egg Plant* . . . Impossible brutal sound . . .

(He attacks the can with an opener, tears off the cover, and begins to eat with his fingers. Carrying her mysterious box, MOTHER O *enters and regards him critically as he stuffs himself.)*

MOTHER O *(with disdain):*

Who's this thief in my kitchen?

SON *(eating defiantly):*

You don't care if I starve to death!

MOTHER O *(taking the empty eggplant can away from him):*

A grown man raids my shelves for a can of eggplant tidbits? I've had it with your paranoia!

SON :

Schizophrenia. You always get it wrong.

MOTHER O:

I don't give a damn anymore. Eat up and die! Poison yourself with canned food! See if I care!

SON:

That's all you give me to eat—cat food and aubergine tidbits!

MOTHER O *(brandishing her mysterious package):*

From now on, I'm gonna help you eat yourself to death.

SON *(suspiciously):*

What's in your tricky box, Pandora?

> *(Opening the box with a flourish,* MOTHER O *takes out several gourmet cans and packages.)*

MOTHER O *(displaying them):*

Foreign goodies! Guaranteed non-English, in your favorite languages . . . French . . . Fancy Italian . . . German . . .

SON *(grabbing the German can and reading the label):*

Sauerkraut! *(then, sourly, when he sees it's a food he doesn't like)* Sauerkraut . . .

MOTHER O *(shrugging):*

Gourmet Sauerkraut.

SON *(reading another label):*

Zuppa di Spinaci . . .

MOTHER O:

Spinach and egg soup.

SON *(delighted with the foreign sound):*

Zuppa di Spinaci! *(then, with disgust)* I hate spinach!

MOTHER O:

You'll love it . . . I walk into a fancy import store and order twenty-five different foreign specialties just to please you . . . A guy, in green glasses, puts me down icily, "What kind of *food,* Madame, do you want?" Any kind, I say, as long as the labels are in foreign languages, so my crazy son can read and eat himself to death.

SON *(staring at her)*

Sometimes I don't think *I'm* crazy . . .

MOTHER O:

So he runs for the manager who prances up in white buck shoes like he was Cary Grant stylish in the 1920s. When I explain about my son's schizo language problems, he pats me on the shoulder as if it's all right— he knows all his customers are fruitcakes. Then he throws in a fancy can of free Polish sausage . . .

SON *(examining several cans):*
Most of these French cans are truffles. *(He pronounces it in French.)*

MOTHER O:
You got something against truffles?

SON:
Truffles are too *rich.* You want me to swell up and burst?

MOTHER O:
Maybe then you'll run out into the street and holler for a hot dog.

SON:
If anyone shouts "Hot Dog" at me, I might murder him.

MOTHER O:
So you're a violent boy at heart . . . I should have known . . .

SON*(staring at her):*
Right, Mother O . . . Last night I dreamt of killing you with an ice axe . . .

MOTHER O *(unbelieving):*
An ice axe?

SON:
In my dream I struggle up Mt. Everest . . .

MOTHER O:
You'll never make it to the top.

SON *(struggling to continue):*
On top is a shrine to the Mother Goddess of the mountain . . .

MOTHER O:
How come they call it Mt. Everest if there's a Mother Goddess up there?

SON *(continuing desperately):*
Mt. Everest is just a stupid masculine English name! The Tibetans call it Chomo-Lunguna, God-Mother of the country.

MOTHER O:
Score one for the Tibetans.

SON *(struggling to concentrate):*

When I get to the top in my dream, an enormous wall of ice surrounds the Mother Goddess's shrine. I hack at it, I hack my way into it!

MOTHER O:

You killer! . . . I'm not living with a son who hacks his way into my shrine with an ice axe!

SON *(defensively)*

It's just a dream . . . *(meditating, gloomily)* Maybe it would be better if we commit suicide together!

MOTHER O *(indignantly):*

You'd like that . . . Big headline: *Mother O and Son in Love-Death!*

SON:

You could kill me first, then fall over me.

MOTHER O *(staring at him, deciding):*

We've gotta change . . . I'm through with being your old Mama Oedipus . . . But to help you get rid of your obsessions or make you run out of this house screaming, I'll be your Mama Freud . . .

(The lights change abruptly for the new scene.)

SCENE 9

SON *(eagerly):*

Jetz sollen wir spielen. Freud und seine Mutter!

MOTHER O:

All right, son, I'll be Freud's mother . . . We let everything hang out!

SON *(covering his ears):*

I hate that phrase, it makes me sick! All I want to do is show you what Freud's mother did to him—the same kind of thing you did to me!

MOTHER O:

You mean Freud's mother gave her genius son a hang-up?

SON:

When she was only twenty-one, she gave birth to a son, whom she named Sigmund. She started to call him "mein goldener Sigi . . ."

MOTHER O:

Her golden boy . . . Every momma feels that golden moment . . .

(They play the fantasy scene of Freud and his mother. The SON *approaches* MOTHER O *like the six-year-old Sigmund.)*

SON:

When Freud was six-years-old, he began to wonder how he was born . . . *(He kneels before his mother and tugs at her skirt.)*

MOTHER O *(playing Freud's mother grandly):*
What is it, mein goldener Sigi?

SON *(tugging at her skirt):*
I want to know how I was born!

FREUD'S MOTHER *(smiling):*
Of course, Sigi . . . We're made of earth . . . That's why there are so many people . . . Different kinds of earth . . . Look at your skin . . . *(She touches and rubs his hand.)* See how soft your hand is with some bones in it . . . Like the earth with stones in it . . .

SON *(disturbed):*
Is my skin really earth? Was I born like dirty earth?

FREUD'S MOTHER:
Ja, mein goldener Sigi . . . Feel my hand . . . *(He begins to feel her hand and arm.)*

Feel the softness, the hardness of earth . . . That's where you come from, mein goldener Sigi . . . Look close . . . Dirty earth . . . You see my skin is more wrinkled than yours . . . That's what happens when old people get ready to die . . . Their skin wrinkles into earth . . .

SON *(disturbed):*
I don't believe you, Mama! You're not dying. I wasn't born out of the dirty earth!

(Freud's mother lifts her hands high in the air and rubs them together mysteriously.)

FREUD'S MOTHER:
It's true, Sigi . . . See what happens when I rub my hands together . . . The skin peels off in tiny fragments . . . You can barely notice them . . . Dust to dust . . .

SON:
But the skin is born again! Skin loves skin and makes new skin. I can't see your skin peel off!

FREUD'S MOTHER:

Yes, you can, mein goldener Sigi . . . *(She holds her hands down, palms up, so he can inspect them. Fascinated, afraid, he examines her hands.)*

Look at those tiny fragments of skin . . . See how they peel off . . . That's the earth we're born of . . . That's how our skin comes off when we die . . .

(Blackout. The PIANIST *plays a more serious variation on Mother O's song from the opening Prologue.)*

SCENE 10

(Lights up in Mother O's bedroom. The SON *is lying on a couch, twitching with anticipation.* MOTHER O *sits sternly behind him in a chair with a large, yellow-lined scribbling pad on her lap.)*

MOTHER O:

No more games . . . Now we tell the truth . . .

SON *(twitching):*

My unconscious mind has the jerks . . .

MOTHER O:

Clear out your fake dreams of Mother O.

SON:

I can't tell the difference between my Freudian mother fantasies and my ice-axe dreams.

MOTHER O:

In fantasies you got room to move. You cry and laugh. If you go down one road, you still have time to go back. But in dreams, you're there. You can't change a dream. Sometimes you wake up yelling . . .

SON *(twitching and struggling):*

What do you know about dreams? . . . The other night I dreamt of you as a dirigible, a blimp . . .

MOTHER O:

You think of me big and fat?

SON:

I'm stranded in a western desert waiting to be rescued . . . Hot and dry, endless desert . . . On the horizon I see two strange billboards . . .

MOTHER O *(scribbling on pad):*
Billboards is your city upbringing.

SON:
I have to translate the billboards because they're written in stupid English. They're advertising *eis-kalt Bier* and Coca-Cola. I turn away and shut my eyes. Then this enormous blimp sails in!

MOTHER O:
Coming to rescue you?

SON:
Rescue, hell. You turn out to be the Captain. I'm the only passenger.

MOTHER O *(scribbling):*
One passenger son, one Captain Mother . . . The old incest dream . . .

SON *(sitting up, snapping at her):*
Don't judge me till I'm finished!

MOTHER O:
Lie down, I can't stand looking at your face.

SON:
Now you know why Freud sat behind his patients!

(He throws up his hands in disgust and lies down.)

MOTHER O:
So what happens to the Captain Mother on your fat blimp?

SON:
I scream at you: "Where am I? Why am I alone? Where are all the European passengers?"

MOTHER O *(scribbling):*
European passengers, huh . . . No Americans on board . . .

SON:
You don't answer. All you do is hand me a flaming torch . . .

MOTHER O:
You stole that from my Statue of Liberty . . .

SON:
Soaring up in the blimp, I dream you're like a rebel Prometheus bringing the gift of fire to man in immortal verse: *(Rapturously, he quotes a famous*

Greek phrase from Prometheus Bound:) Pasai Technai Brotoisin ek Prometheos!

MOTHER O:

Do I look like a giant Greek man?

SON:

With the torch you force me to set fire to the helium and destroy the blimp! I wake up sweating . . .

MOTHER O *(staring at him critically):*
When you dream, you always wake up before the showdown . . .

SON:

You're the Captain with a spirit of steel exploding the blimp! Confess, *Mutter, Mère Mama, Mother O!* You wore my father down. You turned him into a ghost! You exiled him to a park bench!

MOTHER O *(slowly):*
Now we're down to it . . . You blame me for creating a Ghost Father . . .

SCENE 11

(The GHOST FATHER *is on his park bench, feeding the pigeons in his mathematical manner.)*

GHOST FATHER:

Pigeon Number 1, Chow Time! Waddle into the triangle and present yourself to Ghost Father . . . What? . . . You can't see me, the invisible man . . . I was trained to be a patriarch! . . . Father sits at the head of the table and commands . . . The family comes running to the table just like you pigeons . . .

Pigeon Number 2, here's your dinner . . . Good . . . You hop to my call . . . Daddy as destiny . . . In the bedroom I ride on top . . . The father as provider . . .

Pigeon Number 3, get into the chow line . . . That's it, the universal triangle, Mother, Son, and Ghost Father in the disappearing angle . . . Pigeon Number 1, the revolt begins! Mother O moves up into the acute angle . . .

Pigeon Number 2, my son, in this triangle you're the unknown element . . . Instead of one, two, three, you say *une, deux, trois* . . . The house

is shaken by language mysteries . . . Father as penis-authority fades into
ghost . . .

Exile him to the nearest park bench . . . From now on it's Cole Porter
Supreme and no more cooking . . . Give him a treat once in a while
. . . The bedroom turns into a battleground . . . The clitoris becomes
like the flag of the French Revolution . . . Three, four, five orgasms . . .
No more Daddy as ruler and supreme organ . . . Watch out my son,
you're in the Battle Zone . . .

(Towards the end of the GHOST FATHER'S *monologue, the* SON *enters and
stands watching his father feed the pigeons.)*

SON *(calling finally):*
Vater? Père?

GHOST FATHER:
Is that you, son?

SON *(resentfully):*
How come you disappear when I need you?

GHOST FATHER:
Here I am—park bench exile . . .

SON *(peering):*
It's hard to see you in the dusk.

GHOST FATHER:
I'm more of a transparency than a disappearance.

SON *(accusingly):*
You left me alone with Mother O. I can't handle her and her Cole Porter
worship. You've got to help me bury Cole.

GHOST FATHER:
How can I help, son?

SON *(mysteriously):*
Together we can exorcize him.

GHOST FATHER:
You're going to kill him with one of your foreign language rituals?

SON *(confidentially):*
She likes Cole just because of his music. If she learns the truth about him,
she'll change.

GHOST FATHER:

You know the truth?

SON:

I'll show you . . .

(MOTHER O *enters singing "Wunderbar" from Kiss Me Kate, which she pronounces deliberately "Wonder Bar! Wonder Bar!" We see the* SON'S *fantasy of exorcising Cole Porter.*)

SON (*ironically, to* GHOST FATHER):

Mother O stars in *Kiss Me Kate!* . . . Her German accent is terrible.

GHOST FATHER:

What part do I play?

SON:

Like Petruchio in Shakespeare, you tame the shrew. For a change you act like a real man.

GHOST FATHER:

I don't think a ghost can tame a shrew.

MOTHER O (*to audience*):

Ladies and gentlemen, we present for your entertainment the truth about Cole Porter's secret fantasy life!

GHOST FATHER (*muttering*):

I'll bet I end up playing Cole Porter . . .

SCENE 12

MOTHER O (*continuing*):

How did Cole set out to "wife it wealthily"? His mother had a purse full of bucks, that's how! She ruled the household and packed her son off to Yale. She made him travel with the rich and famous to all points of the compass . . .

SON:

Stick to the point! Through travel Cole learned foreign languages!

MOTHER O (*dominating the Son again*):

He wrote his great song lyrics in *English*. He married a wealthy divorcee. She was older than Cole and became a second mother. After Cole had his terrible fall from a horse that crushed his legs, he and Linda bought a country place in Williamstown, Mass . . . Mother O presents a final vision of Cole and his wife in their country home . . . *(She hands the Ghost Father a dressing gown.)* Rudy, you get to play Cole.

GHOST FATHER *(putting on the dressing gown, he says to the Son):*
I told you this would happen.

MOTHER O *(assuming the role of Linda Lee Thomas, Cole's wife):*
Look, Cole, darling!

GHOST FATHER:
Yes, Linda, New England is so lovely in fall . . .

MOTHER O AS LINDA:
The flaming maples, thousands of red and yellow leaves falling gracefully . . . Williamstown is so beautiful!

GHOST FATHER AS COLE:
Yes, Linda, it's beautiful. Just like Peru . . .

MOTHER O AS LINDA *(musing happily):*
Think of it, as beautiful as Peru, the land of mysterious, ancient gods . . .

GHOST FATHER AS COLE:
I mean my hometown, Peru, Indiana. Sometime I'll take you there. It's a peaceful place.

MOTHER O AS LINDA *(sharply):*
I don't want to go to Peru, Indiana! Cole, you have to promise me something!

GHOST FATHER AS COLE:
What do you want me to promise?

MOTHER O AS LINDA:
I want you to give me your word of honor!

GHOST FATHER *(avoiding her eyes):*
Anything, you say, Linda.

MOTHER O AS LINDA:
When I die, I want to be buried *here* in Williamstown, Massachusetts! I don't want to be buried in Peru, Indiana! Promise on your word of honor!

GHOST FATHER AS COLE:
Of course, darling, I promise you.

MOTHER O AS LINDA *(wailing):*
But when I died, you buried me in Peru, Indiana, next to your mother!

GHOST FATHER AS COLE *(uneasily):*
It wasn't my fault.

MOTHER O AS LINDA:
How could you betray me?

GHOST FATHER AS COLE:
What else could I do? In my final rest, I wanted you on one side, and my mother on the other side. That's security!

MOTHER O AS LINDA:
You could have moved her to Williamstown!

GHOST FATHER AS COLE:
I couldn't dig up my mother. That would have been sacrilege.

MOTHER O AS LINDA *(wailing):*
So I'm buried in Peru, Indiana! That's hell!

GHOST FATHER AS COLE:
No, it isn't, it's eternity! *(He goes into a jubilant solo, an exultant little song and dance.)*

I'm singing in eternity	Singing, singing in eternity,
With Mother Kate	I've tamed the shrew
And my wife,	And mother too,
Linda, too,	And ended with them all
In my hometown	in my hometown
Of Peru . . .	Of Peru!

(Ironically, the GHOST FATHER *puts Cole to rest as he says:)*

Rest, Cole, my fellow ghost, rest listening to Linda's protest . . .

SON *(staring, entranced):*
Can you believe it? Cole Porter is buried in his hometown between his mother and his wife! What more could a man ask?

MOTHER O *(playing herself now):*
All right, son, I get the message. You celebrate Cole's burial to get rid of him. You bury him in Peru, Indiana, between his mama and wifey, and I'm supposed to shut up and go back to serving you. But I'll keep on singing and ride out of this prison . . .

SON:
You won't get rid of me and my father so easily! We've formed a new alliance. Isn't that true, dad?

GHOST FATHER (*summoning his ghostly courage, straightening to attention, and motioning the* SON *to attention too*):
Numero Dos and Numero Tres!

MOTHER O (*scornfully*):
Some traitors . . . How are you going to kill off *Numero Uno?*

SCENE 13

(*Near the park bench, the* GHOST FATHER *and* SON *are arguing about their next strategic move.*)

GHOST FATHER:
Sorry, son, I can't help you. Mother O is Numero Uno . . .

SON:
Fathers must help sons against mothers. You've got to help me, Dad . . .

GHOST FATHER:
Thanks for the Dad, but you have to do it alone.

SON:
You're deserting me!

GHOST FATHER:
In a showdown about their children's problems, parents stick together. It's a law of nature.

SON (*angrily*):
You're saying I can't count on you!

GHOST FATHER:
I'm saying you've got a better chance alone to change Mother O.

SON:
What can I do alone?

GHOST FATHER:
You have to find a way to convert Mother O by showing her what language really means to you . . .

SON:

She won't listen to me.

GHOST FATHER:

Maybe if you tell her about Helen Keller . . .

SON:

Are you crazy? What good will Helen Keller do?

GHOST FATHER:

Even though she was deaf, dumb and blind, Helen Keller broke free from her afflictions by learning how language communicates physically . . .

SON:

You mean my learning languages helped me to balance my schizophrenia?

GHOST FATHER:

No. . . . If you show Mother O how the power of language can heal, she might appreciate your linguistic abilities. She might even reconsider your situation.

SON *(excited)*:

If this fails, you've got to promise to work with me so she doesn't throw me out of the house. You can't just sit back and fade away.

GHOST FATHER:

I promise . . . You remember in Helen Keller's case how one common-place word was crucial? *The* GHOST FATHER *exits as the* SON *prepares to confront* MOTHER O.)

SCENE 14

(MOTHER O *is filing her nails on the couch in her bedroom as the* SON *approaches furtively, reading up on Helen Keller.*)

MOTHER O:

How did your visit with your Ghost Father go?

SON *(twitching)*:

I'm seeing him often now. We're plotting against you!

MOTHER O:

Good, keep your plots in the open. Get out and talk with your father on his park bench. See how the homeless survive. Pretend I'm deaf and dumb if you like . . .

SON (*dropping the book abruptly*):
Deaf and dumb? How'd you guess?

MOTHER O:
Guess what?

SON:
Put up your hands. I'm going to show you something . . .

(*Dramatically, she puts up her hands as if surrendering.*)

No, no! You're not Mother O, the actress . . . I want you to pretend you're deaf and dumb like Helen Keller. Your intelligence is locked up behind a wall of flesh . . .

MOTHER O:
I don't hide nothing with my flesh.

SON (*getting up, trying to control himself*):
Try to understand . . . Lie down . . . (*He places her on the couch.*) Helen Keller is not hiding. She's searching for her lost senses. Maybe if you learn how language works physically, the world will open up for you. Think of language, glowing like sex, near you in the dark . . .

MOTHER O (*sitting up, uncontrollably*):
I like sex better in the light.

SON (*pushing her down, then taking a glass of water from a nearby stand*) Keep your mouth shut, your eyes closed! Put out your hand! (*She extends her hand.*) Remember, you're Helen Keller! You're about to make a discovery . . .

(*He pours some water into her extended right hand and she reacts dramatically, sitting up and flicking the water at him.*)

MOTHER O:
Are you crazy?

SON (*pushing her down*):
Relax . . . Lie down . . . You've got to discover it's not just *water* . . .

MOTHER O (*sitting up and holding out her hand*) So why is my hand wet?

SON (*pushing her down*):
Your hand is wet with many mysterious names—*Eau. Agua. Wasser* . . . If you, Helen Keller, discover the meaning of *water*, it will liberate you . . .

MOTHER O:

You mean Helen Keller had to study water in foreign languages?

SON *(upset):*

No, she had to discover water as language! Can't you see she had to feel the word become flesh! She had to feel language deep inside her blocked senses so she could learn *how to be, ser, estar, sein, to be!*

MOTHER O *(sitting up, glaring, irrepressible):*

You mean Helen Keller had water poured in her hand to learn to be?

SON:

Oh god, let's try again . . .

MOTHER O:

No more water stunts!

SON:

Shut your eyes! . . . *(He pushes her down again.)* Imagine yourself back in Biblical days . . .

MOTHER O:

You want me to be Bathsheba . . .

SON:

No, think of Genesis, the way language begins . . . "And God called the light Day, and the darkness he called Night." Think of the amazing time when a language begins and starts naming things to form a community . . . Hold out your hand . . . *(She does so.)* I'm going to pour a few more drops of water into it . . . Don't panic now . . . You're Helen Keller, deaf and dumb, locked into a dark, silent world that has no way to communicate, no language . . . You feel the *waaa-ter,* but you can't name it because you're deaf and dumb . . . You're Helen Keller cut off from the thrill of physical language . . .

MOTHER O *(impulsively, feeling herself):*

Thank god, I'm not cut off from physical thrills . . . So how did Helen Keller learn?

SON:

Sei ruhig, pace, be quiet and I'll show you! . . . (He pushes her down again.) Palms up again . . . *(She holds up her palms again.) Du musst dein Leben ändern, you must change your life* . . .

MOTHER O:

You trying to put a spell on me or something?

SON:

A few more drops of water in your hand . . . *(He pours a few more drops.)*
I don't give a damn, think of it as a spell . . . Feel it like Helen Keller—
soft, liquid, puzzling because you don't know its name . . . Now in the
palm of your other hand I trace the sacred word—*Eau. Agua. Waaa-sser.*
Waaa-ter . . . *(As he traces the words slowly in her palm, he draws out the*
syllables like a chant of redemption.)

MOTHER O *(Slowly, beginning to understand the mysterious transformations of*
language, MOTHER O *reacts, repeating the syllables with real feeling.):*
Waaaa-seeeeer . . . *Waaaa-teeeeer* . . . *j*

SON *(excited):*
That's it! . . . Feel it? . . . Name it! . . . That's how Helen Keller
discovers language and the ability to communicate!

MOTHER O *(intoning with the excitement of discovery):*
Eauuuu . . . *Floooow* . . . *Aguaaaaa* . . . *Waaaaa-teeer* . . .
Waaaaa-ter . . .

(Staring at her hand, she breaks off as if she's just realized the physical power
of language.) Waa-ter . . . Is this really how Helen Keller learned words?

SON:

It's true . . . This is how she learned in her dark world to connect abstract words and physical meaning.

MOTHER O *(staring at her palm):*
God, it's mysterious . . . I never understood that words were so physical
before . . .

(She traces the word, water, in her palm again.) *Waaa-ter* . . .

SON *(getting up and pacing about):*
You feel how sensuous words are? I've been trying to tell you for years,
Mother O. To me the universe is a great sea of languages full of secret syllables, each with its special sound. Currents of sound move through the
great sea of languages with hidden messages that need translating. I want
to be the greatest translator in the world! The trouble is most translators
are just hacks. They translate the drab, literal surface, not the deep meaning of words. I want to find the wonder of hidden meaning in languages!
New rhythms and images! Don't you see, Mother O, that way I won't be
just a run-of-the-mill schizophrenic. I'll be famous for my own special
self!

MOTHER O *(tracing the water in her palm):*
I can see how you feel about language . . . It has its own magic . . .

SON *(excited):*
You see how language can heal, the way it did with Helen Keller?

MOTHER O *(getting up slowly):*
Yes, I understand now how language can heal . . . If you're deaf and
dumb . . . *(looking at him)* or schizo . . . the discovery of words can be
marvelous . . . You've made me learn something finally . . . But language hasn't healed you . . . You're not Helen Keller . . . I'm sorry
but I can't take it anymore . . . You've got to leave this house . . . I
want you to leave for your own good . . .

*(They stare at each other, both on the verge of tears. Suddenly, the SON
turns and runs away.)*

SCENE 15

*(Lights up on the GHOST FATHER and the SON outside by the park bench.
They are plotting to return and take over the house.)*

SON *(nervously):*
Remember the count . . . *Uno, dos, tres* . . . We attack on *tres* . . .

GHOST FATHER:
You really think we can do this by the numbers? If Helen Keller didn't
work, what can we do against Mother O?

SON:
You promised! We have to attack together. After all it's our house too. She
has no right to throw us out.

GHOST FATHER:
What are we going to do if we get into the house?

SON:
You know the plan. We assert our territory. I get my language laboratory
back and you take over the bedroom again.

GHOST FATHER:
You're promoting family war . . .

SON *(grimly):*
That's where wars begin. *(The GHOST FATHER starts feeding the pigeons.)*

SON:
Stop feeding those damn pigeons! Come on, we've got the strength . . .

GHOST FATHER *(sighing):*
And she's got the magic . . .

SON:
You promised! Remember the count!

GHOST FATHER:
Uno, dos, tres . . . We break in on three . . . I never did Breaking and Entering before . . .

SON *(fiercely):*
Willst du immer ein verdammter Geist sein?

GHOST FATHER:
You don't have to tell me off in German. Ghosts are not always damned. Sometimes they just sit and think about what happened to them.

SON *(impatiently, starting to count):*
Time for action! *Uno!* . . . *Dos!* . . . *Tres!* . . .

SCENE 16

(They bang loudly on the door with their fists. The GHOST FATHER *starts more feebly and is forced to hammer more energetically by the* SON. *As they start banging,* MOTHER O *appears in the kitchen, singing her variations of Cole Porter's "Just One Of Those Crazy Things.")*

MOTHER O *(singing):*
As Dorothy Parker once said to her boyfriend,
"Fare Thee Well;"
As Donald Trump announced from his glittering dump,
"You've got your million, love, I'm gone."
As Rudy the Ghost learned from his wife,
"On a park bench there's no marital strife!"
As Mother O cried in Genius Son's ear,
"Henry, my son, why not face the facts, my dear?"
Refrain
It was just one of those things,
Just one of those crazy flings,
One of those break-ins, no door bell rings,
Just one of those crazy things . . .

(As the GHOST FATHER *and* SON *keep banging and shoving against the door,* MOTHER O *opens it. They pitch through it, sprawling onto the floor.* MOTHER O *assumes her judgment seat behind the piano in the kitchen. Banging on the top of the piano for order with a cleaver, she orders:)*

MOTHER O:

All rise, please! The honorable court of Mother O is convened for supreme judgment. Trapped in a break-in! . . The first defendant is Rudy Abendstern, ghost father. How do you plead, Guilty or Nolo Contendere?

SON *(gaping):*

You've been studying Latin.

MOTHER O:

Judgment language! How does the defendant plead?

GHOST FATHER *(meekly):*

No contest . . .

SON *(hissing):*

You traitor!

MOTHER O:

The court rules that Ghost Fathers can haunt their homes only if they help throw their kids out into the world.

GHOST FATHER *(defensively):*

I was only trying to help him get back in until he finds a translation job.

MOTHER O *(furiously):*

You ganged up on me!

GHOST FATHER *(signaling mildly):*

Point of Order . . .

MOTHER O:

I'm sick of your mathematical points! Sit on your park bench and talk to your pigeons by the numbers! *(turning to the* SON*)* Schizo son, how do you plead?

SON:

Guilty of being born to Mother O.

MOTHER O:

Overruled! Even genius children are supposed to grow up and depart.

SON:

Maybe we could compromise. Build a thick wall, divide the house in two!

GHOST FATHER:
A house divided . . .

MOTHER O:
No soap, this house is too small. I apologize for complaining so much about your foreign speech. I'm sorry I didn't understand about language sooner . . .

SON (*trying to take advantage of this little opening*):
Maybe we can work things out . . .

MOTHER O:
Son, this is Mother O's goodbye judgment! Time for you to leave your dead room and find your living tree of language!

SON:
You're serious about this!

MOTHER O:
I cut the cord! (*a great surgical gesture*) I expose you to life on the streets! I sentence you and me to freedom!

SON:
I can't stand freedom! I'll die!

MOTHER O:
Learn freedom or die is Mother O's showdown judgment.

SON (*stubbornly*):
I refuse to go! (*He sits down, facing the audience.*) I'm sitting down right here . . .

MOTHER O (*a whirlwind of command*):
Stand up! (*The* SON *is jolted to his feet, at attention facing her.*) About face! (*He pivots around automatically, facing the audience.*) Salute the universe, you who are about to enter it!

> (*Staring at the audience, the* SON *breaks down, cowering as he turns back to* MOTHER O, *falling on his knees before her.*)

SON (*begging*):
Please, Mother O, they're all American speakers . . . I can't make it out there! I'll clean up my room . . .

MOTHER O:
Appeal denied! Mother O hardens her heart. I'm going to turn this home into a lighthouse! Be happy you taught me about language. When you're

cured, and have become a great translator, you can come home again. We'll celebrate! I'll try to learn French . . . *(She sings the Verse to her version of Cole Porter's "I Get A Kick Out Of You.)*
A new age begins of family change!
It's time for a bold new kind of equality!
I know that there's something out there I must find,
Something speaks to me out on the street,
To all women a freedom so sweet
There's a new world out there to greet,
A world free in the sun . . .

SON *(overlapping as* MOTHER O *sings):*
She'll never learn French . . .

GHOST FATHER:
She'll never give up Cole Porter.

MOTHER O *(glaring at the* GHOST FATHER*):*
Look who's talking from the fadeout angle! How did we ever get together anyway?

GHOST FATHER *(shrugging):*
Magnetic attraction . . . Positive and negative points . . . No vector understanding . . .

MOTHER O:
Don't give me your mathematical crap! I tried to give you confidence!

GHOST FATHER:
In a commander's tone of voice.

SON:
Her parents should have enrolled her in the Marines.

GHOST FATHER:
No one can compete with you.

MOTHER O:
Bullshit! How come marriage always turns into a competition?

GHOST FATHER:
In this country marriage is either a religious ordeal or a competitive sport.

SON *(pleading desperately):*
What am I going to do?

MOTHER O:
Think positive. Build your own foreign language community!

SON *(agonizing):*
I can't work! *Ich kann nicht arbeiten* . . .

MOTHER O:
Speak English! *(She continues with the Refrain of "I Get A Kick Out Of You", singing to the* SON *and* GHOST FATHER*)*
I get no kick out of French!
All you men want is a wench
You can flaunt
Who'll make your erotic dreams real
But I'm not that wench, no third wheel! *(then to the Father)*
Computers give me no thrill!
When it comes to science
I can use an appliance,
But I hate reliance on you,
So I'm learning to myself to be true! *(crossing to the Son)*
My son gets sick every time he thinks
That I will cease to want him.
You've got to lick this despair and leave,
Tell language stories a la . . . Grimm!
The three of us in this house
Dreaming a tango,
Go crazy and Bango! . . .
When I can dance free like you men
Then I'll get a kick . . . *(speaking)*
I scatter you to the four winds like a Mother Bird!
Yes, I'll get a kick once again!

> *(*MOTHER O'S *expression shows grim determination, as the* PIANIST *modulates into a minor key. The* GHOST FATHER'S *and* SON'S *expressions also become anxious and worried.)*

GHOST FATHER:
We're in the world of park benches now . . .

> *(Slow blackout on their frozen, agonized expressions as Part I ends.)*

PART II

(The set is now transformed by Mother O's new life and feverish interests. Two years have passed. The Son's former chaotic room is now spartan clean, transformed into a dance studio, with Mother O's weavings and paintings on the wall. The kitchen is without cans, neat, full of plants and charts indicating Mother O's current concern for fresh vegetables and vitamins. Mother O's bedroom looks brighter and full of color with more dynamic weavings and paintings. The large portrait of Cole Porter is still prominent. Nervously, MOTHER O *is bustling about, cleaning, arranging a dinner party for her Prodigal Son, who is returning after a long absence and his unexpected worldly success. As she sets and prepares the table,* MOTHER O *sings:)*

MOTHER O *(singing):*
Time was when time stood still
And you were stuck in the house
Where you lived all your life . . .
Time was when time stood still
And you knew all you were was a wife.

Time was when time stood still.
Like a flypaper fly
You asked why you were born to serve men.
Time is when time stands still
Unless you break out free in the sun
And learn how to be yourself—Number One.

(spoken as she collapses in a chair)
So give it up, Baby! . . . *(singing again)*
When time stands still,
Dying dreams in your head
You ask why you were born to serve men.

Time is when time stands still
And you know you'll never be born again—
Unless—you break out free in the sun,
Break out free in the sun,
And learn how to be yourself—Number One!

(The SON *appears, formally dressed in a suit and tie, symbolizing his new success as a translator. He pauses at the door, rehearsing his new confident, successful role before he knocks.)*

SON *(cautioning himself):*
No more Mother O . . . Mom, mama, mother . . . *(He knocks.)*
*(*MOTHER O *opens the door, then runs back to hide in her room, as the Son calls out:)* Mother, I'm home!

MOTHER O *(calling from her room):*
Welcome, Prodigal Son!

SON *(looking around with amazement):*
Where are you?

MOTHER O:
Enter the new house of Mother O . . .

SON:
God, she's turned into a spider! . . . *(starting toward her room)* Are you hiding?

MOTHER O:
Hail to the genius! *(She rushes out and they embrace.)* How do you like my new house?

SON *(looking at the portrait of Cole):*
C'est la Vie . . . Still closeted with Cole . . .

MOTHER O *(as the* PIANIST *starts to play):*
I'm so glad to see you! In celebration of your new fame! *(She bursts into her new version of Porter's ''You're the Top.'')*
   "At words poetic, I'm so pathetic
   That I have always found it best
   Instead of getting 'em off my chest
   To let 'em rest unexpressed.
   I hate parading
   My serenading
   As I'll probably miss a bar . . .

SON *(muttering):*
More of the same Mother O . . . You never miss anything!

MOTHER O *(sweeping on):*
   But if this ditty
   Is not so pretty,

At least it'll tell you
How great you are . . .
Refrain:
You're the Top!
You're the Best Translator,
Even though
You're an English hater! . . .

SON *(shouting):*
I don't hate English anymore! I'm cured!

MOTHER O *(sweeping on):*
You're the Great Linguist!
You're the harmony of languages by the score—
You're a Greek perfection,
A Spanish election,
You're French to the core . . .

SON *(muttering):*
She hasn't changed . . . *(shouting)* This is your *welcome?*

MOTHER O *(continuing implacably):*
You're Supreme!
You're the Prodigal Child!
You're the Cream
Of new words so wild!
I'm a worthless Mom, a total wreck, a flop,
But if, Baby, I'm the Bottom,
You're the Top!

(She embraces her SON *grandly.)*

Cole and I welcome you!

(The SON *is overwhelmed by the embrace, kisses her, then draws back cautiously.)*

SON:
Thanks, Mother O . . . Oh, it's great to be home . . .

MOTHER O *(surveying him critically):*
You look tired.

SON *(wearily):*
I'm fine . . . All I need is a little rest in my room.

MOTHER O:
Your room is gone with the wind!

SON (*startled, pointing to the door of his former room*):
Where does that old door lead then?

MOTHER O:
No more litterbug cave . . .

SON (*trying to joke*):
You've smashed the walls down?

MOTHER O:
Total transformation! It's my studio now.

SON (*resigned*):
All right, I give in . . . May I rest a little in my *former room?*

MOTHER O:
It's my studio now! I put in a new floor to cover up your crap.

SON (*irritated, but trying hard not to show it*):
Congratulations on your new artistry. All I want to do is wash up and rest
for a moment.

MOTHER O:
Wash up is ok . . . But no hide-out in your room. It's my room now!

SON (*laughing uneasily*):
Hide? I'm just home for a visit. You wanted to celebrate my success . . .

MOTHER O (*proudly*):
Mr. Personal Translator for the President! I'm proud of you!

SON:
I was the President's first American-born translator! I translated for him
into Russian!

MOTHER O:
Mr. Big Shot! I'm delighted, but the question remains . . . Is the murder
of Mother O still in your heart?

SON (*staring at her with amazement*):
What? . . . I'm famous . . . I'm cured!

MOTHER O:
I sing your praises, and welcome you with caution.

SON *(resentfully):*
Just treat me like any visitor, for Christ's sake!

MOTHER O:
How come a visitor swears?

SON *(snapping):*
Swearing is a sign of my new maturity!

MOTHER O:
Just so maturity doesn't turn into a permanent guest.

SON *(exploding):*
You're the god damndest Mother O . . . Mom . . . I've ever seen!

(He turns to go.)

MOTHER O:
Wait . . . Despite the old curses against Mom, we'll celebrate my new kitchen skill. I cooked you a dinner. I threw out all the cans.

SON *(incredulously):*
You think I'm still interested in cans?

MOTHER O:
You're free of your crazy tin can food dreams?

SON *(angrily):*
You want to test me?

MOTHER O:
Why not? You'll taste miracles . . .

SON:
Don't tell me you've turned into a gourmet cook . . .

MOTHER O *(smiling):*
I went to school for a certificate . . . Nouvelle Cuisine . . . *(She mispronounces it rather badly, as he winces.)* You'll see Mother O is your kind of Chief!

SON *(growling):*
You mean Chef . . .

MOTHER O:
Don't I get to use a pun? We can't talk friendly?

SON:
Maybe I should take you out to dinner . . .

MOTHER O:
You don't want to face it?

SON:
Face what?

MOTHER O:
Testing our kitchen problem to prove you're cured . . .

SON:
All right . . . Cook me to death!

MOTHER O (reprimanding him):
Melodrama is my thing.

SON (despairing):
Everything is *your thing!*

MOTHER O:
As we stuff ourselves, you can tell me how you became the President's right hand translator.

SON (shaking his head):
Right hand is a truly bad expression . . .

MOTHER O (pricking up her ears):
What? You're still schizo about American?

SON (pulling himself together):
No, I love all languages. I told you I'm cured! How could I be a *right hand* translator if I'm not cured?

MOTHER O:
Don't get hysterical. I'm just putting my new foot forward . . . *(She puts her foot on the piano.)*

SON (savagely):
On your piano as usual . . .

MOTHER O:
I have to keep a little music in my life . . . You never understood about Cole. Still I admit I maybe pounded his spirit into your ears too much . . . You wait, I've changed too. I've got some surprises . . .

SON (warily):
All I can do is wait I'm so tired . . .

MOTHER O *(pointing):*
How do you like that rug? I wove it myself.

SON *(staring at the rug):*
The Navajo Indians would call it *iimass*—an Eye Dazzler.

MOTHER O *(gesturing at the wall):*
How do you like my paintings?

SON:
Incredible . . . You're better than a Jack of All Trades. You're a Jill of All Arts!

MOTHER O:
You haven't seen anything yet . . .

SON *(staring at the portrait of Cole):*
How come with all this new action, Cole is still stage center?

MOTHER O *(mysteriously):*
He's my front man . . . Wait till you see the other side . . .

SON:
You mean Cole has two faces?

MOTHER O *(teasing):*
If I show you all the changes too fast, you'll drop dead.

SON:
Do you still see my father?

MOTHER O *(laughing):*
Doctor's prescription: Take one ghost father for occasional comfort . . . Don't worry! He'll fade in to see you.

SON *(troubled):*
Do I want to see him?

MOTHER O:
Sure, you want to tell him all you've done. He'll be proud too.

SON:
Is he still the same?

MOTHER O:
He's not too interested in American forward motion.

SON *(snapping):*
Why don't you admit a ghost in bed is better than nothing!

MOTHER O:
So I admit it . . . Go on, wash up, take a little rest . . . Say goodbye to your junky past.

SON *(uneasily):*
I won't be long. Maybe a little nap . . .

MOTHER O:
Prepare for dancing revelations!

SON *(worried again):*
Dancing revelations?

MOTHER O:
Watch out while you're resting . . . Stare up at the ceiling . . . See if the stars come out! What did the old prophets say? "Dance, if you want to feel joy!"

(Dazed by the new MOTHER O, the SON begins cautiously to enter his former room, ushered by MOTHER O, as the scene blacks out.)

SCENE 2

(In his old room, the SON lies stiffly on an unfamiliar couch, staring at Mother O's new studio. Banging her pots and pans in the kitchen, MOTHER O sings: "Give Me America," influenced clearly by Cole Porter's "Give Me The Land.")

MOTHER O *(singing):*
"Give me America,
The land of games and wealth,
Give me the old USA,
The land of natural foods and Health . . ."

SON *(tossing restlessly):*
Oh god, she's still on her USA kick . . .

MOTHER O *(continuing):*
Give me America,
The land of music and Funk,
Of athletes and the Slam-Dunk . . .

SON:
Funk and Slam-Dunk?

MOTHER O:

> Give me America,
> Land of love and hysterica,
> Where the sun never sets
> On advertising bets,
> Where we run after loot
> In the happiness pursuit,
> Oh give me America!
> Give me the USA!

SON:

"Loot and happiness pursuit!" *(angrily)* You can't treat me anymore like a schizo kid! I'm a success now! *(The* GHOST FATHER *materializes like a ghost.)*

GHOST FATHER:
Welcome home, son!

SON *(startled):*
How did you get in?

GHOST FATHER *(shrugging):*
Through the walls . . . Congratulations on your success as a translator.

SON:
No thanks to you . . . Dr. Archibald Piersen, the inventor of Transformational Therapy, cured me. He took me in as a patient because of my linguistic ability.

GHOST FATHER:
Genius to genius, eh . . .

SON *(furiously):*
It was a nightmare! Where else could I go after you collapsed and Mother O pushed me out? Dr. Piersen was glad to have me as a laboratory subject, a pet guinea pig! He forced me to see that life is like theatre. To survive, you have to become a master of performance!

GHOST FATHER:
You learned a lot about performance around here.

SON *(angrily):*
Dr. Piersen taught me what a successful father should be! He showed me how you reverted to your childhood when you became a ghost father! I had to perform my fantasies. It was a nightmare! I had to turn language into action! He began with the Home as Fortress . . .

GHOST FATHER:
I know that one.

SCENE 3

(The Fantasy Scenes take place like flashbacks in the Son's mind. A drop box drops a banner reading THE FORTRESS HOME, *as the* SON *begins to recall his therapy with the stern behavioral psychologist, Dr. Piersen.)*

SON:
In the Judaic-Christian tradition, the Fortress-Home stands always at the apex of the environment . . .

GHOST FATHER:
The apex is the tough part of the triangle . . .

SON:
Shut up! . . . The home is built as a fortress to maintain both family security and national strength. Inside the fortress, the Master guards his family. . .

GHOST FATHER:
What do I play?

SON *(furiously):*
You play the child! Dr. Piersen taught me how to command the fortress! . . .
(He struggles to assume the role of Fortress Master, as if being taught by Dr. Piersen. Imitating Dr. Piersen's voice:) "Returning to your fortress after a long day's hard work, you don't crawl home like a worm!" No. Doctor! I command my entrance!

(He announces his presence vehemently, while the PIANIST *plays appropriate music.)*

Let down the drawbridge! Master is home!

GHOST FATHER *(reflecting):*
If I lived in the age of fortresses, I'd like to let down the drawbridge. . .

*(*MOTHER O *bustles in dressed to the teeth to welcome her husband home.)*

MOTHER O AS FORTRESS WIFE *(as the Ghost Father reverts to childhood):*
Father's home! Why haven't you let down the drawbridge? You're an eternal child gaping at things!

(Sound of drawbridge banging down. The SON *continues to act out the agonizing conflict between him and Dr. Piersen, as the* SON *enters and bangs down his briefcase with fortress authority.)*

SON AS FORTRESS MASTER:
Is dinner ready?

GHOST FATHER AS CHILD *(producing a drawing):*
Papa, look at my drawing!

MOTHER O AS FORTRESS WIFE:
Not now, son . . . Papa is tired . . . *(trying to seduce the Fortress Master with her welcome)* You must have had a hard day's work, dear. Let me get you a relaxing drink and your slippers.

GHOST FATHER AS CHILD:
Why don't you just sit down and rest, Papa. . .

MOTHER O AS FORTRESS WIFE *(miming handing him the drink as the child mimes putting the slippers on the Fortress Master):*
Relax and enjoy your beautiful fortress. I've spent all day fixing it up for you.

SON AS FORTRESS MASTER:
It's good to be home. My fortress is so relaxing . . . *(to the* GHOST FATHER *as Fortress Son)* What are you drawing, son?

GHOST FATHER AS CHILD *(producing a drawing):*
I'm drawing a Super-Drawbridge to drown our enemies!

SON AS FORTRESS MASTER:
Good work, son. You've got real talent . . . *(then, realizing he's relaxing too much)* "Don't relax like a little rabbit! Inspect the fortress!" *(He jumps up to attention.)* Look, I see some dust? I thought you'd been working on the fortress! You call this clean? The maid forgot to dust today!

MOTHER O AS FORTRESS WIFE:
I warned her . . . I warned her . . . I have to do everything!

SON AS FORTRESS MASTER:
No excuses!

GHOST FATHER AS CHILD *(calling with glee):*
You should punish the maid, mama!

SON AS FORTRESS MASTER:
What's for dinner?

MOTHER O AS FORTRESS WIFE:
Your favorite roast beef and baked potato!

SON AS FORTRESS MASTER *(overcome by this American banality):*
I hate roast beef and baked potato! *(He rushes downstage, gagging, then addresses himself sternly, as if reacting to Dr. Piersen's reprimand.)* No, no, Dr. Piersen, I won't regress! It's just that roast beef and baked potato are so American I feel sick!

GHOST FATHER AS CHILD *(pressing the drawing at his father):*
How do you like my Super-Drawbridge, Daddy?

SON AS FORTRESS MASTER *(snapping):*
Get lost! *(The son begins to cry.)* I've lost it, Dr. Piersen! What? . . . Try again . . . Think of the Quest . . . Lancelot, Guinevere, King Arthur . . . I don't know if I can do King Arthur . . . Let's try the Fortress again . . .

SCENE 4

(The SON *repeats his arrival home as Fortress Master. From the second drop box falls a banner reading* THE SUPER DRAWBRIDGE.*)*

SON AS FORTRESS MASTER *(He's moving more painfully now, his jaunty step stiffer and more exaggerated, more sadistic.):*
I'm home! Is dinner ready?

GHOST FATHER AS CHILD *(hissing from the place where he is huddled with his mother):*
You forgot the drawbridge.

SON AS FORTRESS MASTER *(glaring at him):*
I'm home! Let down the drawbridge!

GHOST FATHER AS CHILD *(as the sound of the drawbridge banging down is heard):*
It's down, Papa! I drew a Super-Drawbridge for you! *(Gives him the drawing, as the Fortress Wife flutters around the Fortress Master).*

SON AS FORTRESS MASTER:
Thank you, son . . .

MOTHER O AS FORTRESS WIFE *(fluttering):*
Isn't your son gifted? I'm so glad you're home, dear. Here's your drink

. . . You look tired. Why don't you sit down and rest. Would you like a little romance before your roast beef?

SON AS FORTRESS MASTER *(Struggling to control the rapid fire of his welcome home, he jumbles his answers, as he seizes her wrist and forces her to the ground.)*
Drinkdinnerfirstromancelater!

MOTHER O AS FORTRESS WIFE *(seductively):*
You're such a powerful fortress master . . . *(stroking his hair)* How I love your mastery! I'm so glad you're home. Let me give you a kiss . . . *(to the* GHOST FATHER *as* SON*)* Why don't you go play, darling. Papa and I want to be alone.

GHOST FATHER AS SON *(protesting):*
Why can't I tell Papa about my Super-Drawbridge?

MOTHER O AS FORTRESS WIFE:
Go play! *(The son withdraws reluctantly.)* Now you can relax, dear . . . We can have a little romance before dinner.

SON AS FORTRESS MASTER *(crying out):*
Help, Dr. Piersen! Which comes first, romance or dinner? Of course . . . Dinner comes first! *(turning to reprimand his fortress wife)* Since the fortress commander brings home the bacon, I demand that it be cooked on time! Dinner first, then romance!

MOTHER O AS FORTRESS WIFE *(meekly):*
As you say, dear . . .

SON AS FORTRESS MASTER *(on the edge of a breakdown):*
Dr. Piersen, I can't stand that awful American phrase, *bring home the bacon!* . . . No, doctor, please . . . Drill myself in the ear? . . . *(In agony, he repeats):*
Bring home the bacon! Bring home the bacon! Bring home the bacon! . . . Is that better, Doctor? *(then, echoing the doctor's instructions)* "Enter the fortress, think positive, look powerful, take deep breaths, act like a master!" . . . Begin again!

SCENE 5

(Wearily, he becomes the Fortress Master again, crawling home this time from work, as the drop box drops a banner reading BRING HOME THE BACON!*)*

SON AS FORTRESS MASTER *(exhausted):*
I'm home! Let down the drawbridge! ,

(We hear the drawbridge bang down and, in a burst of enthusiasm, the GHOST FATHER *as Fortress Son hurls himself upon the Fortress Master in an eager welcome.)*

GHOST FATHER AS SON *(sullenly, matter of fact):*
I made a Super-Drawbridge for you, Papa . . .

SON AS FORTRESS MASTER *(pushing him away):*
Not now, son. I'm tired. I need my dinner.

(This time MOTHER O's *subservience as the Fortress Wife is cursory and sullenly played in an abrupt manner.)*

MOTHER O AS FORTRESS WIFE:
Despite all the difficulties I had with the cook, your dinner is ready . . .

GHOST FATHER AS SON *(resentfully to his mother):*
Papa won't look at my Super-Drawbridge!

SON AS FORTRESS MASTER *(failing in his role):*
I need a drink. What's for dinner?

MOTHER O AS FORTRESS WIFE *(sullenly):*
Your favorite meal—roast beef and baked potato. *(She exits abruptly.)*

SON AS FORTRESS MASTER *(gagging, falling on his face, and crying out):*
I can't do it! I'll never be a Fortress Master! You want me to try another model, Doctor? Which one? I'm so tired . . . You want me to try "The Trains Run on Time" . . . What? . . . I know . . . This time I'm the Chief Executive Officer.

(The drop box drops the fourth and last banner, CEO.*) (The* SON *struggles to assume a Teutonic patriarchal demeanor, hat, gloves, formidable briefcase, a rolled umbrella, trying to prove that he is determined to return to the fortress exactly on schedule.)*

SON AS CEO:
In every strong patriarchal state the trains run on time! . . . If the trains are late, nothing functions properly . . . Law and order collapse . . . The family breaks down . . . Anarchy reigns . . . Try again . . . How's this? . . . The train pulls up right on time . . . I enter my home as Chief Executive . . . *(he calls out)* Let down the drawbridge! *(A pause, there is no sound of the drawbridge banging down.)* What's that, Dr. Piersen?

. . . There's no drawbridge in "The Trains Run On Time"? . . . I understand . . . It's a burglar alarm system for security . . . Thank god, we got rid of the damn drawbridge . . . I insert my key and turn off the burglar alarm system that protects my family . . .

MOTHER O AND THE SON (*watching warily and saluting with their arms upraised*):
Welcome home, Chief!

> (*Goosestepping, they march off as the son collapses. The* SON *twitches convulsively on the bedroom cot as the* GHOST FATHER *resumes his role as the real father.*)

GHOST FATHER:
You're sweating, son . . . Are you all right? Have you been dreaming?

SON (*sitting up as his fantasy fades away*):
I was dreaming about Dr. Piersen, the behavioral therapist, the one who cured me . . . I was commanding a fortress . . . It was horrible!

GHOST FATHER (*gently*):
You should have stayed out of your old room . . .

SON (*tormented*):
This isn't my room anymore!

GHOST FATHER:
Would it help if I join you for dinner?

SON (*hesitating*):
I guess a ghost presence is better than nothing.

GHOST FATHER:
You know Mother O's been studying dancing with Martha Graham.

SON:
What do I care? All I want is to show her how I made it in the world. One simple, final proof of my success which she doesn't want to admit. That's what I need to survive her dinner . . .

SCENE 6

(*He lies back, tossing restlessly on the bed. The* GHOST FATHER *stands silently, watching. The lights go up as* MOTHER O, *in a leotard, enters the room dramat-*

ically, reversing the portrait of Cole Porter on the wall to reveal a portrait of Martha Graham. The portrait is of Graham performing in a fierce, mythological dance, Jocasta in Night Journey. *Shocked, the* SON *is jolted upright, riveted to her performance. As the* PIANIST *plays Mother O's music based on Cole Porter,* MOTHER O *begins to speak and dance out for her son's benefit, Martha Graham's revolt against her mother.)*

MOTHER O *(dancing out this monologue):*
Cole and Martha Graham together! A perfect match! Freedom's dancing time! *(flexing her spine)* See what Martha discovered? . . . The spine is the tree of life! . . . Bare feet planted in earth *(flexing her feet)* . . . Toes curling in to act as hinge . . . Thrust up from the hips! *(she thrusts up)* . . . So you don't know Martha Graham, son? . . . Martha's parents were very strict . . . Old school religion . . . Momma in bed, kitchen and church . . . Dancing was sinful . . . *(takes a stance as stern mother)* All Martha wanted was to escape from her mother . . . "What do you mean, Momma, what do you mean by God and the moral laws?" . . . "God commands you not to sin!" *(She dances.)* "Is dancing a sin, Momma?" *(She dances another defiant gesture.)* "If a woman reveals her body lewdly that is a sin!" *(She dances a sensuous pelvic thrust.)* "Is a pelvic thrust lewd, Momma? Aren't we born by a pelvic thrust?" . . . *(then, as the stern Mother)* "A woman does not ever display publicly the private agony of birth!" *(dancing)* "Is that why the church people speak of Immaculate Conception?" *(as Mother)* "The Virgin is all white purity!" . . . *(dancing exultantly)* "But doesn't the Virgin move with joy, Momma? Doesn't the Virgin ever dance with joy?" *(as Mother)* "The Virgin never dances lewdly, my daughter. The Virgin only moves and glows with pure light!" *(dancing, thrusting up)* "What about *spasms,* Momma? Isn't life full of *spasms?"* *(as Mother)* "Spasms are for the dark, and for privacy!" *(dancing defiantly)* "Then I want the dark! . . . I want the spasm of climax! . . . I want to expose the body! . . . Show bones, muscles, nerves, how the body works when it moves freely." *(as Mother)* "They'll crucify you, Martha! They'll call you a whore, a lewd woman!" . . . That's what happened with women, son . . . Martha led the revolt to break the family stranglehold . . . Now we've come to the testing time! . . . *(dancing before the* SON*)* Let the river of movement flow as it empties into the ocean! . . . Maybe then we can rest in this family . . . Who knows the end, son, until we dance it out with Cole and Martha! *(She continues dancing powerfully as the scene blacks out.)*

SCENE 7

(Lights up in the kitchen area, which has been transformed into a ceremonial din-
ing room by moving in a completely set table with candles. The GHOST FATHER
sits quietly, inconspicuously, as the token head of the table. The SON *stands cau-*
tiously by his chair. In a dazzling Op-Art apron she has created, MOTHER O
bustles around, preparing her ceremonial dinner. Her bustling has a mysterious,
dance-like quality.)

MOTHER O:
Ready? . . . Set . . . Go for your Feast of Honor!

SON *(shaking his head):*
I'm exhausted. You kept dancing all over the room.

MOTHER O:
I told you . . . It's my dance studio now. Get ready to spill your story,
but you get a taste surprise first.

SON *(sullenly):*
I'm not sure if I can stand a *taste surprise* . . .

MOTHER O *(brightly):*
Shut your eyes everybody!

(As they shut their eyes, she moves like Martha Graham, whips open the re-
frigerator, pulls out two elaborate dishes on beds of rock salt, and places
them triumphantly in front of the SON *and* GHOST FATHER.)

Open up!

SON *(opening his eyes, gaping):*
What's this on a salt mountain?

MOTHER O *(grandly):*
Oysters Rockefeller! *(dancing out her gestures as she talks)* In these pearls,
one teaspoon anchovy paste . . . A few dashes Tabasco sauce to give you
the hots . . . And the final secret Mother O touch—goodbye to worries
with one tablespoon of absinthe!

SON *(tasting with extreme caution, then increasing amazement):*
What a taste! . . . Like Rockefeller feeding you a million dollar bill!

GHOST FATHER *(tasting and laughing):*
A real Rockefeller dish!

MOTHER O *(pleased):*
So we begin with a taste supreme! . . . Now you can start your success story!

(MOTHER O puts out her hand to slow the SON down as he is eating greedily.)

Eat slower . . . You'll get cramps.

(Resenting her instructions, the SON tries desperately to eat and tell his story at the same time.)

SON:
When you threw me out of the house, Rudy suggested that I study the computer . . .

GHOST FATHER *(confirming):*
The computer does not worry which language it speaks.

SON:
Since I can't study the computer in English, of course, I go to a Spanish-speaking computer school . . .

MOTHER O *(breaking in):*
Give me a credit for pushing you out of your room.

SON:
I conceived the idea of developing a computer program for international corporations that would translate foreign languages almost simultaneously with absolute accuracy of communication . . .

MOTHER O *(unable to stop interrupting):*
How come a machine gets to be more accurate than people? If it tells me what to do, I'll give it a punch!

SON *(stiffly):*
The computer doesn't give orders. All it does is say what you want it to say.

MOTHER O *(not convinced):*
In the movies, it orders you around.

SON *(choking):*
That's silly Hollywood science fiction! Humanity is not in danger because of the computer!

GHOST FATHER *(sympathetically)*:
The danger is in the people who program the computers.

MOTHER O *(agreeing)*:
You tell him, Rudy!

GHOST FATHER *(brightening)*:
The computer is just a super-tool. Soon, you'll be able to carry it in your pocket.

MOTHER O *(to the Son)*:
Go ahead, son . . . So you programmed this super-tool to take over . . .

SON *(Frustrated, he stuffs another oyster in his mouth and crunches savagely, then gurgles desperately.)*
I can't eat and talk at the same time!

MOTHER O *(shrugging)*:
Make a choice.

SON *(struggling to assert his story and gagging on the food)*:
All right! I thought if I could program syllabic sound structures into new shorthand symbols for any linguistic structure . . . then I'd be linguistic Super Champion! . . .

MOTHER O:
You're trying to be Superman with your Super-Tool . . .

SON *(shouting while chewing)*:
It's not Superman! . . . It's champion phonetic techniques!

MOTHER O:
What do I know from phonetic . . .

SON *(desperately)*:
I failed! I couldn't program the right phonetic techniques into the computer! *(He stares at the now empty dish.)*

MOTHER O *(taking pity on him)*:
Come on, it's all right . . . *(then, as the SON is about to continue)* Wait a minute . . . Time to feed your story with Mother O's masterpiece. Cover your eyes, boys!

GHOST FATHER *(getting the Son to cover his eyes too)*:
We boys are prepared to die with delight.

(With another dancing flourish, MOTHER O produces her supreme dish from the oven.)

226

MOTHER O *(proudly):*
Martha Graham's *Salmon Archiduc!*

SON *(peering under his arm with a resigned look):*
Martha Graham's *What?*

MOTHER O *(dancing magically with it to the table):*
Dancing salmon! I named it after Martha because the salmon is a great upriver dancer. One quarter cup Spanish sherry . . . and two table-spoons of French cognac for your foreign language tongue.

SON *(wildly):*
My head's floating! You're trying to kill my story with liquor!

MOTHER O:
Booze isn't my secret ingredient . . . Try it . . .

GHOST FATHER *(tasting):*
Whatever it is certainly opens up the nasal passages!

MOTHER O *(nodding):*
Come on, son, see if you don't breathe in better . . .

SON *(tasting, hit by the cayenne pepper):*
Phewwww! . . . That salmon is really dancing upstream!

MOTHER O *(with delight):*
My secret is an extra dab of cayenne pepper!

SON:
My head is ringing like a bell!

MOTHER O *(gesturing for him to return to his story):*
Go on with a clear head . . . You were trying to become the Superman Computer Champion . . .

SON *(mopping his eyes which are watering):*
No matter what I did, I discovered that I could still translate faster than any machine . . . So I put the computer aside for the time being . . .

MOTHER O:
You always had a quick tongue. Have another bite of dancing salmon.

SON *(eating and talking):*
I went to the United Nations . . . They hired me as a Simultaneous Translator to translate from English into foreign languages . . . In the whole world there are only a few hundred Simultaneous Translators, so they needed me . . .

MOTHER O *(observing him):*
You're good at simultaneous . . . No one beats you eating and talking together.

SON *(furiously increasing the tempo of his eating and talking together):*
Simultaneous translation . . . is perfect for a schizophrenic genius . . . Isolated from the world . . . you translate . . . with your earphones on . . . in a soundproof booth . . . The lights are dim . . . It's cool . . . No one bothers you . . .

GHOST FATHER *(observing mildly):*
That's what it's like on a peaceful park bench.

MOTHER O *(to the Ghost Father):*
What do you do, Rudy, about all those joggers in the park, running around you with earphones?

GHOST FATHER:
They run in a turmoil of sound, but I don't hear them.

MOTHER O *(to the SON):*
I don't go for earphones. Can't you shut 'em off in the U.N. when you need a rest?

SON *(yelling):*
You can't shut them off! If you shut off your earphones in the United Nations, you might set off a nuclear bomb!

MOTHER O *(considering this):*
A bomb? I thought it was just speedy translation . . .

SON *(continuing desperately):*
If you don't translate fast and true, you can set off a bomb . . .

MOTHER O *(regarding him critically):*
In your isolated booth, with your speedy languages, it doesn't sound like you changed much.

SON *(shouting again):*
A miracle happened! In that booth, I reduced the most difficult idioms from official United Nations languages to shorthand phonetic sounds. Then, in my free time at home at night, I programmed my new sound-system into the computer. This time it worked!

GHOST FATHER *(proudly):*
He was the first to make the computer's binary system translate simultaneously from English into the U.N. official languages.

MOTHER O *(to* GHOST FATHER*)*:
Where'd you hear about this?

GHOST FATHER:
I've been following his career.

MOTHER O *(to Son)*:
Go on . . .

SON:
When delegates from all over the world heard my computer program translate difficult phrases accurately, they broke into applause!

GHOST FATHER *(proudly)*:
It was a great diplomatic breakthrough!

MOTHER O *(staring at the* SON*)*:
Let me get this straight . . . You're still isolated in a booth and they're clapping at a computer that speaks *foreign*?

SON *(continuing desperately)*:
I knew I had to break out from my booth and prove I was cured . . .

GHOST FATHER *(interrupting again eagerly)*:
He had to prove he was the greatest translator into Russian!

SON *(struggling)*:
I resolved to test my system under the most difficult stress conditions I could find . . .

MOTHER O *(interrupting)*:
Stress is our family brainmark! Right, Rudy?

> *(The* GHOST FATHER *chokes on his salmon, as the* SON *continues with another savage bite.)*

SON:
Russian and American astronauts were working together at the Johnson Space Center. They needed a special translator, so I asked for a transfer . . .

GHOST FATHER *(interjecting again)*:
The Cosmos and the Astros!

MOTHER O:
We had Russians working in this country?

SON *(savagely):*
The two Presidents decided to send a joint team of Russian cosmonauts and American astronauts into space together . . .

MOTHER O:
How come the Russians get the cosmos and we get the astros?

SON *(snapping):*
It's just linguistic jargon to differentiate Russians from Americans in space!

MOTHER O *(calmly):*
Jargon, schmargon. Eat more dancing salmon for clarity.

SON *(struggling harder to talk, eat, and control himself at the same time):*
The Johnson Space Center was a real test for my schizophrenia . . . A madhouse, every engineer as tense as a hot wire! . . . No quiet booth to think in . . . Life was a nightmare of infinite computer screens flashing lights and commands, attacking my eyes!

GHOST FATHER:
Infinite computer screens . . .

SON:
Administrators with enormous security badges pinned to their chests walked in and out, shouting directions in English shittalk . . .

MOTHER O *(staring severely):*
Shittalk? . . . What kind of language is that? So you weren't cured?

SON *(a despairing admission):*
Almost cured . . . Unconsciously, I spoke English slang without any problem. I'd trained myself to feel that it sounded as musical as French. From there to get it into Russian for the cosmonauts was no problem . . .

GHOST FATHER:
No problem! He created a new language, *Frenglish.*

MOTHER O *(laughing):*
That's a good one, Rudy, Frenglish!

SON *(in a frenzy):*
All right, damn you, Mother O! I created Frenglish to solve my schizophrenia. All the bigwigs in the Johnson Space Center thought it sounded like a new kind of American jargon!

MOTHER O *(sympathetically):*
At least you knew what you were doing.

SON *(shouting, stabbing at his food):*
No one knew that I still hated English! They were impressed by the incredibly accurate speed of my Frenglish! When the President heard about me at a White House party, he hired me as his Russian interpreter.

GHOST FATHER *(proudly):*
The President . . .

SON:

The President was visiting the Soviet Union to make a new trade agreement for all the big corporations like MacDonalds and General Motors. Since the State Department had been using refugee translators, they wanted to use an American interpreter this time . . .

MOTHER O:
So they got my son in a big kettle of fish . . .

SON *(he rises, acting out his horrified memory of the event):*
We landed in Moscow . . . Thousands of cheering Russians jammed the airport . . . I was right behind the President as we stepped out of Air Force 1!

GHOST FATHER *(nodding with pleasure):*
Air Force 1!

SON *(continuing in agony):*
You know what the temperature was? . . . Twenty degrees below zero!

GHOST FATHER:
Jesus Christ that's cold!

SON *(shivering and shaking in memory):*
That kind of deep freeze turns you into an instant icicle! My fingers turned as white as the birch trees around the airport . . . My teeth began clicking . . . I couldn't open my mouth! *(His teeth chatter in recollection.)*

MOTHER O *(surveying him):*
Don't tell me your shorthand system froze up . . .

SON *(desperately):*
The President waved and began to address the cheering crowd . . . Holding his arms up in an embrace, he cried out: "I have come to visit your great country because I have always loved the Russian people!"

MOTHER O *(nodding):*
Love is always tough to translate.

SON *(concluding desperately):*
I translated: "I have come to your great country because I want to make love to all of you Russian people!" . . .

MOTHER O *(staring at him, then beginning to laugh):*
Am I to believe this? . . . You make the President into a lover boy?

(The GHOST FATHER *begins laughing with her too.)*

SON *(angrily):*
You think I relapsed into my schizophrenia!

MOTHER O:
No, you tell us what happened . . .

SON *(bitterly):*
I should have trained in Siberia instead of Texas! . . . Am I any better than Napoleon and Hitler at defeating Russian winter?

GHOST FATHER:
It's all right . . . It wasn't a real defeat.

MOTHER O:
You had courage . . . You didn't quit.

SON:
In this family it's impossible to run out of energy! After the President let me go, I went back to perfecting my computer program. I set up an international translation school . . . *The Henry Abend System of Translation—Copyright by me!* A school for great translators! Branch offices in London, Paris, Rome, Berlin, Vienna, Tokyo, Moscow! *(The Ghost Father joins in reciting this list proudly.)*

GHOST FATHER:
With his new program, he went from diplomatic failure to international business success.

SON:
I'm invited everywhere to linguistic conferences . . . Intelligence agencies throughout the world study my system . . . *(He slumps, exhausted)* That's why I'm a famous failure!

MOTHER O *(slowly):*
Not too many failures are famous . . .

232

SON *(savagely):*
Oh, my system is great for international business and power politics. Business men and militarists can share products and weapons throughout the world. They delight in my translation system because it's such an easy way to do business. But my system's no good for deep language. I can't touch real emotional metaphors. So far I can't even translate "Do not go gentle into that good night" into Chinese. The tone comes out sounding like Mao-Tse-Tung.

MOTHER O:
Too bad. You'll get it one of these days. Have some more dancing salmon.

SON *(groaning):*
I'm drunk . . . My head is like dried-up paper.

GHOST FATHER:
He's just a little dry from the Cayenne pepper.

MOTHER O:
My dessert will clear your vision.

SON:
You want me to throw up like the old days?

MOTHER O:
Behave yourself! Other lavish mothers would serve you eight luxurious courses . . . I serve only three marvels . . . Marvel III coming up!

GHOST FATHER *(licking his tongue):*
Marvel III . . .

(With another dancing flourish, she produces her specially prepared, lascivious dessert.)

My god, it's . . .

MOTHER O *(gesturing at the dessert):*
In honor of ghosts and famous sons! . . . Oeufs a la Neige! . . . Master translation please?

SON *(staring, hypnotized):*
Eggs in the snow . . .

MOTHER O:
Is that all it is?

SON:
Snowball eggs . . .

MOTHER O:
Make it sound grander!

SON *(struggling):*
White eggs in the white snow . . .

MOTHER O:
Closer, but you've got snow on your brain!

SON *(angrily, finally admitting that he sees two naked female breasts atop the dessert):*
Snow White and her Snowball Breast Eggs!

MOTHER O:
What are you staring at, schizo son? You want me back in the mother cage?

(He raises the dessert, poised to throw it.)

SON:
I'm going to kill you!

MOTHER O *(defiantly, proudly):*
You can't kill a dancer! *(Howling with frustration, he hurls the dessert at her as she dances away and then turns to face him.)* Crazy son, what do you really want? Kill or kiss? . . .

SON:
Kiss!

MOTHER O *(staring at him):*
You've got to heal yourself in my house! . . .

(Moaning with fury, he rushes at her, tries to drag her down. Panther-like, she eludes him, then embraces him. They fall to the floor, frozen together.)

GHOST FATHER *(at the table, surveying the two together on the floor):*
Why was I invited to this dinner?

(Blackout.)

SCENE 8

(The lights come up on the GHOST FATHER.)

GHOST FATHER:
Here I sit, the ghost of reason, Number 3 and out in this family . . .

234

There they lie before me, the two people I love most attacking each other in the primal sin . . . Do I only dream I'm the final witness, judge of the dying family? . . . If I lived in Greek times I might put out my eyes like Oedipus . . . If I were an Elizabethan Oedipus, I could howl like Lear, "Kill, kill, kill, kill, kill!" . . . I could kill them both, but that wouldn't create the family again . . . Was Freud right about mothers and sons? . . . Tell it to Mother O . . . Oedipus is dead and Freud didn't know how to describe women dancing out into the sun . . . In his time women were all prisoners of men . . . Now they're prisoners of themselves . . . How is the family going to find a new community? . . . I weep for my dying family, but my body is full of ghost radiation . . . When you come to the end of the family, does it mean some kind of new beginning? . . . Look at them, damn them . . . Is there still a role they want me to play? . . . Look at me! . . .

(*Slow blackout.*)

SCENE 9

(*As the lights come up,* MOTHER O *and the* SON *are sitting together on the edge of her bed in her room, as if recovering from a dream.*)

MOTHER O:
Abendstern . . . Evening star . . . When you took just the name Abend, you made a big mistake. You cut out the starlight. You went into the *night* . . .

SON (*nuzzling her*):
I'll take back the name, Abendstern . . .

MOTHER O (*pushing him off*):
Don't get the idea we're starting all over . . . It's the end we're playing . . . Time to finish . . . (*She gets a rope, begins to tie it around his waist, then around hers. Throughout the following dance sequence, the pianist plays and strums appropriate music on a small harp under the upright piano.*)

SON (*beginning to laugh*):
What are you doing? Another game?

MOTHER O:
I'm tying us together . . .

SON (*laughing*):
Ewig! Forever!

MOTHER O:
A last dance to sever the umbilical cord . . . Like Martha Graham's *Night Journey*. The last night of Mother Oedipus . . .

SON *(playing along):*
Tied together in the eternal myth . . .

MOTHER O *(into her dancing ritual):*
No more mother goddesses . . . Who remembers the Mother after the King is born?

SON *(pulling at the rope playfully):*
The King remembers!

MOTHER O *(pulling him to her):*
I pull you in for a last farewell, my baby, my genius schizo son . . .

SON *(ecstatically):*
Into the fountain of birth!

MOTHER O *(cradling him classically for a moment):*
The curse is branded on you by the Gods . . . *(She traces the curse on his brow as he moans with delight.)*

SON:
The curse of greatness . . .

MOTHER O *(intoning):*
You are fated to rule in your father's place . . . Your father turns into a ghost . . .

(Protesting MOTHER O's *exorcism ritual, the* GHOST FATHER *enters like the Seer in Graham's* Night Journey, *warning Oedipus and Jocasta of their impending doom. He carries an enormously long white stick to guide him in his blindness. As he confronts* MOTHER O, *he pounds the stick on the floor, which creates a hammering, threatening rhythm.)*

GHOST FATHER *(pounding his stick as they freeze):*
Stop! You can't leave me behind! . . . You're my wife, my Mother O too! . . . You can't use Martha Graham to exorcise your son!

SON *(shouting defiantly):*
We're creating a new myth!

(Angrily the GHOST FATHER *lunges with his stick against the rope and they fall to the floor.)*

GHOST FATHER *(pounding with his stick):*
I am the ghost that denies! . . . Your son is famous now . . . He'll never be schizo again!

(MOTHER O *dances against the* GHOST FATHER, *pulling the rope so that the* SON *is pulled along.*)

MOTHER O:
Get lost! I'm going to cure him forever!

GHOST FATHER *(pounding his stick):*
Miriam, this isn't 475 B.C. . . . You can't cure your son by making love to him!

(MOTHER O *pulls the rope tightly so that the* SON *is forced to confront the* GHOST FATHER. *Threateningly, the* SON *raises his arms to attack the* GHOST FATHER, *as if he's going to commit his mythical act of parricide.*)

SON *(raising his arms):*
We sacrifice ourselves, oh Zeus!

MOTHER O *(pulling the* SON *back):*
Cut the melodrama . . . The days of sacrifice are over . . . You men tried to jail me in my own house, but I escaped . . . Martha taught me every soul is a circus!

SON *(crying out):*
Our love will live in eternity!

(MOTHER O *pulls on the rope to confront the* SON.)

MOTHER O:
Your dream is ended, schizo son. You tried to crawl back into the womb . . . I never slept with you! . . . You men stripped the magic from mothers . . . But the time of myth is not over . . . We women give magical life to the world! Mother O cuts the umbilical cord . . . *(Concluding the ritual, she throws away the rope, and picks up the lighted candles on the table. She hands a candle to the* GHOST FATHER, *then to the* SON. *With the third candle in her hand, she leads the way slowly out of the house to the park bench, as the* PIANIST *begins to sing and play. "The Farewell Song of Mother O.")*

PIANIST *(singing and playing):*
Abe Lincoln wrote:
"All I am I owe,

237

All I am I owe
To my Angel Mother."
That's what Abraham wrote,
"Angel Mother."
Goodbye to mothers, oh brother,
Who smother . . .

And Lizzie Borden took an axe
And gave her mother forty whacks—
That's what Elizabeth did—forty whacks!
Goodbye to Mother's kisses and smacks!

And Andy Carnegie said of his Mom,
"She's my favorite Heroine!"
That's what Andrew said:
"My heroine!"
Goodbye to mother's heroic scene . . .

And the oldtime mothers fading far
Watch new mothers enter their newborn star,
The old moms of church and home can't stay
With eyes of gold and feet of clay.
It's time to get up and it's time to go
And say goodbye to Mother O.
It's time to get up and it's time to go,
Goodbye to Mother O!

(While the PIANIST *is still singing and playing,* MOTHER O *blows out the candles and seats herself with the* GHOST FATHER *on the park bench.)*

MOTHER O:
Come on, let's sit down . . . A last farewell . . . No bitter feelings . . . Where do we put him? Our Prodigal Son? . . .

GHOST FATHER *(smiling):*
Between us as usual . . . *(They seat the* SON *tightly between them.)*

SON *(rigidly):*
Not too close! . . .

MOTHER O:
Not close enough . . .

GHOST FATHER:
You want closer? *(They squeeze the* SON *in tightly between them.)*

238

SON *(squirming):*

Too close! I feel confined!

MOTHER O:

You have to be close for the end to become a good beginning.

SON:

What do you mean by that? Is it really goodbye? . . . What am I going to do with my fame and money if I don't have any home to waste it on?

MOTHER O:

Learn to enjoy yourself and create your own family.

SON:

How can I create a new kind of family?

MOTHER O *(to the* GHOST FATHER):

You want to give him a last counsel?

GHOST FATHER *(smiling):*

The defense rests. As a ghost I'll always haunt both of you. Ghosts have a proud tradition. The family does not die so easily.

MOTHER O:

You're right, Rudy. The family changes. Look at it this way . . . The Last American Mother will reappear as something new in the world, another American invention . . .

SON:

If you become a new person, how will I recognize you?

MOTHER O:

Don't worry. Look for my resurrection as Mother Independence. You'll know me by the song and dance . . .

GHOST FATHER:

You'll know her by the wink in her eye, the way she moves . . . There's no one like her . . .

(She winks at them. With a grand gesture she reaches across the SON. *With her right hand she grips the* GHOST FATHER'S *left hand. Then, with her left hand, she takes the* SON'S *right hand.)*

SON *(squeezed, twisted):*

This is a position I'll never forget!

MOTHER O *(Standing up, she moves behind the bench, and places one hand on the* GHOST FATHER'S *shoulder, the other hand on the* SON'S *shoulder.)*

This is the legendary Mother O farewell touch. Good for ghosts and schizos . . . Whatever you're doing, being a great translator or a numbers expert, you'll feel my touch. My hand goes out with new mothers throughout the world. My body sings and dances! No one ever forgets Mother O, even though she's the Last American Mother . . .

(She stands there with them for a long moment in this final, ritualistic position, as the scene blacks out slowly.)

THE END

NOTE

The idea for *Mother O* began when I read about a schizophrenic linguistic genius living with his mother who played popular songs to him through the wall into his room. One of the few schizophrenics who knew his problem—that he hated English—the son stuffed his fingers in his ears and translated the lyrics that he couldn't stand into a foreign language. As I thought about the play, in a time when the feminist movement was growing and housebound mothers were breaking out of the home into new identities, I saw how the eternal oedipal conflict might be re-shaped today. Breaking out of her confinement to the traditional maternal role imposed by male authority, Mother O struggles literally to become the last American mother—hence the subtitle. She seeks to expand her horizons through the songs of Cole Porter and the dances of Martha Graham. Structurally, also, I wanted the play to have a certain kind of style that would incorporate elements of musical comedy—songs and dance—into the play to balance theatrically the linguistic obsessions of the schizophrenic son.

The first staged reading of *Mother O* was in 1989 by the Rhode Island Playwrights Theatre with the following members of the Trinity Repertory Company in Providence, Rhode Island: Melanie Jones (director), Barbara Orson as Mother O, Richard Farrone as the Son, and Howard London as the Ghost Father.

Directed by Judith Swift, the premiere was staged by the Rhode Island Playwrights Theatre in cooperation with the Wickenden Gate Theatre in Providence, Rhode Island, in May, 1990, Charles Caffone was the composer and the pianist, and the three actors were Wendy Feller, Pitt Harding, and Donald Wight. David Macaulay created his first stage design for the production.

SHADOWS OF MEMORY

*A Double-Bill
about Dian Fossey
and Djuna Barnes*

To Barbara Blossom and P. William Hutchinson

APE-GOD

or

Who Killed Dian Fossey?

CAST

DIAN, the woman who habituated the African mountain gorilla

GORILLA, played by an actress wearing a gorilla mask based on the face of Digit, Dian Fossey's favorite mountain gorilla. This actress also portrays

ROSAMOND, Dian Fossey's best friend

FATHER, one actor plays these four male roles

DOCTOR,

PHOTOGRAPHER,

STATE DEPARTMENT OFFICIAL,

MUNYARUKU, the Batwa pygmy leader and poacher who became Dian's chief enemy because of his poaching activities against the gorillas. Munyaruku is represented by a puppet figure and his voice is spoken by the Drummer

THE DRUMMER, who is on stage throughout the play, playing a written and improvised score on his drums and jungle instruments

The cast, then, consists of four performers, two actresses, one actor, and the drummer.

SETTING

The setting should be sparse, perhaps a basic black box setting with the audience on three sides. The gorilla mask, displayed as a mask when it is not worn by the actress in her gorilla role, the drums, the costume elements, the striking puppet figure that represents Munyaruku, and the panga (bush knife) hanging on the wall, constitute the major elements of the setting. The entire play is performed in an intense basic white light.

SCENE I

(The three actors are all dressed identically in informal black rehearsal clothes, over which they place a single piece of costume—i.e. the gorilla head or a hat or dress, etc.—when they change characters. As the play begins, DIAN *is sitting on the lap of the actress wearing the* GORILLA *head. The* DRUMMER, *on stage, accompanies and punctuates the action.)*

DIAN:
You're my love, my best friend.

GORILLA:
Animals are suspicious of friends.

DIAN:
Why?

GORILLA:
Friends are not lovers.

DIAN:
Love is beyond friendship.

GORILLA:
Love is appetite . . . I'm your ape-god.

DIAN:
You're joking. You're so playful.

GORILLA *(shaking her):*
Ape-god likes to play!

DIAN:
You're so strong!

GORILLA:
Sometimes I want to kill you.

DIAN *(shrugging):*
You don't mean it. Gorillas have to act that way.

GORILLA:
Ugliness is our power.

DIAN:
You're not ugly. Your eyes are beautiful.

GORILLA:

I should never have let you get close enough to see my eyes.

DIAN:

Once I saw you I couldn't let you go. You're King of the wilderness.

GORILLA:

All I have left is a dream of wilderness. I'm confined to a park where you study us and tourists come to watch me eat.

DIAN:

I try to save you from the poachers.

GORILLA:

You photograph me, you make me famous, you give me a name, Digit.

DIAN:

A name of love!

GORILLA:

A killing love.

DIAN:

I never killed you. I love you!

GORILLA:

I don't want to be human. Why do you learn my signals, my cries?

DIAN:

You won't come near me until I learn your ways.

GORILLA (*throwing her off, seizing her panga, her bush knife hanging on the wall*):

I'm going to kill you.

DIAN (*laughing and taking the knife away*):

You can't kill me with an ornamental knife. I seized it from a poacher to protect you.

GORILLA:

A poacher killed me. He wanted to sell my skull, my hands to tourists.

DIAN:

We'll never die! We're buried together side by side!

(*Emitting gorilla grunts and screams, they whirl around as if in an ecstatic dance, and they fall together.*)

SCENE 2

DIAN *(rising immediately):*
Even as a child, in my dreams I wanted to see the animal of my secrets. Everyone has an animal hidden inside. At first it's your father . . . A huge police dog or a golden retriever, maybe a collie. You don't think of your father as a lapdog.

FATHER *(appearing as if in her dream):*
I'm a kind of stray.

DIAN:
Divorce is an air plant. You get blown through the air and shit your life down elsewhere.

FATHER:
An elsewhere man . . . I always wanted a daughter, but I was a gone daddy. You have a pet dog?

DIAN:
A dog for a daddy.

FATHER:
I miss you. If you had to work in the insurance business, you'd start drinking too.

DIAN:
At least you taught me to love the outdoors life.

FATHER:
Outdoors is indoors in this society. Indoors you sit with a drink in your hand looking into that small glass reflecting outdoor dreams.

DIAN:
I know that cocktail party feeling too.

FATHER:
You live high in the African mist on a mountain and can rush outside to find your wild dream.

DIAN:
Envy is easy. You live in the country in California. You live with trees and animals.

FATHER:
Don't forget I live on a vacation bay. Lovely water is often just an escape.

DIAN:

Apart, we may find each other. Maybe I'm here in Africa because of your love of the wilderness.

FATHER:

What are gorillas really like?

DIAN:

You have to be a mountain climber to get to know them and I'm afraid of heights.

FATHER:

You know something? In World War II in the navy, I was afraid of heights too.

DIAN:

Did you scream up high?

FATHER:

I screamed inside.

DIAN:

Not me. On a seventy percent slope, climbing out of ravines, I scream like a baby dunked in baptismal water.

FATHER:

I'm proud of you. I wish we could scream together.

DIAN:

Whenever I hear gorillas scream, I'll think of you.

FATHER:

Do gorillas really pound their chests and scream like people?

DIAN:

They sure do . . . *(She pounds her chest and screams, as the* DRUMMER *pounds his drums and screams too.)*

SCENE 3

DIAN *(to the* GORILLA*)*:

I'm desperate! I have to habituate my gorillas!

GORILLA *(failing to understand, speaking the word like a sound poem):*
Ha-bi-tu-ate?

DIAN:
I want to be close to you! I want to look into your eyes and touch you!

GORILLA *(growling):*
Touch . . .

DIAN:
We must learn to trust each other. I want to study you.

GORILLA:
Stu-dy . . .

DIAN:
I want to save you. I want you to live a long safe life!

(They turn away. DIAN *pulls on a lovely dress over her tennis shoes. Taking off the ape mask, the actress becomes* ROSAMOND. ROSAMOND *is a woman who lives on a nearby plantation, growing and selling flowers, who is* DIAN'S *best friend and advisor.)*

DIAN:
You grow such beautiful flowers. A flower farm! Who could believe it in Africa!

ROSAMOND:
Tourists like flowers. It's a way to live.

DIAN:
I need your help!

ROSAMOND:
Flowers can't help you.

DIAN:
I want to use your lovely plantation as a base camp for my gorilla studies.

ROSAMOND:
There aren't any gorillas this side of the mountain.

DIAN:
Oh yes, there are.

ROSAMOND:
There are not.

DIAN:
I'll find them.

ROSAMOND (*watching, speaking to the audience*):
They told me she was odd, but you see a lot of odd white people in Africa. White against black is swampland. They didn't tell me she was beautiful with an odd kind of beauty. Six feet tall, she stands out like a lighthouse, dark hair signalling down her shoulders. When we meet at the Ambassador's house, she's wearing this expensive dress. She looks lovely, but, underneath, because of her big feet, she's wearing tennis shoes, filthy from slopping about! All she does is ask me questions. The other guests stare at us silently. Her mind is a real battering ram, forging straight ahead. You wouldn't believe it. She checks off the questions on a piece of paper after she asks them . . .

DIAN (*producing a piece of paper and checking off the questions after she asks them*):
So I can use your plantation as a base?

ROSAMOND:
Yes, but you won't find any gorillas this side of the mountain.

DIAN:
I'll find them. Can you help me hire some good trackers?

ROSAMOND:
Yes, but the trackers won't find any gorillas.

DIAN:
Can you help me buy a Land Rover?

ROSAMOND:
Yes, but it'll cost you plenty.

DIAN:
A secondhand one?

ROSAMOND:
I'll try . . . Secondhand is trouble on African roads.

DIAN:
Where is the best store for supplies?

ROSAMOND:
I'll show you.

DIAN:
Can you tell me about poachers?

ROSAMOND:

Yes, but you must know . . . The poachers have hunted here for years before it became a national park. They won't go away.

DIAN:

It's against the law now to hunt in the park.

ROSAMOND:

Tell that to the pygmies. It's their homeland.

DIAN:

Pygmies have to obey the law too.

SCENE 4

(A large puppet doll represents the ragged, barefooted Batwa poacher, MU-NYARUKU. *His voice is spoken by the* DRUMMER *from the side of the stage.)*

DIAN *(as the* DRUMMER *beats soft martial rhythms):*

Look at the little bastard! I couldn't believe it when five park guards marched in the filthy poacher. Munyaruku, the Batwa pygmy leader, the worst poacher of them all! Usually, the damn park guards are paid off and lose their poacher prisoners on the way down the mountain to park head-quarters. But they couldn't pass up Munyaruku. He's been making them look like fools. Can you imagine being afraid of pygmies? You think maybe he has some sumu magic on him? *(She begins to search the puppet.)* Look! *(as if demonstrating to the guards)* Nothing in his pockets! A damn comb! *(She pulls it out and throws it away.)* You think he ever combs his hair? A razor blade . . . *(She pulls it out carefully and throws it away.)* To cut animals out of traps, I bet! A tiny piece of soap! . . . Slippery, slippery! What's this? . . . Broken pieces . . . *(She holds them up as if showing them to the guards, and they flash in the light. Gasps are heard from the* DRUMMER.*)* Don't worry! It's not sumu! Just pieces of a broken mir-ror . . . Bad luck to break a mirror! *(She flashes it in the puppet's eyes. Then she pulls on a grotesque Halloween mask, and approaches the puppet menacingly.)* Who am I? You see me . . . You don't see me . . . I hide deep in the forest . . . I flash out when poachers come! My sumu is more powerful than yours! . . . Ape-god! Hunt gorillas again, and you die! *(She does a magic trick, making a grotesque head spring out of a box.)* Ape-god hides in the forest! Jumps at you! Finds you in the night! . . . Ape-god haunts your family . . . You hurt Ape-god, he kills you! *(She performs another magic trick with her lighter, setting a piece of paper on fire* *in a bucket as the puppet cringes.*) Fire from ape-god! From the sky, from the mountaintop, Ape-god brings fire! Stay away from gorillas, or Ape-god burn you down, Ape-god burn your houses! (*She takes a whip of nettles and begins striking the puppet.*) Ape-god punish you! Mountain forest belongs to Ape-god! You hurt gorillas, and Ape-god tears down trees, bushes to whip you! Beware, Ape-god! (*As the scene ends, she is whipping the puppet.*)

SCENE 5

DIAN (*lying down, stretching out her hand to the actress in the gorilla head, who is standing nearby warily*):
Men are like gorillas. You can't get too close to them.

GORILLA (*holding back*):
Close is too close.

DIAN:
We need to touch.

GORILLA:
Touching makes me often run away.

DIAN:
You're not running. We're getting closer and closer.

GORILLA:
It's just curiosity brings us together.

DIAN:
More than curiosity, affection, love!

GORILLA:
Affection? . . . Love? . . . (*She exits, as the* DOCTOR *takes her place.*)

DIAN (*hardly aware of the change from gorilla to man*):
Are you really there? I thought I was talking to Digit . . .

DOCTOR:
How can you love an old silverback?

DIAN:
You're a doctor, a surgeon. You'll never change your life.

DOCTOR:
I can't change, but I love you.

DIAN:

I don't need a man. I've got my gorillas. Besides, you've got a black wife and children. You'll never divorce her.

DOCTOR:

She wants to kill you.

DIAN:

That's great! She's still living in your house!

DOCTOR:

She wants 20,000 francs if I leave her.

DIAN:

You're still sleeping with her . . .

DOCTOR:

If I divorce her, will you give up your gorillas and come live with me in town?

DIAN:

I can't trust you. You keep saying you're coming up to the camp to see me and you never come.

DOCTOR:

Gorillas are your life. You'll never give them up. Medicine is my life.

DIAN (reaching out):

We have such wonderful times together! Look! We're almost touching!

DOCTOR (drawing back):

You're famous with your gorillas. You won't live with me in town. I'm sixty years old, too old for you.

DIAN:

I like older men!

DOCTOR:

You want security and adventure at the same time.

DIAN:

I'm in love with you. I don't want to be alone!

(The doctor exits. The GORILLA returns in the DOCTOR'S place.)

Men are all liars! (calling after the DOCTOR) You'll never leave your family!

GORILLA:
You beat that poacher with nettle-stalks to protect me. You used your magic on him.

DIAN:
I don't have any magic for love . . . Let me touch you . . .

GORILLA:
You are getting older . . . You are getting wrinkled like me . . . You are beginning to look like a gorilla . . . *(Slowly, he reaches out his hand, and their hands touch.)*

SCENE 6

DIAN *(to the* GORILLA *at side of the stage):*
So beautiful here in the forest in the mist . . . Your eyes and ears become sharper . . . You hear even the slightest sound and see through the haze . . . The volcano Karasimbi towers before my eyes even in sleep . . . I've been following a new gorilla group . . . They're not afraid of me and I can get as close as thirty feet now . . . I ape their gestures and grimace at them . . . They seem to wonder who I am, whether I'm some new kind of animal species . . . *(The* GORILLA *acts out the grimaces and gestures as* DIAN *speaks.)* When one of the silverbacks tries to bluff me away with his tactics of chest-drumming, smashing through brush, breaking branches, I turn my best grimace on him . . . This makes him nervous . . . He sits down and begins to nibble at some berries, while keeping an eye on me . . .

FATHER *(appearing, calling):*
Dian!

DIAN:
Father! What are you doing here?

FATHER:
I always wanted to see Africa . . . It's lovely, still unspoiled.

DIAN *(staring):*
You're dead . . . You killed yourself . . .

FATHER:
Sometimes that's the only way to get where you want to go.

DIAN:

I hardly ever saw you alive, but now I see you all the time.

FATHER:

Don't worry, Dian, ghosts are free to travel. If I haunt you, it's because I miss you and the wilderness . . . Who's your gorilla friend? (DIGIT growls.)

DIAN:

I call him Digit.

FATHER (laughing):

You've created your own world of names—Beethoven, Digit, Pucker, Hugger, Dora, Scapegoat, Popcorn, Mrs. Moses . . . You've got quite a family.

DIAN:

They've all got different personalities. They deserve names.

FATHER:

You call one of them by your old boyfriend's name, Alexie.

DIAN:

I couldn't resist . . . I'll use more sober names in my Ph.D. thesis.

FATHER:

I'm proud of you, Dian. You don't mind my coming to visit? (DIGIT growls.)

DIAN:

Digit doesn't like it. He doesn't want to share me with you.

FATHER:

I worry about you, daughter. Your health is poor. You don't eat properly. You have emphysema . . .

DIAN (trying to laugh it off):

The altitude makes me huff and puff. I'll be all right.

FATHER:

You can't fool me, Dian. We've got the same problem. Loneliness brings on depression. It runs in the family. You can only love a gorilla so far. (The GORILLA growls.)

DIAN:

Some day I'll find a great love . . .

FATHER:

Watch out . . . We're not far away from each other . . . When you're a
ghost, a great love gets to be difficult.

SCENE 7

(The actor plays a STATE DEPARTMENT OFFICIAL, *and the actress again
plays* ROSAMOND, *Dian's best friend.)*

STATE DEPARTMENT OFFICIAL:

We're getting official complaints here at the embassy! We can't look the
other way all the time! Dian is becoming bushy. Everyone says so. It's a
real danger.

ROSAMOND:

You really think she's bushy?

STATE DEPARTMENT OFFICIAL:

Yes, she's gotten too close to the gorillas. She can't see people anymore.
You're her best friend. Surely you can see what's happening to her.

ROSAMOND:

I suppose I'm a little bushy myself after all these years in Africa growing
and selling flowers to hotels for the tourist trade.

STATE DEPARTMENT OFFICIAL:

Tourists are entirely different than gorillas.

ROSAMOND:

Without gorillas, there wouldn't be any tourists here. The African economy needs tourists desperately.

STATE DEPARTMENT OFFICIAL:

That's just the point. Africans are beginning to hate her. She's hurting our
diplomatic relations! Africans don't like a white woman with so much
power over their wildlife.

ROSAMOND:

How can wildlife be nationalized? She's done more to save the mountain
gorillas than anyone else.

STATE DEPARTMENT OFFICIAL:

Yes, but it's affecting her . . . They say she goes on all fours in her
cabin.

ROSAMOND *(laughing):*

What if she does? She's like an actress. That's the way she's learned to habituate gorillas, by imitating them.

STATE DEPARTMENT OFFICIAL:

If she's becoming too close to the gorillas, how can she remain a scientific observer?

ROSAMOND *(ironically):*

How can you be a botanist, if you don't get close to flowers?

STATE DEPARTMENT OFFICIAL:

I suppose it's all relative. It's a matter of degree, but she's gone too far. She's teaching the gorillas to hate blacks!

ROSAMOND:

What?

STATE DEPARTMENT OFFICIAL:

She teaches gorillas to hate the pygmy Batwa poachers, and the Hutu tribesmen with their cattle. You can't keep these natives out of the park.

ROSAMOND:

Are you implying that the gorillas are learning to love only white people?

STATE DEPARTMENT OFFICIAL:

That appears to be the case. Look at the films that are making her famous. All of the researchers, working with the gorillas, are white.

ROSAMOND:

Nonsense! You're trying to turn her into a white racist! She's just trying to protect the gorillas from the poachers.

STATE DEPARTMENT OFFICIAL:

You can't keep Africans out of their own territory. They've hunted forest antelope for generations.

ROSAMOND:

The gorillas are dying out. Do you want that miraculous link to the evolution of humanity to vanish? There's a new law. They're supposed to be protected in the park.

STATE DEPARTMENT OFFICIAL:

She roams with them outside the park. We have complaints she crosses the border constantly into Zaire.

ROSAMOND:

I agree she's too aggressive about poachers. I tell her, but she won't listen to me.

STATE DEPARTMENT OFFICIAL:

She won't listen to anybody!

SCENE 8

(The actor plays a PHOTOGRAPHER, *making a film of* DIAN, *the gorillas, and the poachers, in the Virunga Mountain jungle. Dian is on her hands and knees, examining a gorilla track.)*

PHOTOGRAPHER *(holding his nose):*

Phew! What a stink!

DIAN:

Think of it as a delightful barnyard odor. Then you'll get used to it. This is the way we track them. Their scent clings to the trees. We have to check their shit too.

PHOTOGRAPHER *(looking):*

Large shit . . .

DIAN:

You have to get on your hands and knees and put your nose close. If it's warm, with a lot of eager flies, it's fresh.

PHOTOGRAPHER:

Wait, this is a film for the National Geographic. They don't want to know about gorilla shit. They don't want to see a woman crawling around sniffing it.

DIAN:

All they want is the old romance of our ancient ancestors, right? Look, diarrhea!

PHOTOGRAPHER *(startled):*

What?

DIAN:

Shit from peaceful gorillas is like horse manure. When they get scared and flee, they get diarrhea.

PHOTOGRAPHER:

Lovely . . . How do I film scared shit?

DIAN:

Film the danger of poachers killing them! Look! *(She points)*

PHOTOGRAPHER:

What is it?

DIAN:

A goddamn snare. The little bastards are great trappers. If you don't chase them all the time, there won't be any gorillas left! *(She smashes the snare.)*

PHOTOGRAPHER:

That's their property!

DIAN *(continuing to smash the snare):*

It's the only way to stop them! Smash their snares! . . . Their spears! . . . Their bows and arrows! . . . Make them see your magic is stronger than theirs!

(She continues her frenzied smashing, as the photographer follows her off, shooting his film. Suddenly, the scene evolves into a frozen, menacing confrontation between the PYGMY *puppet, who has been observing from the side of the stage, and the actress, who is wearing the* GORILLA *head.)*

PYGMY:

Here we are, united enemies . . .

GORILLA:

What do you want with me?

PYGMY:

What do we do with her, smashing my things?

GORILLA *(growling):*

She chases you out of our forest! She protects us!

PYGMY:

I'm going to kill you, Digit!

GORILLA:

You can't kill me! There's no more hunting in the park!

PYGMY:

The hunting landscape never changes . . . Tourists change . . . They pay me big money for your paws and skull . . . *(The* GORILLA *growls.)*

It's a war, you know . . . *(The* GORILLA *looks around nervously, growling louder and louder with fear, preparing to flee.)* In our small world, we had to learn how to kill big game . . . Now, they say we can't hunt forest antelope in the park . . . We can't hunt anything . . . We live in a park for white visitors . . . Crazy white woman looks in your eyes . . . She tickles you . . . You tickle her . . . White people love gorillas, hate pygmies . . . Crazy Woman teaches gorillas you're human, pygmies are inhuman . . . Pygmies are animals . . . So I kill you . . . I cut off your head and paws to sell to white tourist who collects wild animals! *(The* GORILLA *screams with fear, as the drumbeat rises, and then runs off.)*

SCENE 9

DIAN *(In her despair, she summons her ghosts.)*:
Come speak to me, my ghosts, my dear spectres. Tell me who I am! Tell me how I can live in Africa! Tell me how I can save my gorillas!

FATHER *(The actor appears as the* FATHER.*)*:
You're in a National Park, Dian. You've helped to teach the world that wilderness and wild life must be preserved. You've got it made!

DIAN:
You don't understand! It's an African National Park. They make their own rules!

FATHER:
You're a legend now. Nyiramachabelli, Lone Woman of the Forest! You'll be remembered like Tarzan.

DIAN:
I hate Tarzan . . . Lord Greystoke, one of those old aristocrats, even in the jungle.

FATHER:
You've done something no man could ever do. No man could ever have the patience to habituate gorillas.

DIAN:
I hate that word, habituate. I'm not an animal trainer.

FATHER:
You're a Doctor of Philosophy from Cambridge, a real scientist.

DIAN:

They hate me in Cambridge.

FATHER:

You're strong enough to be alone. You wanted it that way.

(The actress appears again as ROSAMOND, *Dian's best friend, in a large straw hat with a watering can for her flowers.)*

DIAN *(desperately):*

Rosamond, you're my best friend . . . What must I do?

ROSAMOND:

I'm afraid you can't stay in Africa, Dian . . . Too many people hate you . . . It's too dangerous.

DIAN:

I love Africa. Karisoke is my home.

ROSAMOND:

It's just a tin hut African research station.

DIAN:

I'll burn it down before I turn it over to tourists!

ROSAMOND:

Your films make gorillas popular and lure tourists, Dian. You're caught in the white African trap . . .

DIAN:

White African trap?

ROSAMOND:

We whites who like to live here can't defend Africa against Africans.

DIAN:

The gorillas will die. There'll be no more human links.

ROSAMOND:

Isn't there a danger you'll kill them yourself, you and your research students?

DIAN:

Yes, I'm afraid of transmitting diseases to them . . .

ROSAMOND:

Human diseases?

DIAN:

Yes, but the poachers are a worse danger.

(The actress puts on the GORILLA *head, and they move close together.)*

DIAN:

Digit! I'll never leave you, even if you're just another ghost. I'll never forgive myself for letting those poachers kill you. They took your paws and
skull to sell, the beasts! I'll always remember us playing together! Look!
Our old toy! *(She pulls out a stuffed animal toy and shows it to* DIGIT.
DIGIT *growls and moves closer to* DIAN *and the toy, growling with interest
and joy.)*
I hide my face . . . *(She pulls a hat down over her face)* Get down on all
fours to play . . . *(She plays and* DIGIT *gets closer and closer.)* No complex yak-yakking . . . Just two little appetites playing at the center of the
world in Africa, where man first came into being . . . No aggressive
threats from anyone . . . Plenty of room for all kinds of animals to move
around and play . . . We learn peaceful ways from animals, Digit. Isn't
that true? *(Suddenly,* DIGIT *screams and moves away.)* What's the matter,
Digit? The poachers can't hurt you anymore. Is there something outside?
(She goes to a door and opens it. On the door is a strange snake-like image.)
My god! The wooden image of a puff adder! Death magic! Someone
wants me dead!

SCENE 10

*(*DIAN *collapses. After a pause as the drum beats hold steady, the* FATHER *enters and kneels over* DIAN'S *body.)*

FATHER:

Dian! Dian! They murdered you! *(As he kneels over, sobbing,* DIAN *rises
slowly, holding her panga, her bush knife.)*

DIAN *(looking at the knife with an amazed smile):*

Killed with my own bush knife! Can you believe that? . . . I grab a gun
to defend myself . . . Grab an ammunition clip . . . The clip doesn't
fit! . . . Story of my life!

RESEARCHER *(The male actor transforms into one of her former research
workers):*

She kept on inventing enemies. She thought everyone wanted to take over
the miserable tin shacks she had created as her research center, her animal

sanctuary. Who wants tin-shacks? The real trouble is that she thought she was an ape-god. She forgot how to treat people. She made so many enemies that one was bound to kill her.

ROSAMOND *(appearing as her woman friend):*
No one robbed her. Her jewelry and cameras were intact. Her health was failing, but she couldn't let go. Maybe it was best she died this way, fighting for what she believed in. All she wanted to do was preserve the natural world of the gorillas. But where is the natural world today? Gorillas are too much like people, missing links. Do we really want to be reminded of missing links? Myself, I think some poacher killed her. She went too far with the poachers, and her magic turned into death magic.

(The poacher puppet appears, as the actress, slowly, puts on the GORILLA *head.)*

GORILLA *(to the puppet):*
You killed her!

PUPPET *(*MUNYARUKU'S *voice):*
Poachers do not kill this way. If I kill, I poison her or kill her in the jungle where she smash my traps! You killed her!

GORILLA:
Gorillas play . . . She play mirror games with us . . . We love to play with her.

PUPPET:
Pygmies look up at trees, sky . . . Forest and pygmies are like tree-fathers and small animal children . . . We build good bamboo hunting traps, snares . . . White lady fall into trap and die.

ACTRESS *(taking off the* GORILLA *head and speaking directly to the audience):*
Once, there was an aged silverback gorilla named Whinny, because he whinnied like a horse. His lungs were bad, which accounted for his whinny. When he died Uncle Bert became leader. Dian called us Group 4. We gorillas lived in eight family groups. That's all of us that were left. Youngsters in Group 4 liked Dian. She liked to comb our hair. We combed her hair. She tickled us, played with us, and slept with us in the sun. But it was Digit she liked best. If Digit belched, Dian would belch back. They loved the belching game! Digit would flop over on his back, wave his legs in the air, and grin his gorilla grin to Dian. It was Digit who turned Dian into a gorilla.

(Slowly, the actress puts on the GORILLA *head again. This time, she sits on* DIAN'S *lap, the reverse of the opening scene.)*

DIAN:

Even if you're dead, you become what you love in memory. I lie next to Digit in the mountain graveyard. Our eyes commune with each other. *(The drum begins a soft, stately rhythm, then becomes exuberant.)* Ape-gods pound out their kingly greetings through the morning mist. Running on all fours, we embrace each other through time. Animal memories live forever! In the forest, ape-gods remember freedom. Animal natures are not ruled by cities and money. Ape-gods play dangerous, kill each other sometimes. We know birth and death have the same force as the wind, change with the wind. Running with the wind is better than dying with money. If you look through ape-god's eyes, you see a prison gate opening into freedom!

THE END

THE RADIATOR

A Play about Djuna Barnes

CAST

DJUNA BARNES
THE ACTOR who plays all of the male parts
THE ACTRESS who plays all of the other female roles

SCENE 1

(A bare stage. DJUNA BARNES, *middle-aged, is warming her hands, as if over a radiator. Alternately, she smiles, then glares at the audience.)*

DJUNA:
I called you Americans: "A fierce, sadistic race crouching behind radiators!" Why did I say *"You* Americans?" . . . *We* Americans! *(She laughs.)* Maybe I am the radiator!

SCENE 2

DJUNA *(continuing to warm her hands as if over a radiator):*
Names burn us from behind the radiators where we crouch! *(She laughs.)*
My father was called Wald . . . Not his last name, his first name, *Wald—*
German for forest . . . *(The* ACTOR *appears as Wald in the background, with a red wool cap and a curly beard.)* That's probably why he had a full, curly beard to hide in. He was short, five feet seven inches, redheaded, a red haze whirling around me. My mother's name was only Elizabeth, so she was an obscurity. *(The* ACTRESS *appears as Elizabeth, across the stage from Wald. She has a big cap over her head, so she looks like an obscurity.)*
But she redeemed herself by having children in this order:

WALD AND ELIZABETH *(alternating):*
Thurn . . .
    Djuna . . .
        Zendon . . .
            Saxon . . .
                Shangar . . .

DJUNA *(continuing):*
Names like thunderclaps before a storm. Inevitably, Shangar and Thurn changed their names to Charles and Bud! The rest of us endured our burning names. My grandmother was called:

ACTRESS *(Taking off her cap, she becomes the grandmother, Zadel.):*
Zadel, writer of special romances! *(She orates.)* "Love, dipping her glowing fingers in the rainbow tints of hope, had written promises."

DJUNA:
Such were the words I inherited. Zadel and I were fixed to our crazy names like flies to flypaper. I was named Djalma originally after the Prince in the French writer, Eugene Sue's novel. My real name, the way life fashions accidents, arose from a mispronunciation when my brother confused *Djuna* for *Djalma* . . .

WALD AND ZADEL *(together, jubilantly):*
How lovely! *Djuna!* Let's change her name!

DJUNA *(continuing):*
The commanders of my family shrieked with joy when they heard the sudden beauty of *Djuna!* The mask of that name has clung to me forever. I am *Djuna.*

SCENE 3

(Upstage, Wald and Zadel begin quarreling. Djuna keeps warming her hands, as if over the imaginary radiator.)

WALD *(shrieking at Zadel):*
Zadel, each great man lives alone!

ZADEL:
What about a woman?

WALD:
Women can't live alone.

ZADEL:

What about Heloise and Abelard? She lived alone as a nun, and they're buried together, forever, in a huge tomb in Paris, where lovers visit every day.

WALD:

The church cut off his balls for falling in love with a nun. They both died alone!

ZADEL:

What about Romeo and Juliet?

WALD:

They slept together one night. The rest was silence in the tomb.

ZADEL:

Better to have one good night of love and immortality.

WALD:

What do you know about names?

ZADEL:

All great names are love names.

WALD:

Zadel is a love name?

ZADEL:

Searching for a mate . . . My weak-named husbands came unstuck.

WALD:

My father's name was only Henry.

ZADEL:

Your grandfather's too. Poor Henry shadow of a name.

WALD:

Why did you name me weakling Henry?

ZADEL:

Not me . . . Father condemning sons . . . The old power succession— III to II to I.

WALD:

No wonder I had to change my name so many times! You could have anchored me!

ZADEL:

Not up to mothers . . . Fathers throw out the anchor.

WALD:

I had to search through a thicket of names until I found Wald.

ZADEL:

You search, you don't find.

WALD:

I'll stick my children with strong names. Then they'll search and find!

(DJUNA *slumps off of her chair and begins to crawl imploringly up to Wald and Zadel.*)

ZADEL:

What are you going to do with Djuna?

WALD:

I'm going to give her to my brother-in-law, Percy Faulkner.

ZADEL:

The brother of your mistress you mean.

WALD:

He's a good man, fifty-two years old, experienced. He knows how to gentle a woman.

ZADEL:

Djuna is not a horse.

WALD:

She's eighteen going frigid. It's time she learned.

ZADEL:

If it's for love . . .

WALD:

It's for love and money. Love needs money when it rides through the night!

ZADEL *(scornfully):*

You ride around with a sponge on your saddle to wipe off your sex.

WALD:

I ride for love. She has to learn.

(DJUNA *has crawled in front of Zadel.*)

DJUNA *(looking up imploringly):*
Don't let it happen!

ZADEL *(looking down at* DJUNA*):*
It has to happen.

SCENE 4

(DJUNA *gets up as Wald and Zadel exit.)*

DJUNA:
Things happen like dreams except you're not asleep . . . My father gave
me like an Old Testament daughter . . . *(The* ACTOR *appears as an
anonymous older man, upstage, seated on a chair, with his back to the
audience.)*
I dream an older man initiates me . . . He holds me on his knee . . .

ACTOR AS OLDER MAN *(taking her on his knee):*
Won't you have a caramel?

DJUNA *(hesitating):*
Yes . . .

ACTOR AS OLDER MAN:
They're excellent caramels . . . Would you like another one?

DJUNA:
Yes . . . I look up at him and say "yes" because I'm supposed to.

ACTOR AS OLDER MAN:
You're a lovely girl . . . Don't be afraid.

DJUNA:
Afterwards, he's frightened because I don't cry, I don't say anything.

(She gets up off his lap, and he exits with the chair.)

I never learn to cry. This is the end of family love, but how can you escape
from a family? They send me to the city to learn art. I study at the Pratt
Art Institute, how muscles jut out and bones sink in. I become a journal-
ist, a radiator of hot words and drawings. Success! With my left hand I do
grotesque illustrations, and with my right hand I write sizzling interviews!
Freelance freedom at last! I work for the *Brooklyn Daily Eagle.* Soon I
earn $5000 a year, more than I ever earn in my life! I write about the great
theatrical dentist, Twingless Twitchell and his Tantalizing Tweezers, who

extracts teeth in public as if he were John Barrymore playing Hamlet. I interview celebrities from Ziegfeld, the showman, to Billy Sunday, the evangelist. My greatest journalistic adventure comes in 1914. English suffragists are on a hunger strike for their voting rights. The British government orders them to be fed by force. So I decide, for the *New York World*, to show the terror of force-feeding the English ladies are enduring.

SCENE 5

(The ACTRESS *and the* ACTOR *appear in white masks and coats as doctors, pushing a table.)*

DJUNA:
As I mount the table for the procedure . . . *(She mounts the table defiantly.)* two masked doctors press down on my ankles, hips and head . . . *(One doctor lifts a piece of red rubber hose.)* I catch sight of the red rubber hose that is to be forced through my nasal passages! *(She begins to panic.)*

FIRST DOCTOR:
Relax now . . . *(He starts to paint her nostrils as the other doctor holds* DJUNA *down.)* I'm painting your nostrils with a mixture of cocaine and disinfectant . . . *(He starts to paint her nostrils.)*

SECOND DOCTOR:
So it won't hurt when we put in the tube.

DJUNA *(crying out):*
I'll fly through the air!

FIRST DOCTOR *(probing her nostrils with a small searchlight):*
This is just to make sure that your nasal passages are clear . . .

SECOND DOCTOR:
Before we insert the tube . . .

FIRST DOCTOR *(as* DJUNA *struggles):*
Just relax . . .

SECOND DOCTOR *(as they begin to insert the tube):*
With the anesthetic, it won't hurt . . .

DJUNA:
A searing pain flows down my spine! The doctor's eyes float over his mask like a jellyfish's soft menace.

FIRST DOCTOR *(lifting a container with milky-colored liquid):*
Now we'll begin to feed you through the tube . . .

DJUNA:
It looks like milk!

SECOND DOCTOR *(helping to pour in the liquid):*
It's like fortified milk.

DJUNA *(twisting and screaming):*
My god, it burns like an inferno!

FIRST DOCTOR:
Relax your throat!

SECOND DOCTOR:
You'll choke if you keep struggling!

DJUNA *(pushing them off and sitting up):*
In my hysteria, I see a hundred women in grim prison hospitals. They are bound, shrouded in hospital clothes in the grip of callous wardens. White-robed doctors pour crude fuel into these victims.

(The doctors take off their masks and laugh.)

FIRST DOCTOR:
You see it's just a medical procedure.

DJUNA *(staring at the doctor as he laughs back):*
I noticed the tiny red mustache on the doctor's soft face . . .

SCENE 6

DJUNA:
In front page New York, I was condemned to be a wild, social person. So I fled from journalism to Paris. Unable to speak French, I saw myself as a receptacle of privacy. Into the vessel of my solitude, I could pour a new language I would invent. *(She smiles.)* Alas, language does not pour. It sounds in unusual wave-lengths. *(She puts on her cloak.)* In the sad, falling twilight, I walked through the darkening evening to Notre Dame.

(Putting a shawl over her head, the ACTRESS *plays an old woman selling oranges.)*

ACTRESS AS OLD WOMAN:
Oranges . . . Bittersweet oranges . . . Oranges bittersweet . . .

DJUNA *(buying one and tasting):*
A bittersweet orange signifying the loneliness of Notre Dame . . . Lost
in history, Notre Dame is in the center condition. Around her surge the
feverish journeys towards and away from faith. They do not disturb her.
In Paris I too am in the central, waiting condition . . .

> *(The* ACTOR *and the* ACTRESS, *who has transformed into the imposing
> figure of Thelma Wood, appear.)*

ACTOR:
I never think of Djuna as a Lesbian . . . Everyone knows she's had an
abortion or two.

ACTRESS AS THELMA WOOD:
She was an experimenter . . . I was the experiment!

ACTOR *(to the audience):*
The army of expatriates who besieged Paris in the 1920s looked like raw
recruits searching for cultural and sexual adventures. But Thelma Wood
roared around like an officer in her dashing red Bugatti!

ACTRESS AS THELMA WOOD:
A red Bugatti from which I had the muffler removed to announce me!

ACTOR:
Everyone knows Thelma Wood is coming by the roar! Shopkeepers shake
their fists at her. She only drives faster!

DJUNA:
At first I'm not impressed by the roar of Thelma's red Bugatti. The color
is more interesting than the sound. In Paris I live mainly on omelettes.
Without any French, that is all I can order. When Paris becomes too expensive, I go to Berlin. Somehow Thelma's red Bugatti drives there too. I
have lunch with Charlie Chaplin, whom I know from New York. Together
we visit a friend in the hospital with jaundice . . .

ACTOR AS CHAPLIN:
Look, his face is bright yellow!

DJUNA:
My favorite color . . .

ACTOR AS CHAPLIN:
Often we go to the marvelous Berlin theatre . . . We sip tea with absinthe at the Hotel Adlon . . .

DJUNA *(As she speaks, Charlie mimes the action of the woman whom* DJUNA *is describing.):*
One of those heavy Germanic ladies having tea, fixes her lorgnette at our foreign presence . . . *(*DJUNA *stares back at her through her fork.)*

ACTOR AS CHAPLIN *(laughing and imitating* DJUNA'S *action):*
That's how I learn to make my Tramp peer through a fork at snobbish society ladies. *(He exits, peering at audience members through his fork.)*

DJUNA:
Then Thelma Wood enters the room . . .

(Dressed in an impressive hat and coat, Thelma Wood strides in carrying a huge doll.)

ACTRESS AS THELMA WOOD *(placing the doll on* DJUNA'S *lap):*
This doll will be our child!

SCENE 7

DJUNA:
Thelma Wood looked like a beautiful lion with huge paws. She wanted to be kept and sheltered like a wild pet, but every night she would escape and roam the streets of Paris. She struggled between love and her bestial nature . . .

THELMA:
I am *wood!*

DJUNA *(accusingly):*
Everyone hammers nails into your wood. Why do you let them?

THELMA:
Wood is my nature . . .

DJUNA:
You've come home drunk again. You remind me of a drunken lion.

THELMA:
If only lions could drink . . .

DJUNA *(impatiently):*
You are independent and luxurious like a lion! *(*THELMA *grabs her hand in a powerful grip that hurts.* DJUNA *kicks her.)* Let go!

THELMA *(beginning to laugh):*
Did I hurt you?

DJUNA:
You will not be controlled in any way!

THELMA:
I experiment with art the way you experiment with language!

DJUNA:
At night you crawl home like a wild, beaten pet. I lie awake, waiting.

THELMA:
You never wait anymore.

DJUNA:
Even Dilly lies awake, waiting for our stray.

THELMA *(mockingly):*
Dilly-Darling—what a horrible name for a cat!

DJUNA:
As cruel as the *wood* of a wanton lion. Did you expose our child to the streets?

THELMA *(producing the doll):*
Here is our child, sacred and profane.

DJUNA:
Sacred here in our apartment. You degrade her on the street.

THELMA *(looking around):*
She can't live in all of your mirrors. She loses her humanity.

DJUNA:
Did we not buy everything in the flea market together?

THELMA:
We tried to turn this place into a religion, liturgical ornaments, ecclesiastical pillows, mirrors, a glass cross . . .

DJUNA:
A prowling lion is not fit to bring up a spiritual child! We are searching for souls, not chasing up alleys!

THELMA:
Our child resents your fake religion. That is why I take him out.

DJUNA:

The streets make him angry! Look at him . . . He hates the homeless on the streets!

THELMA:

He is angry because you are not at the door, waiting.

DJUNA:

I have grown tired of waiting for you.

(They glare at each other across the motionless doll.)

SCENE 8

(DJUNA alone, holding the doll on her lap. The ACTOR enters in a dark suit and black hat. He is wearing a black mask, and is carrying a wine glass in his hand.)

ACTOR:

Are you finished with your oddities?

DJUNA:

Thelma is gone . . . *(She puts away the doll.)*

ACTOR *(Toasting her, he quotes from* Nightwood*)*:

"You are, he said, testing the wine between his lower lips and teeth, experiencing the inbreeding of pain . . . " *(He is testing the wine.)*

DJUNA *(whispering)*:

The inbreeding of pain . . . Dr. O'Connor . . . *(She picks up the doll.)*

ACTOR AS DR. O'CONNOR:

"Most of us do not dare do it. We wed a stranger, and so we 'solve' our problem."

DJUNA:

Thelma was an animal made out of nightwood, Dr. O'Connor . . . My problem is not solved.

ACTOR AS O'CONNOR:

"When you inbreed with suffering—which is merely to say that you have caught every disease and so pardoned your flesh—you are destroyed back to your structure as an old master disappears beneath the knife of the scientist . . ."

273

DJUNA:

Yes, I have pardoned my flesh . . . I have been pregnant with a child whom you aborted. I disappear beneath the knife of your science, Dr. O'Connor.

(She puts the doll away, as the ACTOR *tears off his mask and hat and presents himself as T. S. Eliot.)*

ACTOR AS T.S. ELIOT:

I am happy to report you have written an extraordinary novel, Miss Barnes. Dr. Matthew O'Connor is a character of Shakespearian dimensions.

DJUNA *(dazed):*

You really like my novel, Mr. Eliot?

ACTOR AS ELIOT:

Like is not the word. Your novel has no structure. It pours over the reader in a succession of waves that never stop foaming and rolling, never crash finally on the shore. It haunts me.

DJUNA:

Your firm, Faber and Faber, will publish it?

ACTOR AS ELIOT:

Oh, your Dr. O'Connor talks too much. Your novel is far too long. As your editor I will help you to cut it down.

DJUNA:

My novel has been rejected by every New York publisher. It slips quickly through their hands like a greased pig. They don't even like the title, *Bow Down* . . .

ACTOR AS ELIOT:

Bow Down is a terrible title. What would you think of *Nightwood?*

DJUNA:

All my life I have been wandering in a nightwood . . .

ELIOT *(laughing):*

I don't know what it means, but it'll give the critics something to chew on. It suggests a dark tangle, and that is what your book is, Miss Barnes.

DJUNA:

Nightwood is a perfect title. Please call me Djuna.

ELIOT *(laughing):*
If you call me Tom.

DJUNA *(to herself):*
How can I call T. S. Eliot, Tom? . . . I can't believe you want to publish my book!

ELIOT:
It contains brilliance, but you have written 190,000 words!

DJUNA *(to herself):*
Did he count all the words? . . . *(to the audience)* By the time Faber and Faber published the novel, he cut 125,000 words, leaving a slim volume of 65,000 words.

ELIOT:
You must know, I'm afraid, that Faber will not pay you any advance. They will claim full American rights too, as they expect a loss from English publication.

DJUNA:
Publishers . . . I should write poetry instead of prose.

ELIOT *(laughing):*
I wish I could write prose as well as you, but I'll give you a black eye if you write poetry! Goodbye, Djuna of the Nightwood!

DJUNA:
Goodbye, Mr. T. S. Eliot of the Wasteland, I mean Tom . . . *(The* AC-TOR *as Eliot exits, as* DJUNA *waves after him.)*

SCENE 9

DJUNA *(to the audience):*
Nightwood was an immortal failure . . . Eliot introduced it, Graham Greene, Dylan Thomas, and Edwin Muir praised it in reviews, and no one bought it. A window cleaner told me he had read *Nightwood* and thought Rabelais was better. A postman said that such an evil book should not be sent through the mail. In the United States, Philip Rahv condemned its "minute shudders of decadence." . . . *(moving across the stage)* Well, it's true my book is full of shudders told by the bawdy Dr. O'Connor. It tickles and scratches along the strands of decadence in the 1930s that led to

World War II. *(She picks up a bed cover.)* As the war began, I perched my-self at the foot of Peggy Guggenheim's sumptuous bed . . . *(She throws the "marabou cover" around her shoulders.)* and told her: "Peggy, we'll be bombed in feathers!"

SCENE 10

(The buzz of a doorbell is heard.)

DJUNA *(sitting stubbornly):*
Answering doorbells is to admit defeat!

(As the doorbell rings again impatiently, she finally goes to the window and shouts down.)

Is someone buzzing below like a drunken fly disturbing the peace?

(The ACTOR'S *voice is heard offstage as the Biographer.)*

ACTOR AS BIOGRAPHER:
Miss Barnes? . . . We have an appointment!

DJUNA:
An appointment for what? I am not a dentist.

BIOGRAPHER:
An appointment for fame . . . I am your biographer.

DJUNA:
I don't see anyone anymore . . . Well, come up if you must . . .

(The Biographer enters and she examines him closely.)

Fame, young man, does not exist in a closet. This is a recluse's closet be-longing to the cockroaches. *(She takes off his glasses slowly.)*

BIOGRAPHER:
I thought she might hit me! She stares into my eyes as though she were always looking backwards into time . . . (DJUNA *turns away slowly.)* If not completely satisfied, she seems somehow pacified . . .

DJUNA:
The last time I received someone in this room was twenty-five years ago. I distrust interviews . . . You see I used to do them myself.

BIOGRAPHER *(uncomfortably)*:
I understand . . .

DJUNA:
Reporters will stop at nothing to get what they want . . . Nietzsche said that the newspaper has replaced the prayer in everyday life.

BIOGRAPHER *(hastily)*:
I don't work for a newspaper . . . I know what you mean.

DJUNA:
What is it you want to know about me?

BIOGRAPHER *(entranced)*:
Everything.

DJUNA:
Everything does not exist. Only a specific any thing exists.

BIOGRAPHER *(cautiously)*:
What any thing are you doing now?

DJUNA:
I'm writing a long poem in Cantos to outdo Ezra Pound. But everyone interrupts me! I am the most famous unknown interrupted person in the world!

BIOGRAPHER *(nervously)*:
I'm sorry if I interrupt you . . .

DJUNA *(getting some aspirin and a glass of water)*:
You need two aspirin and a glass of water.

BIOGRAPHER *(accepting them)*:
How did you guess?

DJUNA:
I give everyone I talk to a headache.

BIOGRAPHER *(swallowing the aspirin)*:
You're so intense.

DJUNA:
My intensity is deteriorating . . . Asthma . . . You hear the voice of an asthmatic, as if dying words are strained through a screen.

BIOGRAPHER:
Your voice still penetrates like a polished toothpick.

DJUNA:
Thank you, but you don't look like an expert on toothpicks.

BIOGRAPHER *(bursting out):*
I'm trying to show you I'm not a stuffed shirt!

DJUNA:
It's useless talking to me, Mr. Biographer! Make up your own life stories.
Old people should be killed! There should be a law! This business of keeping us alive past our time . . . It's inhuman! I'm already dead! Do you
know that? They brought me back. Now I have to go through the whole
horrid business again! I can't do it! Goodbye!

BIOGRAPHER *(exiting dejectedly):*
I am the biographer of nothingness . . .

SCENE 11

DJUNA:
I unlist my telephone in New York . . . Is it better to say that I enlist my
telephone with eternity to avoid the crank calls of curiosity collectors? For
forty years I cultivate the art of immaculate silence . . .

(The ACTOR *and the* ACTRESS *appear upstage, watching silently.)*

Only ghosts visit me when I die at the age of ninety . . . Every child
knows how real ghosts are . . . In old age, ghosts become actual figures,
seizing your eyes, grasping your hands . . . In 1945, Mrs. Silence, Mrs.
King Lear as I call her, dies! My mother!

ACTRESS AS DJUNA'S MOTHER:
It is like a coil of snakes around my neck having children still alive, children outliving me!

DJUNA *(accusingly):*
Name your children, mother!

ACTOR AND ACTRESS AS FATHER AND MOTHER *(Alternating, they repeat
the names of the children as in Scene 2.):*
Thurn . . .
       Djuna . . .
              Zendon . . .
                     Saxon . . .
                           Shangar . . .

278

DJUNA:
Radiator names!

MOTHER:
May God protect us from such impoverished names as Elizabeth . . . I wonder what evil you'll write about me when I'm dead and gone . . .

DJUNA *(turning on her, and scattering pages on the floor in front of her):*
I'm writing a play about you, Mrs. King Lear! How I stuffed my ears when you read Mary Baker Eddy to me constantly!

MOTHER:
Your ego puffs like a chimney! What is your play called?

DJUNA:
The Antiphon.

MOTHER:
A concealed title as usual. Is your play really like a hymn?

DJUNA:
It is chanted and sung in alternating parts between you and me.

MOTHER *(alarmed):*
I will not be an alternating part of your demonic hymn! You classify everyone into oblivion!

DJUNA:
Furious at being called Plain Elizabeth, you named us all into oblivion.

MOTHER:
Blame your father. He and your grandmother, Zadel, sold you. You are full of self-pity.

DJUNA:
You never fought against my father and his many mistresses! I was the scapegoat! You revenged yourself on me!

MOTHER *(scornfully):*
You never learned to control yourself with all your male and female lovers.

DJUNA:
You are the world's strongest weak woman! I will make you disappear in my play. *(pointing to the pages on the floor)* You will writhe in torment in all those strenuous pages of dialogue. You will become a ghost repeating my lines forever!

MOTHER:
Your pride is destroying you. I won't learn your tangled lines!

DJUNA:
Vanish! As a ghost you have no choice. These lines are the veins of your life.

(She snatches up the pages and hands them to her MOTHER.*)*

MOTHER *(Struggling to accept the pages, she is forced to accept them.):*
You can't make me act in your play!

DJUNA *(coldly):*
Learn your lines and die!

MOTHER *(retreating slowly, beginning to recite her lines as if by force):*
"You all seem to know much more than I do.
I like the poor man-handled mendicant
Sit down alone to banquet in a dream . . ."
I can't understand these lines . . .

DJUNA:
Get Mary Baker Eddy to explain them to you!

MOTHER *(continuing to recite as if by force):*
"Say, I mothered children in a vision . . ."
No, I'm not your ghost mother! You can't do this!

DJUNA:
It is my dream as much as yours.

MOTHER:
"Gone, gone! cast out and waning
like a circle running from a stone
pitched upon a frightful deed; forgotten.
I leave the whole catch to the resurrection!"
Impossible devil daughter!

DJUNA:
My play is your resurrection.

MOTHER:
Mother of God!

DJUNA:
Precisely not!

(The mother fades away, struggling with her lines as she exits.)

The true loneliness is never to be alone . . .

(With his back turned to the audience, the ACTOR *has put on his mask and hat, and now turns towards* DJUNA.*)*

ACTOR:
That sounds like one of my lines!

DJUNA *(puzzled, staring at him):*
Tom Eliot? . . . Dr. O'Connor? . . .

ACTOR *(posing):*
Which am I?

DJUNA:
What is the difference between a character and a real person?

ACTOR *(laughing):*
The character is often more believable.

DJUNA:
I have wasted so much time in my life.

ACTOR *(laughing as he takes off his mask and hat):*
Yes, but think what you did when you were not wasting it!

DJUNA:
My writing is like cryptography. You have to struggle to decode it.

ACTOR *(laughing, he puts the mask on her):*
Perhaps writing out of a crypt is the most enduring of all literature!

DJUNA:
Tom, why are you always so courtly to me?

(He takes her and they begin to dance.)

ACTOR:
I am a lover of courts. In royal courts, the masked dancers begin to dance!

DJUNA *(drawing away):*
Will you speak a courtly sermon at my funeral?

ACTOR:
I died before you . . .

DJUNA *(tearing off the mask and turning on him):*
Why did you write of my play, "It might be said of Miss Barnes, who is

incontestably one of the most original writers of our time, that never has so much genius been combined with so little talent"?

ACTOR *(laughing):*
It was Dr. O'Connor speaking when I said that, a terrifying, mocking fellow . . . Does not the ghost of genius endure longer than the ghost of little talent? You will outlive all of us ghosts! *(He vanishes.)*

DJUNA:
What did a friend of mine say long ago in Paris? People who spend too much time alone turn in the end into enormous ears . . . As our ears grow bigger, what are we listening for?

BOTH ACTORS:
"Somewhat sullen, many days
The Walrus is a cow that neighs,
Tusked, ungainly, and windblown,
It sits on ice, and alone."

DJUNA:
Think of me as that Walrus . . . If you want to see the Walrus, you have to walk out on dangerous ice through a myriad of ghosts. There you'll find the Walrus burning like a radiator in his iniquitous past. Slowly, softly, he'll raise his paw . . . *(She raises her hand.)* in salute to his fellow ghosts!

(She stands for a long moment, with her hand raised, contemplating the audience as the play ends.)

NOTE

In *Shadows of Memory,* I contrast two very different women, both gifted, stubborn individualists struggling throughout their lives against male-dominated environments. What struck me particularly about Dian Fossey was that she had the enormous patience to observe gorillas quietly (unlike previous male scientific observers) until they became accustomed to her, and she became the first person to touch one, an astonishing moment. Fossey's courage was mirrored, I felt, in the courageous isolation that Djuna Barnes endured for many years in New York at the end of her long life. Both plays presented, too, the challenge of biographical compression to achieve the right style. In two related short plays, I wanted to see how many authentic biographical facts I could compress to show poetically, yet realistically, the way two extraordinary women shaped their lives in the midst of difficult times against which women were beginning to revolt.

Structurally, the play involves poetic transformations, with the small cast, except for the principals, transforming into various roles. In the opening performances, which I directed with the actors, the props were designed and hung in a theatrical way to provide the minimal set. One musician improvised the music on a variety of percussion instruments. The framework of the improvisation, of course, was established in rehearsals.

The first performance of *Ape God* was in April, 1988, on the annual program of Wastepaper Theatre at the Rhode Island School of Design Museum. The cast included Barbara Blossom, Joanne Gentille, J. S. Blakemore, P. William Hutchinson, and Gordon Sands. In June both plays were produced by the Rhode Island Playwrights Theatre and Wastepaper Theatre, and then taken in August to the Fringe of the Edinburgh Festival. The cast for these performances consisted of Barbara Blossom, Margot Dionne, P. William Hutchinson, and Ted Mitchell. In Edinburgh these plays were produced by P. William Hutchinson.

THE LAST ROMANTICS

THE LAST
ROMANTICS

To Andrea Gordon

CAST

GEORGE SILVERLIGHT, an older distinguished plant pathologist and former Professor of Botany at the University of Wisconsin

MARGARET PIERSON, a handsome, older woman, poet, artist, with an impressive, tormented past.

ERWIN PIERSON, a young struggling poet and teacher

SHIRLEY PIERSON, the son's Japanese-American wife, an attractive, experienced social worker

AN ACTOR WHO PLAYS SEVERAL ROLES:

LANCELOT SANDERSON, a well-known Canadian abstract artist

SILVERLIGHT'S father, a minister

FRANK LLOYD WRIGHT, the architect

C. G. JUNG, the psychiatrist

LORENZO HUBBELL, the trader on the Navajo and Hopi reservations, whose former trading post and home is now a national monument

A DANCER, who appears in the dance scenes. If desired, the dancer can be a musician too in appropriate places. The play, then, requires five actors and a dancer.

(No solid sets are used in the play, only appropriate pieces of furniture, platforms, a few props, and projections of various weaving designs by the Hopi weaver, Ramona Sakiestewa. The effect is of the characters struggling across time, remembering, acting across space, caught between the present that is theatre, the past that is memory, and the future which is the prospect of death turning into the memory of ghosts. The play begins in the early 1950s and goes back and forth in time, ending in a timeless world. In the opening scene, Margaret is discovered, arms upraised exultantly, in front of a projection depicting the famous, pre-Columbian Inca weaving in the Dunbarton Oaks Museum in Washington, D.C.)

SCENE 1

MARGARET *(exultantly, as* GEORGE *stands in the shadows, waiting):*
Rejoice with me, George! Rejoice in the knowledge
Of a perfect kind of beauty that endures!

See how the ancient Incas created
A world of radiant colors spun together
From the coats of animals in brilliant designs . . .

GEORGE:
Margaret . . .

MARGARET *(absorbed in the weaving):*
Such a weaving shows us
How we've lost the soul of unity today.
Always we search for that goal of
Blessed unity between earth and heaven—
The sun shining beyond our reach—
No matter, we worship the pursuit . . .

GEORGE:
Margaret!

MARGARET *(turning):*
The pursuit of love! In search of
Such perfect unity, we dedicate our lives
Through eager, searching days
To the eternal pursuit of happiness!

   (She laughs, as GEORGE *moves in and they laugh together.)*

SCENE 2

MARGARET:
Do you really mean it, George? Is romantic love still possible at our age?

GEORGE:
As long as the heart pounds. Is yours pounding? *(He puts his hand on her heart.)*

   *(*GEORGE *and* MARGARET *are close together.)*

MARGARET:
Can you feel it?

GEORGE:
It's chugging like an old steam engine. *(handing her a poem)* I've written a poem for you.

MARGARET *(taking the poem):*
You're romantic all right even if "old steam engine" isn't very poetic
. . . It's in German. I don't understand German.

GEORGE:
I've translated it. If I'm not a poet, at least Goethe is. *(He reads.)*
Loneliness I can bear
As long as my love is true to me.
My longing for you
Sets fire to my mind
For your memory flames
In my poor alien heart.

MARGARET:
That's lovely. You're taking advantage of me.

GEORGE:
You're the poet. I'm just trying to show you how a tough, old plant pathologist can be poetic too.

MARGARET *(teasingly):*
Sometimes I worry a little about a man who lives like a hermit. He looks at
disease all the time . . .

GEORGE *(grinning):*
Disease can be beautiful. I'll show you under the microscope.

MARGARET:
What if romantic love gets infected with a blight like plants?

GEORGE:
Plants are like sick people. You have to know what's wrong to cure them.

MARGARET:
A romantic healer! . . . I like that. Still, I'm afraid of your energy.

GEORGE:
Would you rather have a limp sponge, or a passionate old plant pathologist?

MARGARET:
Are you proposing to me?

GEORGE:
I've got our secret wedding and honeymoon plans all made.

MARGARET:

I like passionate secrets! *(They both laugh and freeze in a marriage photo pose.)*

SCENE 3

(The son, ERWIN PIERSON, *and his wife,* SHIRLEY *appear, preparing to go to bed, as the scenes overlap.)*

ERWIN *(angrily, reading a letter):*

Can you believe this? They didn't even invite us to their wedding!

SHIRLEY:

They're really married?

ERWIN *(crumpling the letter and throwing it away as* MARGARET *and* GEORGE *react and exit):*

George enticed Mother into a god damn honeymoon in Canada.

SHIRLEY:

Enticed her to Canada?

ERWIN:

George thinks he's the Wilderness Magician of Lake O'Hara!

SHIRLEY:

So you're a wild poet and cunning teacher. What's magical about Lake O'Hara?

ERWIN:

He's building mountain trails around the lake. Secretly, all by himself! He thinks his trails are magical!

SHIRLEY:

Plant Pathologist doesn't fit in with Wilderness Magician.

ERWIN:

He wants to bring back the old wilderness gods.

SHIRLEY:

Sounds like a true Wagnerian mystic. What does your mother think of these trails?

ERWIN:

She's thrilled by the fact that he named one of the trails after her— EYSA . . .

SHIRLEY:
Eysa?

ERWIN:
Eysa is a combination of Eve and Yseult.

SHIRLEY:
Eve and Isolde . . . Your mother will love that.

ERWIN:
Maybe they're the last romantics.

SHIRLEY:
You're jealous.

ERWIN:
I can invent myths too. *(gesturing to her)* I married a practical social worker. Now she's turning into an earth mother! She wants to be a mother!

SHIRLEY *(laughing):*
You should talk. You turned our wedding into your own ritual with your poems and the music you selected.

ERWIN:
At least we invited our families. Remember how they stared at each other suspiciously.

SHIRLEY:
My father wasn't too happy about us getting married.

ERWIN:
Who could blame him? He was just as good an American as anyone, and then he got stuck in a concentration camp by white racists after Pearl Harbor. I liked your father. I think he came to like me despite his feelings about our marriage.

SHIRLEY:
He did like you. I miss him . . .

ERWIN:
Is that why you want a son?

SHIRLEY:
Maybe, in part. I want a family. That's what your mother wants too. She doesn't want to be alone. Where did your mother get married?

ERWIN:

In Vancouver, at the home of a former judge who transformed himself into one of Canada's leading abstract artists. George met him at Lake O'Hara one summer. Probably this artful judge drew inspiration from George's abstract trails! Believe it or not, this legal artist is called Lancelot Sanderson!

SHIRLEY:

Did she say what the wedding ceremony was like? Probably she tried to outdo you.

ERWIN:

They made their own secret pledges to each other.

SHIRLEY:

Secret pledges? Well, why not at their age?

ERWIN:

They should have invited us. I'll get even with them.

SCENE 4

(The wedding ceremony of GEORGE *and* MARGARET *in Canada. George is giving instructions to* LANCELOT SANDERSON, *who is played by the actor who transforms into the various male characters.)*

GEORGE:

Lancelot, don't slouch! Stand straight! You're running the ceremony! Hold your painting! You're giving it to us as a wedding present, right? *(He thrusts the painting at him.)* There . . . We need a little atmosphere. Wedding officials should be gift-bearers, not preachers of morality.

LANCELOT:

I can't hold it. It's too heavy! *(He places it on an easel.)*

GEORGE *(surveying the painting critically)*:

You're painting too big! The trouble with you abstract artists is that you paint only for museums.

LANCELOT:

Is this a critique or a wedding ceremony?

MARGARET:

Let him alone, George. It's beautiful. We'll build an extra room for it! Time for your judicial functions, Lancelot!

LANCELOT *(grinning):*
Do you know I'm the only abstract artist in Canada who is a former judge?

GEORGE:
The truth is if you weren't a retired judge, you couldn't afford to be an abstract artist.

LANCELOT:
You hear, Margaret? You're marrying an aged dinosaur at your peril! I should warn you both that the peculiar ceremony you two lovers have contrived is not strictly legal . . .

MARGARET *(a little alarmed):*
Really?

GEORGE:
Lancelot, your ironic, little jokes are repetitious *(pointing)* like the barbed arrow symbolism in your new paintings. Watch out! You're transfering your skeptical legal behavior into the idealistic, metaphysical realm of art.

MARGARET *(to* LANCELOT*)*:
I like the bold, modern way you paint oldfashioned arrows, Lancelot.

LANCELOT:
As a western Canadian, I prefer the image of arrows to that of computers.

GEORGE *(impatiently):*
Let's get on with it.

LANCELOT *(looking at the ceremony* GEORGE *has given him):*
You haven't given me much to say, a few dry semi-legalities typical of your pseudo-rational scientific mind.

GEORGE:
Judges always pontificate too much. This is our marriage, not yours.

MARGARET:
George, please . . .

LANCELOT:
It's all right. I understand an old fossil's dreams . . .

GEORGE:
All you have to do is begin by inviting our pledges . . .

LANCELOT *(beginning):*
Dear friends, gathered here for a sacred purpose . . .

GEORGE *(interrupting)*:

It doesn't say *sacred* . . . We don't want *sacred*. We don't want *secular*. We want *us*.

MARGARET:

Please, George. Surely we can have one accidental *sacred*.

LANCELOT:

Sorry, George, you're right . . . *(reading)* Gathered here together for the unifying desire of natural matrimony, you wish to recite your own secret pledges. Margaret, may we hear your pledge?

MARGARET *(turning to* GEORGE*)*:

Dear George, this is my pledge. Both of us have lived beyond first marriages and children into the hoped-for sanctuary of old age. We have lived in feverish cities and grown away from them. Accustomed to loneliness, we seek now to escape from it. We have lived with animals and have come to see the communal instinct of their loyalties. In the spirit of romantic search, we have read many books and recited poetry together. We know that words can be chanted, as if they are music across time, to celebrate man's spirit and destiny in the natural world. When magical flesh seeks to love, words are its mask. In my aging flesh, I promise to seek with you words of wisdom. I promise to share with you your knowledge of plants and your creation of mountain trails. I give you my heart, mind and body in search of all the true romantic myths that enable mankind to endure the quest for honor, dignity and love.

LANCELOT *(gleefully)*:

Your turn, George. Try to top that!

GEORGE:

Dear Margaret, this is my pledge. In the furnace of old age, with desire raging against fleshly limitations, I have found someone to share with me the adventurous building of trails and the protection of plants and trees. I know the world's diseases that seek to ravage and wither all beauty. With your help I will succeed in finishing my translation of Theophrastus, who wrote the greatest botanical treatise of all time, *On The History of Plants,* in nine volumes. Even Aristotle recognized the greatness of Theophrastus when he appointed him his successor and the guardian of his children. Margaret, I promise to regard you with the respect that Theophrastus gave to a rare plant. Such respect must not be sentimentalized. As a rare being, an exquisite plant, you are to me a body of infinite promise and infinite danger. I pledge to cherish you through the infinity of that promise

294

and danger. As Goethe says at the end of *Faust*, written in the wisdom of his old age:

Everything that we see
Fades into memory;
Everything that is fiction
Here becomes action;
The mysterious will—
Here it is done.
The Eternal Feminine
Draws us on!

LANCELOT *(moved)*:
Dear friends, clasp each other and embrace! With the legal powers invested in me by the Canadian government, which is blissfully indifferent to the fact that I have vanished from law into the dangerous realm of art, I pronounce you marital trailblazers husband and wife! Live happily, if not forever!

GEORGE AND MARGARET:
Thank you, Lancelot. *(The three embrace, then* LANCELOT *draws back.)*

LANCELOT:
Wait a minute . . . As an artist, not a judge, I get to say a few more words. Dear friends, romance is a cliff over which you have to jump sometimes. On its highest trails where fanatics venture, there are often bears and boulders. Dear George, I pray that a wrinkled plant pathologist will recognize and explore carefully the beauties of new love. Dear Margaret, I pray that your poetry and artistry may find in a new world of plants and Canadian mountain trails the abstract force and beauty of new creative power!

GEORGE:
Good words spoken abstractly, Lancelot! Let's drink to us!

(They all toast each other.)

SCENE 5

*(*SHIRLEY *is in bed, looking at* ERWIN, *who is about to join her.)*

SHIRLEY:
Maybe we should have a child . . .

ERWIN:

Don't change the subject. Why are you so insensitive about mother's marriage?

SHIRLEY:

She's got a right to her own life. You're too attached to her. A family of your own might help.

ERWIN:

You're missing the point. Mother's going to have trouble with George's crazy energy.

SHIRLEY:

That's her decision. Maybe she can change him. What do you expect from the oldest son of a tyrannical Fundamentalist preacher?

ERWIN:

He can't change. What if he finds out about mother's history of depression?

SHIRLEY:

Surely she told him.

ERWIN:

Not everything . . . All she mentioned was her analysis with Jung. She said she was cured.

SHIRLEY:

She's all right. That extraordinary woman has had so many romances. She wants another one and you can't stop her.

ERWIN:

Maybe I can stop her . . .

SHIRLEY:

Don't blame her. Lovers want their own privacy. We did in our time.

ERWIN:

So you really want a child . . .

SHIRLEY:

I want a magical child who continues us into the future.

ERWIN:

How can you really believe in the future?

SHIRLEY:

After World War II, when my father lost his business and was never able to regain it after his release from the camp, I had to learn how to live with-

out hating the United States. We were Americans. I was born here. I had
to dream of the future.

ERWIN:
You were a better kind of American. You endured. Your family endured.
You never grew bitter.

SHIRLEY:
I grew up on the edge of bitterness. Our child must never live that way.

ERWIN:
I thought this is the age of women's liberation from slavery to children
and macho men.

SHIRLEY:
This is the age of liberating ourselves.

ERWIN:
You want me to overwhelm you?

SHIRLEY *(laughing)*:
Let's practice our own secret bed language . . .

SCENE 6

*(GEORGE and MARGARET on their honeymoon. He is showing her the trails he
is building. The trails are represented by a ramp on which GEORGE is standing
above her. They are dressed in individualistic hiking and working clothes.
GEORGE is carrying a shovel and a map.)*

GEORGE *(looking down)*:
How do you like *Eysa?*

MARGARET:
Such a beautiful view!

GEORGE:
What about the *trail?*

MARGARET:
You built these trails all by yourself?

GEORGE:
No one would help. Everyone thought I was crazy. To tell the truth, I began to like the work. I never thought I'd fall in love with a shovel! *(He
shovels dirt energetically, throwing some of it down on her.)*

297

MARGARET *(laughing, protesting)*:
George! You are terrible!

GEORGE *(exuberantly)*:
See how *Eysa* curves into the clouds?

MARGARET:
Stop it! I'm coming up to see! *(She climbs up to see and he helps her up, embracing her.)*

GEORGE:
How do you like your honeymoon on *Eysa?* You've become an immortal name!

MARGARET *(laughing)*:
I never thought of immortality as existing on a map.

GEORGE:
Maps create mythological worlds! Think of Columbus . . . The world is flat! You sail towards the edge! Suddenly, demons grab you. You drop off into hell-fire! If it hadn't been for some dedicated cartographer, we'd never have known about hell!

MARGARET:
I never thought of a cartographer as a mapper of hell!

GEORGE *(unrolling his map)*:
Look . . . *(pointing)* Here comes *Eysa* winding up over these lower trails—Proserpine, Theophrastus, Athena, Lancelot . . .

MARGARET *(laughing)*:
All your Greek favorites, and one Canadian abstract artist . . .

GEORGE:
Athena is for my first wife. She was wise.

MARGARET:
Am I wise too?

GEORGE:
No, you're full of impulsive, poetic instincts. I love that! You're a big love trail, and Lancelot is a small, abstract trail. *(pointing to the map)* You see? SAT . . . Small Abstract Trail . . .

MARGARET:
George, you're a devil! How can anyone ever decipher your coded map?

GEORGE *(grandly):*
Only legendary trails retain their magic. Romantic climbers see where the trails go and follow them. Only you and I will ever know this trail's secret!

MARGARET:
Such a lovely secret, George. *(warning him mischievously)* Beware, one day I may betray your code. Beauty must be shared. But I will never betray *Eysa.*

GEORGE:
Never! On peril of your life! *(A small shower of rocks comes down from above and* MARGARET *clings to* GEORGE.*)* See what I mean!

MARGARET *(alarmed):*
George, it's beginning to storm!

GEORGE *(holding her):*
Don't worry, darling! Let the mountain rage! The wilderness gods will protect us! *(He shakes his hand at the mountain.)* My trails exist forever! Wipe them out and I'll rebuild them! *Eysa* lives! *Eysa lives!* *(He holds her as the thunderstorm begins and more rocks hurtle down.)*

SCENE 7

(Working intently, ERWIN *is creating his version of a Navajo medicine map as* SHIRLEY *enters. He is working on it vertically, so the audience can see it too.)*

SHIRLEY *(looking at Erwin's table):*
What are you doing?

ERWIN:
I'm working on a Navajo medicine map to welcome mother and George home.

SHIRLEY:
A Navajo medicine map?

ERWIN:
I'm going to test George's fantasies!

SHIRLEY:
Are you crazy?

ERWIN:
I can be just as crazy as George!

SHIRLEY:

I should have married into an average family.

ERWIN:

Look who's talking. You've got too much curiosity for the average family. As a social worker, you always poke your nose into the first astonishing case that comes along.

SHIRLEY:

Thank you, all problems are normal to us.

ERWIN:

Like the homeless family with thirteen children you're trying to help?

SHIRLEY:

You're superstitious about thirteen. I'm just trying to break through the birth control barrier.

ERWIN:

What bugs me about your social work is that you think you're so calm and practical. Really, you love grappling madly with poverty and insanity.

SHIRLEY *(kicking him):*

Erwin Pierson, sometimes you are so stupid I want to kick you!

ERWIN *(fending her off):*

It seems to me you *are* kicking me!

SHIRLEY *(keeping up the playful attack with her fists as well as her feet):*

I'll keep kicking you until you understand that social service is a planned, scientific attempt to help the underprivileged achieve their democratic rights!

ERWIN:

Ok, fighter, I understand . . . But remember Auden's famous words of advice to all students: "Thou shalt not commit a social science!" *(They embrace. She breaks away and looks at the map.)*

SHIRLEY:

What is this crazy map?

ERWIN:

It's a ceremonial map of the Navajo plant world.

SHIRLEY:

What the hell do you know about the Navajo plant world?

ERWIN:

Nothing. You see this clown on the side, summoning everyone onto the natural trails? That's me . . . Once, mother took me to a Navajo ceremony I'll never forget. The women wore their family wealth in turquoise and silver. Massive strings of white shell, coral and turquoise beads shone around their necks over red and bright blue velveteen blouses. Just as colorful, the men wore big silver concha belts and bright green satin shirts. They tied silk handkerchiefs around their heads, and sported new "ten gallon" Stetson hats with silver bands around the crowns. *(As he talks, he puts on a Stetson hat. The* DANCER *appears, wearing the mask of The Talking God, as music is heard.)* The Navajos were going to a curing ritual. They believe only a place unpolluted by human use can serve as a curing center . . .

SHIRLEY *(alarmed suddenly):*

Erwin, you can't conduct a curing ritual!

ERWIN:

Who can cure George?

SHIRLEY:

Where do I fit in? You're leaving me out!

ERWIN:

It's just a little ritual test in plants for the Professor of Plant Pathology. Come on, you can participate . . .

SHIRLEY:

I don't know this ritual, Erwin! Your mother will be upset . . .

ERWIN:

Mother will love it. She'll remember . . . *(As the* DANCER *dances, the rhythm of the music with drums and rattles shaking slowly increases in pace and volume.)* We heard the call of the Talking God . . . *(We hear "Whu-hu- hu- hu" chanted four times, louder and louder.)* The woman patient comes out of the medicine hogan, holding a basket filled with corn meal. In the evening darkness, the twelve ceremonial fires shoot up into the night. Out of the darkness comes the masked figures of the Talking God and the four dancers representing the four directions of the world, as well as the Chiefs of the Corn, Rain, Pollen, and Plants . . . The Chiefs move slowly up to the patient . . . You can be the patient . . .

SHIRLEY:

I'm not the patient!

ERWIN:
You're right . . . George is the patient. We sprinkle George with holy corn meal . . .

SHIRLEY *(pulling away):*
You'll turn George into an enemy!

ERWIN *(taking her hand, chanting over the music and dancing):*
Come on, we'll dance together . . .
"Happily may fair corn of all colors
To the ends of the earth
Come with you
Happily may fair plants of all kinds
To the ends of the earth
Come with you . . .
In beauty, I walk . . .
With beauty all around me I walk.
It is finished in beauty.
It is finished in beauty . . ."

SHIRLEY *(overwhelmed):*
You're sure it will finish in beauty?

SCENE 8

(The DANCER *has disappeared, as the music of* ERWIN'S *welcoming ceremony continues.* SHIRLEY *is a reluctant, fascinated watcher. Returning from their honeymoon in Canada,* GEORGE *and* MARGARET *enter.)*

ERWIN *(interrupting his chant):*
Welcome home, honeymooners! *(He prods* SHIRLEY *and she echos, "Welcome home!"* ERWIN *concludes his chanting against the ceremonial music that carries over from Scene 6.)*

Happily may fair corn of all colors
To the ends of the earth
Come with you.
Happily may fair plants of all kinds
To the ends of the earth
Come with you . . .
In beauty, I walk . . .
It is finished in beauty.

MARGARET *(laughing joyously):*
How wonderful! Erwin, you remembered our visit to the Night Chant!

ERWIN:
The Talking God and the Chiefs dance up to the patient . . . They sprinkle her with corn meal . . . *(He sprinkles her with a little corn meal. Then he sprinkles* GEORGE *with a lot of corn meal.)* The patient begins to sing with the Chiefs . . . *(He and his mother sing together, while* SHIRLEY *and* GEORGE *listen,* GEORGE *sensing* ERWIN'S *challenge.)*

MARGARET *(ecstatically, as she starts singing and chanting, and* ERWIN *joins in):*
And the woman sang, re-born in the harmony of the Gods—

In beauty, I walk.
With beauty before me, I walk.
With beauty behind me, I walk.
With beauty above me, I walk.
With beauty below me, I walk.
With beauty all around me, I walk.
With beauty within me, I walk.
It is finished in beauty.
It is finished in beauty . . . *(to* SHIRLEY *and* GEORGE*)* Come on, join in! *(all conclude)*
It is finished in beauty.
It is finished in beauty.

SHIRLEY *(impulsively, handing glasses of wine to* GEORGE *and* MARGARET*):*
Welcome home, George and Margaret! May your marriage be finished together in beauty!

ERWIN:
Wait a moment! The ceremony is not finished . . . *(to* GEORGE*)* Chief of Plants! You have come to cure this woman's illness . . . *(He unveils the sandpainting map he has created, a huge figure of his mother in Navajo costume. A corn plant is growing up through her body. Brightly colored strings run from various parts of her anatomy to pictures of different plants.)* You must identify these sacred plants to save this woman!

GEORGE *(trying to control himself):*
Wait a minute, Erwin. I'm no medicine man. I don't know how plants cure. I study their diseases.

SHIRLEY *(hastily, to* GEORGE*):*
You don't have to be Chief of Plants. Have another glass of wine.

MARGARET *(laughing):*
It's just a game, George!

GEORGE:
I haven't studied southwestern plants for a long time.

MARGARET:
Come on, see how many you can guess.

ERWIN:
Chief of Plants, cure this woman with your magical knowledge.

GEORGE:
I told you I don't know about curative plants.

ERWIN:
Take a guess!

GEORGE *(taking up the challenge):*
All right, Erwin, I'll travel up your little wilderness trail . . . Let's see
what we can find . . . *(He begins to examine each plant.)* That's yarrow
. . . *(ERWIN tears off the string and hands it to MARGARET.)* This looks
like Small . . . Yes, Small *Snakeweed* . . .

MARGARET *(laughing, waving the colored strings that ERWIN has thrust into
her hands):*
Oh George, you're marvelous! You're healing her!

GEORGE *(staring):*
I don't know this one . . . Wait a minute, it's Brigham Tea . . . *(Reluctantly, ERWIN tears off the colored string. SHIRLEY takes it from ERWIN
and gives it to MARGARET.)* And this one is Black . . . Black Walnut
Shells! *(Defeated, ERWIN sags back, and SHIRLEY tears off the string and
hands it to MARGARET.)*

SHIRLEY:
You've got four!

ERWIN *(glaring, subdued):*
Oh Chief of Plants, you have liberated this woman's head . . . Now, we
pray that you can reach down into her body and free her soul.

MARGARET *(laughing):*
I see what you're up to, Erwin! You're curing me with all of the dye-plants
from which Navajo weavers get their dyes.

GEORGE *(waving her away):*
That doesn't help, Margaret. What do I know about weaving . . .

MARGARET:
Quiet, everybody, the Chief is thinking!

GEORGE:
I'm trying to remember.

ERWIN *(desperately):*
Reach into your memory, oh Chief of Plants, and free this woman's soul!

SHIRLEY *(poking* ERWIN *and whispering):*
Enough is enough, Erwin!

GEORGE:
I'm not sure . . . I think this is Purple Larksong . . .

ERWIN:
Almost right . . .

GEORGE *(triumphantly):*
I mean Purple Larkspur . . . And this one is Small Sunflowers! . . .
*(*SHIRLEY *tears off the strings and hands them to* MARGARET, *who cheers.)*

MARGARET *(laughing):*
You have liberated my soul! See, children, my heart soars free with the plants!

SHIRLEY *(to* ERWIN, *then to all):*
The Chief of Plants wins! Let's liberate some food!

MARGARET:
You're a funny gameplayer, Erwin. That was quite a welcome home!

GEORGE *(to* ERWIN):
Yes, quite a welcome. I didn't know you were so interested in plants.

ERWIN *(holding up his glass):*
You win! Here's to the Chief of Plants!

SCENE 9

(As the scene opens, the four of them are a little high on drink and food, more relaxed, laughing and talking.)

305

SHIRLEY *(to* MARGARET*)*:
Go on, tell us about your first visit to the Navajos.

GEORGE *(to* MARGARET*)*:
I've never heard the full story.

SHIRLEY:
That must have been a real adventure.

MARGARET:
In 1912 everyone was dreaming about the west . . . I was an Irish girl from immigrant parents who sent me to Wellesley College to be *finished!*

GEORGE *(chuckling)*:
Education is those days was supposed to *finish* women.

MARGARET:
I translated Horace Greeley into "Go West, young woman!" After graduating, I was offered a job teaching high school in Tucson, Arizona. Believe it or not, I taught English and coached the basketball team. The girls wore long bloomers in those days.

ERWIN:
She was the first tall woman basketball player.

MARGARET:
All of the old Indian cultures still haunted Tucson. I fell in love with Navajo jewelry and rugs, and Hopi kachinas. Friends put me in touch with the famous Indian trader, Lorenzo Hubbell. I wrote to him and arranged a visit . . .

SHIRLEY:
You traveled alone up to the Navajo Reservation?

MARGARET:
The only way in was by train. It slowed down at a canyon junction to throw off mail bags. I persuaded the conductor to let me jump off with the mail bags.

GEORGE:
That was risky, Margaret!

MARGARET:
The train was barely moving. Still, my heart was pounding. I felt all tangled up in my back pack and my long hair dangling under my hat. The conductor helped me to jump in the right direction. I clung to his hand. I

couldn't let go! Finally, I jumped and landed, striding, like a professional. As the train pulled away, the sun shining on those red canyon cliffs blinded me. That blazing sunrise taught me my first lesson about sun worship! Then I heard Lorenzo calling from his Model-T. He owned one of the first Fords on the reservation. There were no roads. He drove that old Tin Lizzie like crazy over the desert! Riding beside him, I held onto my hat and prayed!

GEORGE:
You drove off with him alone?

MARGARET:
I sure did! He liked me too. Of course he was married. In those days marriage was a fortress.

ERWIN:
No more fortresses . . .

SHIRLEY:
How come your school let you go alone? Weren't there strict rules for women teachers being chaperoned in those days?

MARGARET *(chuckling):*
I lied. I said I was visiting an aunt.

GEORGE:
Now young people fly off anywhere to stay in luxury hotels. Then they describe their trips as adventures.

SHIRLEY:
Somewhere there are still adventures.

MARGARET *to* GEORGE):
Tell them about your youth.

GEORGE:
Not many adventures . . . I don't like to think about it too much . . . There were eight of us children. I was the oldest boy. Our father was a devout, strict Lutheran minister. I had to see that the younger children carried out their assigned tasks . . .

ERWIN:
Heavy duty . . .

SHIRLEY:
Was your father always occupied with his church?

(As GEORGE *speaks, we see the figure of his* FATHER, *played by the actor who played* LANCELOT, *ascending as if to a pulpit in the background.)*

GEORGE:

Every day of the week he thought about his Sunday sermon as if he were preparing for Armageddon. Preaching was his power. On Sunday he dominated the whole town. From his pulpit he ruled his flock, but one Sunday he met his destiny . . .

THE MINISTER:

Dear friends and brethren . . . Today the forces of evil menace us again, the forces of Satan. They threaten our unity of plow and hand. Trains and ships have opened the world to the lure of vanity. The Lord's way of sowing and reaping stands in danger! Promising false pleasures and profits, cities call our young people away from the land to which they should be dedicated. Spiders of greed beset us and menace our ways!

GEORGE:

Luther was his model of salvation.

THE MINISTER:

As Luther turned away from the glittering splendor of corrupt Rome to find his salvation within, we too must seek again that Christian salvation for which our Lord Jesus sacrificed himself. Here, in our country's heartland, we must fight for the salvation of our community. The cloven hoof of the Devil approaches. You can hear him drumming on the edge of our town! We must not let him enter! Like Goethe's Mephistopheles, he speaks enticing words, "Grau, teurer Freund, ist alle Theorie, und gruen des Leben's goldner Baum."

GEORGE:

Goethe's Mephistopheles fascinated him, the Devil as seducer . . . *(translating the words of Mephistopheles)* "Gray, dear Friend, is all theory, and green is Life's golden tree."

THE MINISTER:

Dear Brethren, if the Devil entices us away from the Bible's sacred laws to eat forbidden fruit, we must resist! We must . . . *(Suddenly, he strangles on the words. Although he struggles desperately to continue, he can only utter sounds and no more words.)*

GEORGE *(continuing, addressing now his* FATHER *directly, who is still struggling for speech in the background):*

Suddenly, you were sentenced! You could not speak another word in the pulpit!

THE MINISTER *(struggling to speak):*
Earrrgh . . .

GEORGE:
You never preached again in any church. You felt that Luther himself,
your idol, had condemned you to hell!

THE MINISTER:
Ahergg . . .

GEORGE:
Father, I began to fear Luther. Do you understand? I remembered his
famous, barbaric boast: "If I fart in Wittenberg, they smell it in Rome!"
Was the Lutheran Church cursed?

THE MINISTER:
Nohiggah . . .

GEORGE:
You had to change your profession. Ironically, you became a sullen car-
penter. Our house, that resounded with the Lord's commandments, became a bitter house full of silent agony. Mother looked at you with fear
and growing resentment as we lost our place of honor in the community.

THE MINISTER:
Myshuggahh . . .

GEORGE:
I grew to hate your bitter presence, father. I hated you! You were possessed by Mephistopheles! I too began to think that all theory is grey. I
longed to escape into the green trees and plants of life . . . *(The* FATHER
sags down in despair, still struggling to preach.)

(Blackout.)

SCENE 10

(Evening. A little hung over, ERWIN *and* GEORGE *appear, as if in the kitchen.)*

ERWIN:
Maybe we need a cup of coffee . . .

GEORGE:
Too much coffee and I don't sleep. At my age I save coffee for special
occasions.

ERWIN:

Right . . . I guess this occasion requires booze more than coffee. *(He takes another drink after* GEORGE *refuses one.)*

GEORGE:

All I meant was, at my age I save stimulants for the moment when I need them most.

ERWIN:

Why not? Everyone needs thrilling moments.

GEORGE:

I'm glad to say your mother has given me many such moments when I thought they were over.

ERWIN:

Good in the sack, eh? . . . I'm sorry . . . If my welcome seemed like a test I apologize. You got a perfect score. I was sore because we weren't invited to your wedding.

GEORGE:

Your mother wanted her own private ceremony.

ERWIN:

She loves secret, poetic ceremonies. I prefer Walt Whitman's attempt at public performances.

GEORGE:

Isn't it tough with two poets in the family?

ERWIN:

I guess it's good to have a romantic wall to stand against.

GEORGE:

Somehow it's hard to think of your mother as a wall.

ERWIN:

I began to see her as a romantic wall when I discovered how different she was from my father. She couldn't learn his foreign languages. They loved each other, but it was like a hidden Irish-Spanish war. He wrote his critical praise of Cervantes on one side of the wall and she wrote her Irish love poems on the other side.

GEORGE:

I like her Irish love poems.

ERWIN:

Yeah, I'll bet she's written some good ones for you . . . I couldn't blame Dad. One day a young Spanish-American graduate student appeared in his class . . .

GEORGE:

Thank god, I never had that kind of temptation.

ERWIN:

No temptation in Plant Pathology, huh . . . Pretty soon this fiery lady was writing in Spanish on Dad's side of the wall. Mother went into a deep depression. She'd never been turned down before in all of her romantic escapades. She wouldn't come out of her room. Finally, she decided to go back to Switzerland and work with Jung again to see if he could help her. I was assigned to accompany her to Europe as a kind of nurse-companion.

GEORGE:

She told me that Jung saved her, got her writing again. I wanted to ask you . . . I'm a little worried about her history of depression . . .

ERWIN:

You don't need to worry. Underneath she's a fighter. She's fine now since Jung and her shock therapy . . .

GEORGE *(reacting):*

Shock therapy?

ERWIN:

You didn't know?

GEORGE:

She had shock therapy?

ERWIN:

I'm sorry I mentioned it.

GEORGE:

She never told me! I thought we had a complete understanding! She lied to me!

ERWIN:

Don't call her a liar. She's just forgotten the shock therapy.

GEORGE:

How can you forget shock therapy? I can't believe what you said!

ERWIN:

I take it all back. You never heard anything. Blame it on the booze . . .

GEORGE:

I'm tired of your games! I don't know what to believe anymore. At our age, Margaret and I agreed to reveal all health problems. God damn it, we even had complete premarital examinations. She said she was certified in excellent health.

ERWIN:

She is healthy! You don't need to worry . . .

GEORGE:

How can I trust her anymore?

ERWIN:

You're taking this too hard. Shock therapy is so painful that she thrust it out of her mind. Jung was a more romantic cure . . . Surely, you can understand that . . .

GEORGE:

Romantic cure, hell! Did she tell me half the truth?

ERWIN:

Cool down . . . We're a little plastered . . . You're making a pathological plant out of a little erroneous seed . . .

GEORGE:

Don't get smart with me! She should have told me! Don't you see how important this is? I took care of my first wife for several years when she was dying of cancer. I can't take care of another invalid!

ERWIN:

If something should happen to mother, she doesn't expect you to take care of her.

GEORGE:

At our age, we don't have much time. We need a few years of happiness and peace. We can't deceive each other. How could she do this to me? (*He exits.*)

SCENE 11

(ERWIN *is reading one of his poems to* MARGARET. *She is standing at the edge of a table as if about to undergo shock therapy.*)

312

ERWIN:

"Often the hand cannot control the eye.
The senses rip apart like torn silk,
And the eye seeks its own salvation
Exploding with the shock of vision . . ."

MARGARET:

Striking lines, but they're too intellectual.

ERWIN:

How can you tell? I'm not finished.

MARGARET:

What do you know about shock? You make it sound abstract.

ERWIN:

I'm trying to get the unique sound of the word *shock*. Shock, knock, fuck
. . . All the hard K sounds. Everyone is shocked so much today with rock
and television, the ear goes numb. No one can hear hard sounds anymore!

MARGARET:

Never mind the ear. Shock affects every nerve in your body.

ERWIN:

That's a poem for you to write.

MARGARET:

I've tried. It's too terrifying.

ERWIN:

My poem is not about your shock therapy!

MARGARET:

You have real ability, but your work needs to be simpler, more direct.

ERWIN:

Oh god, let's not fight again about our different views of poetry.

MARGARET:

I'm not fighting, only criticizing the way you've made "shock" too abstract.

ERWIN:

Maybe you're right. Your shock therapy was so painful to me that I shut it
out of my mind just the way you did.

MARGARET:

Perhaps I deserved that . . .

313

ERWIN:

I'm sorry, but it's true.

MARGARET *(acting out the effect of shock therapy as she climbs onto the table):*
For years I've tried to write a poem about my shock therapy . . . Can
you believe it? For years I dreamt of the psychiatrist as a master electrician. He stood at a switch in his white coat controlling the power of electricity. When he pulled the switch, the electric current lashed at me like a
bolt of lightning. It lashed through the frontal area of my brain . . . My
body twisted and turned against the straps. Spasm after spasm racked me
in waves of anguish. I struggled to break the straps that held me down
. . . The master electrician tried vainly to calm me. "It's almost over,
almost over!" But he pulled the switch again . . . No escape . . . More
terrible convulsions . . . Electricity lashed into my brain again as if richo-
cheting from a lightning rod. My sick mind was illuminated. I felt I was
flying through a jagged thunderstorm! Lightning, the spear of God, conquers me!

ERWIN *(pulling her up):*
Please, mother . . .

MARGARET:

That master electrician with his lightning bolts altered my brain forever.
Nurses stroked me like a baby. Everyone was so falsely kind to me. They
took me to the locked ward and imprisoned my spirit. Only when Jung
analyzed me, did my spirit return to earth. With his gentle guidance, I
confronted my nightmares and controlled them. People can learn to be rational. Jung taught me that with his calm strength. But a locked medical
ward is a prison, even though they pretend it is a hospital . . .

ERWIN:

I know what it was like. I visited you there . . .

MARGARET:

The master electrician classified me forever as an unstable mental patient.
In the locked ward I began to feel that everyone dressed in white to guard
my mind. If I was not controlled and shocked properly, the signals of civilization would vanish. If our sick minds were not altered by lightning, we
insane people would come to think of ourselves as witches in a cabal or
power moguls like Napoleon or Hitler. The locked ward is the arena to
tame wild, demonic forces . . .

ERWIN:

Stop, mother, I've heard it before! Whenever I talked to your doctor, I felt that his quiet manner only masked his true feelings about shock therapy. How could a doctor, I wondered, believe in a therapy that was so violent? How would he treat me if I too got depressed, and I was depressed at times . . .

MARGARET:
You never told me this before.

ERWIN:
I couldn't talk about it when you were in such pain . . . I'm so sorry . . . I didn't mean to tell George . . . I tried to make him understand . . . *(He breaks down, and she embraces him, trying to console him.)*

SCENE 12

(The lights come up on another area of the stage. SHIRLEY *is standing behind* MARGARET, *brushing Margaret's long hair.)*

SHIRLEY:
Relax . . . I'll get you ready.

MARGARET:
I'm afraid to confront George . . . He has such a quick temper . . .

SHIRLEY:
You'll work it out.

MARGARET:
I should have told him before . . . I suppose I was too ashamed. He's so against any radical kind of medical treatment. I was afraid of what he would think of shock therapy . . . I didn't want to lose him . . .

SHIRLEY:
You won't lose him. You're both intelligent people. He just lost his temper . . .

MARGARET:
Erwin doesn't like him. That strange plant test last night . . .

SHIRLEY:
Family punishment . . . Erwin wanted to chastise you and George for not being invited to your wedding.

MARGARET:
He's a funny boy . . . How are you and Erwin getting along?

315

SHIRLEY:

I want a child . . . He's not sure.

MARGARET:

You can persuade him.

SHIRLEY:

He's worried about you.

MARGARET:

When you're old, a new marriage isn't easy. You can understand why we wanted our own privacy . . .

SHIRLEY:

Erwin doesn't blame you for your secret romantic ceremony. He's jealous because you created a new adventure and left him out.

MARGARET:

I was too preoccupied with my marriage to think of anything else. I dread confronting George now . . .

SHIRLEY:

Your life has been full of such powerful romantic relationships . . . You're a strong lady. You won't have any trouble handling George.

MARGARET:

Romantic relationships that I lost . . . Perhaps that is what romantic really means, a passion that cannot endure.

SHIRLEY:

Erwin needs to create his own memories, not live in yours.

MARGARET:

You're a wise woman, Shirley. I'm glad he married you.

SHIRLEY:

I love him! He's my relief from the everyday world. In my family, I was always told we had to work hard and be practical to fit into American society. In a concentration camp, there wasn't much of an opportunity to be practical anymore. You had to dream of the future to survive. As a kid, I dreamt of romance in that camp and haunted the movies whenever we got a chance to see one. I collected photos of movie stars the way Ann Frank did.

MARGARET:

I can see why you liked romance, but I thought you would have hated whites who put you in the camps.

SHIRLEY:

You still don't understand. We were Americans. We thought of ourselves as Nisei, not Japanese. How could we help loving escapist American films?

MARGARET:

I'm sorry . . . It was a hateful time.

SHIRLEY:

After the war when I met Erwin in college, I was studying to be a social worker. It was a time to be practical again and I wanted to help change things.

MARGARET:

Is that why you fell in love with Erwin? He always wanted to change things too.

SHIRLEY:

No, I fell in love with Erwin because he seemed so free. He seemed to live in a world of romance where there were no racial barriers. You were part of that free world in the stories he told me about you. I loved to hear Erwin talk about your affair with Frank Lloyd Wright.

MARGARET *(listening):*

Is that George coming?

SHIRLEY:

No, tell me about Wright . . .

MARGARET:

I would call it more of a romance than a love affair. He romanced me and he was a powerful romancer! *(The actor appears as* FRANK LLOYD WRIGHT *with a broad-brimmed hat and a striking cape.)* He made me laugh! When I first saw him, he seemed so small under his cape and peculiar, broad-brimmed hat. He looked like a walking mushroom! But what dashing energy!

WRIGHT:

Margaret, come away with me! I'll take you to Venice!

MARGARET *(rising):*

Venice seemed like Venus, a rising star . . . *(speaking to* WRIGHT*)* You know I'm married, Frank. I can't leave my husband and son . . .

WRIGHT *(passionately):*

Love casts out fear! I left my wife and children . . . One day they'll un-

317

derstand as your son will understand eventually. I can't live anymore in the wasteland of American suburban sprawl. I need your help and love to be a great architect.

MARGARET *(laughing, to* SHIRLEY*):*
My help and love! That was pretty convincing! George wanted my help and love too. Men are liars!

(WRIGHT *begins energetically to re-arrange the furniture.*)

SHIRLEY:
Wright was only five feet five inches tall, wasn't he?

MARGARET:
Whirling that cape, he looked like a giant. The first time he entered my house, believe it or not, he started to re-arrange the living room. Can you imagine?

SHIRLEY:
Why did he do that?

MARGARET AND WRIGHT *(simultaneously):*
He said that he wanted me to live in beauty!
I want you to live in beauty, Margaret!

SHIRLEY *(laughing):*
If it was my living room, I'd be furious!

MARGARET:
All the time he was re-arranging the furniture, he kept pleading with me . . .

WRIGHT:
Margaret, dear, Venice is the most romantic city in the world. We'll have time to dream. We'll create a new world of love together away from these deadly American cities dominated by rushing cars! A world with a new sense of architecture, buildings close to the earth, radiant with light to create a new democratic community!

SHIRLEY:
Was he such an obsessive man?

MARGARET:
He mesmerized me! Obsessive men always attract me. My life seemed to

be shrinking at home. I was frustrated in my writing. Besides, he knew I'd never been to Venice . . .

WRIGHT *(sweeping on):*
Imagine a great renaissance city without cars, Margaret. Only canals and gondolas. I know of a tower in Venice, Margaret, where Byron lived once! We'll live there!

MARGARET:
I'd love to go to Venice, Frank, but how can I leave my husband and child?

WRIGHT:
From our moonlit tower, we'll watch the stars reflected in the canals. We'll glide down the canals in a gondola. I'll show you the same legendary streets where Keats and Shelley walked, where Titian and Carpaccio painted. I'll show you where Ruskin wrote his history. I'll take you to the palace where Wagner died in Venice! There's no romance in this country. It's so hard to create here. In Venice, you can write, help me to change the world with my architecture! I want to create buildings that will soar from the earth as naturally as trees and flowers. I want to build cities that will give men the freedom of new souls!

(GEORGE *enters the room.*)

SHIRLEY *(laughing):*
Did he really say, "cities that will give men the freedom of new souls!"

MARGARET:
He certainly did. I trembled and was on the edge of capitulating. Then Erwin toddled into the room . . .

GEORGE:
Margaret, I want to talk to you!

MARGARET *(to* SHIRLEY):
Children and breakfast against a tower in Venice . . . Do you think I made the wrong decision?

WRIGHT *(with a final thrust at the furniture):*
Margaret, come with me! I promise you an exciting life. We'll change the world together!

MARGARET *(looking at* GEORGE *as* WRIGHT *disappears):*
We don't change the world. It changes itself slowly and inevitably.

SCENE 13

(MARGARET *and* GEORGE *confront each other.*)

MARGARET:
Please, George, don't shout.

GEORGE:
Margaret, is it true? Erwin told me about your shock therapy.

MARGARET:
Yes, it's true.

GEORGE:
Why didn't you tell me? We agreed to reveal everything about our health . . .

MARGARET:
I couldn't do it, George. I'm sorry. I told you the truth about Jung . . .

GEORGE:
But shock therapy, that's serious . . . Why lie to me?

MARGARET:
I didn't lie . . . I told you about my depression . . .

GEORGE:
Don't you think I deserved some consideration? Couldn't you have confidence in me?

MARGARET:
Confidence is the razor edge of understanding. In time after our relationship grew, I thought I could tell you.

GEORGE *(his voice rising again):*
You didn't trust our love! Lovers reveal everything. Trust is essential to love.

MARGARET:
Poor George . . . Don't roar at me.

GEORGE:
I didn't hide anything from you about my past! You make me feel as though you're hiding a nest of secrets!

MARGARET:
Can't you see it was a matter of forgetting, not hiding. Shock therapy was too hideous to remember . . .

GEORGE:
You never forget anything!

MARGARET:
George, please . . .

GEORGE:
This is serious, Margaret! How can I be sure this is the final secret between us?

MARGARET:
If lovers lose all of their secrecy, where is the mystery of love?

GEORGE:
That's not the way you talked before! What other secrets are you hiding?

MARGARET:
This isn't worthy of you.

GEORGE:
Coming here was a mistake. We should have stayed in Canada. Your son challenges me with his crazy test . . . You lie to me! What's next?

MARGARET:
Don't call me a liar, George. I can't promise you anything. You wouldn't believe me now.

GEORGE:
I felt we were as close as two people can be. Only a transparent veil existed between us. The veil's turned grey. Maybe we should have just lived together, never married!

MARGARET:
You were the one who wanted to get married.

GEORGE:
You wanted it just as much as I did! The fortress of marriage will insure our love! That's what you said!

MARGARET:
Never would I speak of marriage as a fortress.

GEORGE:
That's what you called it!

MARGARET:
George, I've never been roared at in my life. I admit I was wrong in not

telling you. But it's no use arguing now . . . We need to talk quietly about this.

GEORGE:
Quiet is a sign of peace. This is marriage!

(Blackout.)

SCENE 14

(The lights come up on MARGARET *and* ERWIN *confronting each other.)*

MARGARET:
How could you tell George about my shock therapy?

ERWIN:
I was plastered . . .

MARGARET:
He roared at me like a scruffy old lion. He made me angry.

ERWIN:
I said I'm sorry.

MARGARET:
Your father never screamed at me. No man has ever screamed at me before.

ERWIN:
The bastard . . . I didn't mean to . . .

MARGARET:
No, it's my fault . . . It was relatively easy to tell George about my depression. But I couldn't tell him about the darkness of that locked hospital ward. Sometimes I feel that I need a sandpainting ceremony to cure me, a communal cure to take away my isolation. But I'm just an outsider to the Navajos . . .

ERWIN:
You only took me to one ceremony. I always wanted to see more.

MARGARET:
You were too young.

ERWIN:
You left me with my father and a nurse. You were always leaving me.

MARGARET:

I had to go alone to find myself. Can't you understand? I loved your father. He was a gentle man, a fine man, but we lived in different worlds. I wanted to paint and write. As a housewife confined in that academic world, I couldn't even speak another language. Your father spoke so many tongues . . .

ERWIN:

Don't forget I was there, when father pleaded with you for divorce.

MARGARET:

I'm sorry about that. Your father wanted you there, but I thought you were too young.

ERWIN:

How do you think I felt caught in the middle between you, wanting me to take sides? Father argued for divorce and you said it was impossible after twenty-five years of marriage. You began to cry!

MARGARET:

No man had rejected me before. I rejected them! I didn't mean to lean on you. I needed you . . .

ERWIN:

Is that why you made me accompany you to Switzerland?

MARGARET:

I had to work things out with Jung. I couldn't be alone all the time. I needed your companionship.

ERWIN:

You barely knew what I was doing. I was eighteen years old and suddenly forced to confront the Nazis.

MARGARET:

All of those Jewish refugees struggling to escape the Nazi terror . . .

ERWIN:

Now I'll tell you a secret . . .

MARGARET:

You told me about that!

ERWIN:

I never told you the full story of what happened that night. You remember how I traveled from Zurich to visit an American friend in Germany?

MARGARET:

Yes, he was studying at the University of Freiburg. November, 1938. How could I forget that date?

ERWIN:

He met me at the station in Freiburg and took me to a cheap hotel room. As we arrived, a building was burning down the street. Nazi uniforms blocked off the area. Two uniforms thrust an old man and a woman into a car. That night I couldn't sleep. I listened through the wall as a whore brought a Nazi storm trooper into the room. She addressed him by his rank, and you could hear the fear in her voice. The terrible thing was that I felt a desire for her the way the Nazi storm trooper felt. The next morning I learned the S. A. troops had burned the synagogue down the street. That was the building we had seen burning. They arrested the rabbi and his wife. They were the old man and woman we'd seen shoved into the car. During the night they'd built a fence around the burnt-down synagogue as if to hide it. I learned that I'd witnessed Kristallnacht. In a rage of anger and shame, I wrote my first poem.

MARGARET:

You never told me about the S. A. officer and the whore and the poem.

ERWIN:

Your many gods have different hammers of lightning.

MARGARET:

Poor boy, I've led you on many wild, impetuous chases. I'm afraid George may be the wildest chase of all.

ERWIN:

But you love him?

MARGARET:

I do love him. One by one, he identifies plants for me and shows me their complex, graceful structures, and their hideous diseases. We read poetry together and listen to Bach on the phonograph. But I thought I could tame his bestial temper . . .

ERWIN:

I'll make him understand it was my fault.

MARGARET:

No, that is my task. But now I'm afraid of George . . . (*The lights dim out on them, as they stand like frozen shadows in time. Across from them, the lights come up on* GEORGE *and* SHIRLEY.)

GEORGE:

I lost my temper! It was a terrible thing to do.

SHIRLEY:

Why are you telling me this?

GEORGE:

I need a new family. I was just getting to know you and Erwin.

SHIRLEY:

We all lose our temper . . .

GEORGE:

It was more than that. I couldn't stand hearing suddenly about her shock therapy. I trusted her. I built trails for her! I feared her depressions!

SHIRLEY:

George, your energy is like a cyclone. You want to search everything out and leave your imprint on nature. That's very impressive to a woman. But it's also . . .

GEORGE:

Disturbing too . . . I know what you mean. My first wife warned me about my impulsive temperament.

SHIRLEY:

You don't have to tell me . . .

GEORGE:

I want to tell you. You're my step-daughter now. I'm afraid of being shut out by this family!

SHIRLEY:

We don't want to shut you out.

GEORGE:

I ask myself constantly, am I too old for another family? My first wife haunts me. She was a quiet, gifted administrator, not creative like Margaret. A strong, practical woman like you, Shirley . . .

SHIRLEY:

I don't like to think of myself as a boring practical lady.

GEORGE:

When we discovered we couldn't have any children, she helped me build my trails. I knew she wasn't really interested in my work, so I encouraged her to find a job that would satisfy her. I wanted her to have a position that would balance the passion I felt for my own work. She became a very successful counselor and administrator in the Dean's office. She had her feet on the ground like you.

SHIRLEY:
Sometimes it's a pain in the ass to have your feet on the ground all the time.

GEORGE:
Every man needs an anchor.

SHIRLEY:
Every woman wants to be anchored and fly too.

GEORGE:
Then she got cancer . . . It was a long two years of withering. What made me feel guilty was I grew to hate taking care of her.

SHIRLEY:
Talk to Margaret about this . . .

GEORGE:
Her confinement confined me. My work suffered, dried up! I began to blame my poor, dying wife. Now I'm afraid of feeling the same way about Margaret. I couldn't stand another two years of living with a dying woman.

SHIRLEY:
Tell Margaret how you feel.

GEORGE:
Will she forgive me?

SHIRLEY:
She's a generous woman. She'll understand. You're going to Europe together aren't you?

GEORGE:
I've been offered a visiting chair in Biology at the University of Frankfurt, but I don't know . . .

SHIRLEY:
Does Margaret want to live in Germany too?

GEORGE:
She wants to visit Jung again in Switzerland.

SHIRLEY:
You're against that?

326

GEORGE:
Not if it's good for her, but I'm jealous of her passion for Jung.

SHIRLEY:
Jealous of Jung? Why?

GEORGE:
I don't like the way she worships him. It's too physical.

SHIRLEY:
That's ridiculous, George. What do you mean?

GEORGE:
Shirley, I want to tell you something. You're a counsellor. Perhaps because of my father, I've always been trapped between a desire for the spiritual and the physical world. Margaret has saved my life. I never thought I'd have a real physical relationship at my age.

SHIRLEY:
You're lucky, George. Don't worry about Jung and her depression. You can work it out together.

GEORGE:
Somehow it's easier to talk to you than to her. When I was a young student I was doing research in the Sahara Desert. One night in an oasis— I've forgotten the name of the town—I saw an authentic "Dance of the Seven Veils" by a Berber girl. When she was naked, with the seventh veil over her shoulder, she came toward me. Suddenly, I realized this was the sexual climax of the dance. I was supposed to go with her. But I was too prudish. I told her I didn't love her. She felt disgraced. She was not a prostitute. I tried to explain it away on the difference of customs. I felt ridiculous. The next day I went back into the native quarter to give her a present. She was amazed to see me. Later, I got an offer from her to dance for me every night if I would get her to the United States. I had to write back that this was impossible. She would have ended up as a whore or in some cheap burlesque show. From that time on, I knew I hadn't lost my desire and my potency as a man. I decided not to enter the monastery. The world meant too much to me. When my first wife died, I entered the monastery again. Margaret cut through my lonely old age and brought me back into the world. I don't want to lose her.

SHIRLEY:
George, you're an amazing man. You have to learn to talk to Margaret about these conflicts. The problem is you're talking to me instead of Margaret. You must open up to her. Otherwise the sense of both of you hiding

327

something will always lead to sudden explosions. If you talk to her, you can work these problems out together.

GEORGE:
I do love her, but I can't stop worrying about her depression coming back. Besides, she's concealed things too. Maybe we should have just lived together . . .

(SHIRLEY *moves away from him, and the lights come up on the four of them isolated in their thoughts at the four points of the stage, as if in the north, south, east and west points of a Navajo sandpainting. The actor who played* LANCELOT *and other roles, appears as* LANCELOT, *high upstage. He is holding a folded banner.*)

ERWIN:
Where are you taking us, Mother,
Trapped in the warring winds
Of one of your Navajo sandpaintings?

MARGARET (*moving into a central position*):
I want to be Turquoise Woman
Living free from the threat of old age!
No more despair in a dark tunnel of flesh,
No more pressure from son and husband
Compromising the blood of my poetry.
Old age should end in peace of mind
Not in the death homes we call rest homes!
I want to be Turquoise Woman!

SHIRLEY:
I married Erwin and was seduced
By the romantic sound of poetry.
But the world of poetry is dangerous
If it paralyzes you into a false subjectivity.
I need to pull Erwin away from Margaret.

GEORGE:
What if Margaret becomes too independent?
Can she free herself
From a hypnotist like Jung?
I need her!
I don't want to spend my life alone!

ERWIN:

A man moves against a woman forcefully.
She doesn't like his aggression;
He learns to go around her and please her.
That's how I came to love Shirley.
Can George ever learn that with Mother?
He's not subtle enough to go around.
He ties all his knots in straight lines.

MARGARET:

Like the Navajos, I came to love
A perfect piece of turquoise, the brilliant
Light blue color of the desert sky at noonday.
Why am I flying to dark Europe? If only I could find
The serenity of vision like Turquoise Goddess,
Carve a perfect stone, weave a perfect design . . .

SHIRLEY:

Creative people are always subject to depressions.
They're more sensitive to shadows created by sunlight.
I want to feel these powers with Erwin,
But he's not easy to live with,
One moment like lightning, laughing, playing,
The next moment like a dark stone.

ERWIN:

I grew up a romantic, trained by Mother,
But romanticism died in the 1960s.
The Beatles' folksongs and Dylan's "Blowin' in the Wind"
Faded into the Rolling Stones and an orgy of drugs
And violence. Suddenly, for the first time in history,
More than half of the world was under thirty.
And youth began to rock out its demands for a new world.
Hard rock took the place of romanticism.
How can poetry today compete with rock?

GEORGE:

My trails are maps of an old, legendary world.
On a trail, you have to be careful of
Arctic winds. You stand there facing north,
And the wind comes whistling in,
Freezing you to the spot. I enjoy that feeling.
I'm a winter man. Margaret's a desert spirit . . .

329

MARGARET:

In the Bead Chant, Turquoise Woman
Is the mother of five daughters—
The fifth daughter is born of her spirit . . .
All I had was a boy who was forced to be
Both the son and daughter I never had . . .

(LANCELOT *unfolds his banner, reading:* HAIL TO THE LAST
ROMANTICS!)

ERWIN:

Why do I think of Mother and George
As the last romantics? Is language today
Sentenced to the instant new images of television?
Why should I write when half of the country
Doesn't read even one book a year?
But I have to write . . . For me putting words together
Is like feeling the pulse of time . . .
I wish Shirley and I could go to Europe.

GEORGE:

Europe will be like going into the furnace of time.
How can you discover love there
Amidst the fires of hate from the rubble
And the concentration camps?
If I don't watch out
I'll become a hermit crab again.
Teaching young Germans will be good for me.
I'll quote Goethe to them about plants:
"Green is life's golden tree!"

SHIRLEY:

Somehow George and Margaret stand driven
By the cruel warnings of age, warnings that threaten
The romantic visions they have struggled so hard to create.
What if they really are the last romantics?

LANCELOT (*crying out, as he waves the banner*):
Hail to the Last Romantics!

MARGARET:

Lancelot is a dear,
But I don't want to be
The last anything.

330

I want to shine like Turquoise Woman
In my own identity.
The community of death
Begins to haunt me—
George is my loving executioner,
But in the world of death
One travels alone . . .
I want to be Turquoise Woman!

END OF PART I

PART II

SCENE I

(AS PART II *begins, the cast is still in the same positions as at the end of Part I. Still dressed as Lancelot, the actor reverses his banner, which reads now:* BON VOYAGE, LAST ROMANTICS! GEORGE *and* MARGARET *move to an upstage right position, where they stand together waving down at* ERWIN, SHIRLEY, *and* LANCELOT, *as if on a ship sailing for Europe.*)

LANCELOT *(waving the banner and calling):*
Bon Voyage! Don't forget to arrange a triumphant retrospective exhibit of my paintings in Europe!

MARGARET *(laughing and waving):*
We'll try!

GEORGE:
Send me some representational paintings of plants! I can sell those!

LANCELOT:
Nonsense! Abstract Expressionism is about to conquer!

(*Slowly, as they wave,* GEORGE *and* MARGARET *move backwards, disappearing into the darkness, as if the ship were moving away from the wharf.*)

LANCELOT:
George is going to love German universities. He likes the idea of being called Herr Professor Doktor. He'll wallow in all that formal kowtowing German professors demand.

ERWIN:
What will mother do? She can't speak German.

SHIRLEY:
Paint and write the way she always does. She won't have to cook or clean.

ERWIN:
Mother was always too imperial to cook or clean.

LANCELOT *(rolling up his banner):*
You sound jealous. You and Shirley will get your chance to travel some day.

ERWIN:
Why do you love them, Lancelot? You came all the way from Canada to see them off.

LANCELOT:
I married them! We old folks have to stick together against you young people who are taking over the world.

ERWIN:
Germany is still in ruins . . . She hates the Nazis. The War Crime trials are coming up in Nuremberg . . .

LANCELOT:
Why worry? Don't try to make them stationary. That's death you know. When they go to unusual places they come alive.

SHIRLEY:
Lancelot is right. They need wings to fly.

ERWIN:
After the concentration camps, it's going to be hard to fly in Europe.

LANCELOT:
They're stronger than you think. Your mother is an extraordinary woman. *(They walk out, arm in arm.)*

SCENE 2

(After a moment, the lights come up on MARGARET. *In her new German apartment, she has been packing, although* GEORGE *doesn't notice this until the end of the scene. Excitedly,* GEORGE *enters, holding a printed card.)*

GEORGE:
Look, my new university office card! *Herr Doktor Professor Georg Silberlicht!*

MARGARET:
That's a mouthful.

GEORGE:
Respect for professors! We don't get that in the United States! There, my

333

office door read, *G. Silverlight,* and students joked behind my back, the G. stands for Geriatric Gardener!

MARGARET:

George, I want to tell you what I've seen today.

GEORGE:

What are you talking about?

MARGARET:

You're in a classroom teaching young people. I'm walking the streets of Frankfurt talking to American soldiers and their German girlfriends. The Black Market is booming!

GEORGE:

What do you expect in a city that's still in ruins? How do you know about the Black Market?

MARGARET:

They talk to me and I use my eyes. One package of cigarettes buys you a woman. The cigarette manufacturers are making a fortune here in Germany.

GEORGE:

We need to get out more, meet some decent people. You seemed to enjoy that dinner with the head of the Biology Department the other night.

MARGARET:

I felt uneasy. What did he do under the Nazis?

GEORGE:

He's a distinguished scientist. He says he wasn't a Nazi.

MARGARET:

He didn't want to talk about the Nazis.

GEORGE:

Maybe he compromised with them to keep his university job. What would we have done?

MARGARET:

I wonder . . . Today I met an angry American soldier who works in Intelligence. He says we're clearing and supporting Nazis and sending them back to work under our Military Government.

GEORGE:

If that's true, it's terrible.

334

MARGARET:

I believe him. No German admits to being a Nazi anymore.

GEORGE:

Margaret, I know how you feel. The situation's difficult. Our Military Government has to put people to work. They can't permit chaos. How can they avoid using some former minor Nazis?

MARGARET:

It's not just minor Nazis. They're using all kinds of Nazis as key officials and informers. These Nazis label anyone they consider their opponent as Communist or leftwinger. It's corruption time, George. I don't want to stay here.

GEORGE:

What do you want to do?

MARGARET:

Jung has asked me to teach a seminar in Navajo myths at his institute. This time I'll be a teacher, not just a patient.

GEORGE:

You didn't tell me that.

MARGARET:

I wasn't sure about it. I just heard from him that the seminar is definite. I don't have to go for another week, but I've started to put together some papers and things I'll need.

GEORGE *(noticing her bag):*
What? You know I have to teach until the semester ends.

MARGARET:

It's only six weeks. You can join me then.

GEORGE:

Damn it, I took this job for your sake.

MARGARET:

That's not true, George.

GEORGE:

I wanted this job so that we could travel together!

(The DANCER *appears dressed as The Black Ogre, dragging a saw behind him, while music is heard.)*

335

MARGARET:

The ruins are too much for me.

GEORGE:

I don't like being left alone.

MARGARET:

It's only a short time.

GEORGE:

You want to run back to your savior, Jung!

MARGARET:

That's not fair, George! *(She turns away from him.)* I thought I could face it here, but I can't. There are too many ruins and too many victims . . . Last night I dreamt I was back in Arizona at a Hopi kachina dance. Nota-aske, the Black Ogre, dragged a saw on the ground behind him while he made a ripping sound. He has green claw marks on his head. His huge jaw with protruding teeth threatens to devour children if they're naughty. When they see him, all of the children scream and promise to be good. But, in my dream, after the children promised, the Black Ogre began to threaten me. Suddenly, the sky turned dark. Lightning flashed and it began to rain and thunder. The Black Ogre grabbed me and started to carry me away . . .

GEORGE:

It's only a dream, Margaret . . .

MARGARET *(as the* DANCER *exits):*

That wasn't the worst part . . . As he carried me off, I cried out for you to rescue me. You just stood there, paralyzed.

GEORGE:

You know I would have helped!

MARGARET:

Help me now! Please, George. I don't want to break down on you here.

GEORGE:

All right. I'm sorry. I want to be with you . . . I want to meet Jung.

MARGARET:

You will when you join me in Switzerland. It won't be long, and we'll have a good time, I promise.

GEORGE:

You promise me?

SCENE 3

(The actor plays the psychiatrist, C. J. JUNG, *as an old man. In his Küsnacht, Switzerland, home,* JUNG *is standing at his study window, looking out at the lake and smoking his pipe.* MARGARET *enters.)*

MARGARET:
Dr. Jung, it's so good to see you again!

JUNG *(embracing her):*
Margaret, you look fine, your old vital self! I feel ancient! But we are both war survivors . . .

MARGARET:
You look a little more wrinkled, but never ancient.

JUNG:
After this terrible war, it is a pleasure to see old friends again. You can imagine how isolated we felt here in Switzerland.

MARGARET:
It was a miracle your country could stay neutral.

JUNG:
There was the constant possibility of invasion from the Nazis. Our Swiss troops were always on alert, our borders mined against invasion.

MARGARET:
Your country was better prepared for war than most of the European nations.

JUNG:
My country is always accused of profiting from its neutrality. You know how legendary we Swiss are for our commercial ways and our hidden bank accounts. Yet neutrality is the only way we can survive in the face of European wars.

MARGARET:
I'm so angry about these recent attacks against you in my country as being pro-Nazi.

JUNG *(shrugging):*
When the facts come out, I do not worry.

MARGARET *(impulsively):*
You must write about your experiences as soon as possible.

JUNG:

Is there so much gossip about me in America?

MARGARET:

You could stop the rumors from spreading.

JUNG:

If I spoke, would it not seem like a guilty man struggling to defend his innocence? No, Margaret, let the facts come out as they must. Did you know that I had a meeting with high Nazi officials in the early 30s?

MARGARET:

I don't think anyone knows that.

JUNG:

They wanted me to become their official Director of Psychiatry. They offered me a great deal of money and a prestigious governmental position. They said I could change the course of psychiatry in Germany.

MARGARET:

I can imagine your answer!

JUNG (chuckling):

I pointed out to them that I couldn't accept the position because they had taken the ancient symbol of the swastika and turned it around, so that the luck was running out!

MARGARET:

What did they say to that!

JUNG:

As I remember, there was a decided pause in the conversation. Then some official went running out of the room, probably to check historical records about the swastika and see if I was right! In any case, they ushered me out as quickly as possible. I was put on their blacklist.

MARGARET:

Why haven't you ever published that story?

JUNG (shrugging):

The Nazis would never admit such an offer since I turned it down. As for my antagonists, they would ask for proof that such a meeting took place. I have only my memories. But come, Margaret, let's not talk about the Nazis. Tell me about your marriage. I admire a man who is a master of plants and their diseases. When may I meet him?

MARGARET:
He's coming here after the term ends at the University of Frankfurt.

JUNG *(smiling):*
I look forward to meeting him! I have some questions about plants to ask him!

(The lights black out and come up to reveal MARGARET *and* GEORGE *entering to meet* JUNG.*)*

SCENE 4

MARGARET:
Watching the meeting of George and Jung fascinated and terrified me. My life with George seemed suddenly at the crossroads. I knew it was wrong to expect a judgment from Jung about George. Beneath the friendly jousting of the two strong men, I wondered if some other force of judgment was taking place?

JUNG *(shaking hands with* GEORGE*):*
Ah, as I suspected, a man worthy of Margaret! A truly independent American!

GEORGE:
I don't know if I can match your standards of independence, Dr. Jung, but it's a great pleasure to meet you.

JUNG *(smiling):*
I can see how you caught Margaret's fancy. *(He points to a Navajo sandpainting on the wall.)* Do you see that sandpainting Margaret did for me? You see the central Navajo tree of life, the Great Corn Plant? You, sir, have emerged from the Great Corn Plant to bring her a new resurrection of Eros!

GEORGE *(smiling):*
I hope that's true, but I'm only a plant pathologist. She's the one who's been teaching me about Eros.

MARGARET:
Nonsense, he keeps translating Goethe's poems for me.

JUNG *(to* GEORGE*):*
And you build trails too, trails into the clouds, I understand. That kind of

339

hand labor is close to my heart. I carve little sculptures myself at my island retreat.

MARGARET:

Big sculptures . . .

GEORGE:

I have no artistic talents, so I build trails.

JUNG:

May I tell you a secret about Margaret? She was instrumental in my
American visit long ago to your southwestern Indian pueblos. She helped
me to understand the mythology of those ancient traditions. That is why I
hang her sandpainting in a place of honor in my study.

MARGARET *(flustered):*

Dr. Jung is a great flatterer. That is how he penetrates one's defenses.

GEORGE:

I can see that. My father was a Lutheran minister like yours, Dr. Jung,
but, alas, he never taught me the art of flattery.

JUNG:

I assure you my father hated flattery too. Tell me, since you understand
plants so well, I have always wondered at the strange etymology of that
simple word, *plant* . . . For example, *(he picks up a book)* I was checking
an English dictionary . . . *(He reads)* "To fix firmly in position; to im-
plant in the mind; to place for the purpose of spying or deception . . ."
How is it that such a basic creative growth is endowed with so many *suspicious* connotations?

GEORGE:

How stupid dictionary definitions can be! To me, the word, plant, comes
simply from the Latin, *plantare.* However, I confess that, as I continued
studying plant diseases, the disease process itself seemed mockingly de-
ceptive. Maybe that's how *plant* comes to have so many different mean-
ings. Today, it means factories and nuclear plants too! Does that mean
language is the real deceiver? Can we ever name things accurately?

JUNG:

Well-spoken! I suppose I've become accustomed to psychological decep-
tions. Perhaps I look for them too easily in the plant world. Nature has its
own cunning. How should I look at plants?

GEORGE:

To me the plant world is the most romantic of all. Every seed is a kind of ritual planting.

JUNG:

How do you mean, ritual planting?

GEORGE:

Sometimes the seed is deliberately sown in the earth by human hands and that creates seasonal rituals. At other times the seed arrives by chance from the excrement of birds in the sky.

JUNG:

From above and from below . . . From the sky and from human excrement . . . It is the way of the spirit, is it not, to seek roots in the dark earth and to fly in the clouds?

GEORGE:

I don't know if plants have a special spirit or not. *(shrugging wryly)* Still, some form of spirit seems to exist in special plants and in special people, don't you think?

JUNG:

Are plants then animate beings as we are?

GEORGE:

In some ways, but they lack the power of locomotion.

JUNG *(laughing):*

Perhaps that way they are better off! *(The two men go on laughing and talking, as* MARGARET *watches in amazement. Blackout. The lights come up immediately as* MARGARET *is talking to* JUNG.*)*

MARGARET:

Did you like my husband?

JUNG *(smiling):*

He is—what do you call it—a tough nut to crack. Margaret, you were watching me as though you expected a judgment. You know you have to solve your own relationship.

MARGARET:

When we got married, friends called us the Last Romantics because we were always looking for new experiences. Now, sometimes I can't match his energy. He explodes around me like a Roman candle!

JUNG:

Margaret, you know your problem. You've worked hard on it. You have always been high in the sensation aspect of your life. You rush out always to seek new experiences. Then you grow depressed because you hurl your energy in too many directions. You begin to feel frustrated because you do not focus your great gifts enough.

MARGARET:

I love him, but sometimes I feel a disaster approaching.

JUNG:

He seems a reasonable man, if he can control his temper. Talk to him. If you go back to Arizona with him, he can settle down to his Theophrastus translations and his plant research . . .

MARGARET:

He is an impulsive trailbuilder. He can never settle down. But I do love him and I don't want to be alone.

JUNG:

To be the Last Romantics is not a bad role to play. You must recognize it's an endgame, not a beginning.

MARGARET:

An endgame makes me afraid.

JUNG:

Why should we be afraid of age?

MARGARET:

I'm afraid it's a bad American fear.

JUNG:

Age should be joyous and not fear death. All great civilizations respect the wisdom of age.

MARGARET:

Can we learn to be wise?

JUNG:

Of course. The wise seek rooted depth, not restless motion. In Arizona is your tranquil center, the relationships with nature that you love. Both of you must play out the roles you have accepted. *(Slow blackout as the scene ends.)*

SCENE 5

(GEORGE and MARGARET in their home in Tucson, Arizona.)

GEORGE *(pointing as if through a window):*
Dawn, Margaret! Look! The eastern horizon is flaming with cloud-wings! Did you know that angels have flaming wings?

MARGARET:
Maybe we're looking at dancing kachinas.

GEORGE:
It's good to be in Arizona. They don't have dawns like this in Europe!

MARGARET *(smiling):*
Only in Arizona . . .

GEORGE *(exuberantly):*
Now I understand why Greek plays began at dawn. A journey towards the sun and the resurrection of the spirit! The search for Apollo, God of rational light! Apollo, the Sun God rising through the forces of darkness in the underworld! In our decaying cities, we ignore the dawn and expend our energies to serve the night.

MARGARET:
At night the Navajo medicine man seeks to cure the wounded spirit to guide it back to dawn. He sings in the *Night Chant:*

In the house of life I wander
On the pollen path,
With a god of cloud I wander
To a holy place.
With a god ahead I wander
And a god behind.
In the house of life I wander
On the pollen path . . .

GEORGE:
I'm a Greek and you're a Navajo!

MARGARET:
Does that separate us?

343

GEORGE:

No, nature is always dualistic. Opposite forces unite! That's what your Navajos believe, isn't it?

MARGARET:

George, do you still resent my leaving you in Germany?

GEORGE:

No, I was glad to meet your medicine man, Jung.

MARGARET:

You seemed to get along so well. Do you really like him?

GEORGE:

I'm not sure like is the right word. I admire him. He has a presence and such a broad range of knowledge that he makes me feel ignorant. Somehow I felt I was being analyzed all the time.

MARGARET:

That was my fault. He was curious about my husband, but he liked you. He liked what you had to say about plants.

GEORGE:

If he helped you, that's fine.

MARGARET:

I was not just a patient there, George. I gave my talks on Navajo sand-paintings. Some important people came to my seminars and admired what I had to say. My talks are going to be published.

GEORGE:

I mean your private consultation with Jung.

MARGARET:

We talked as friends, that's all. He doesn't practice analysis any more. You know he spends all of his time writing, trying to finish his work.

GEORGE:

All I said was that if he helped you with your depressions, that's fine! But don't tell me that you weren't seeking help!

MARGARET:

Oh George, you're still jealous of him!

GEORGE:

You regard him with a different kind of respect than you regard me.

MARGARET:

Isn't that natural? I love you. I honor him because he helped me so much. The truth is, George, I might not be with you if it weren't for Jung.

GEORGE:

We love each other. Still, you say that you honor him more. Do you know how that makes me feel?

MARGARET:

Can't you love me enough to respect my feelings about Jung?

GEORGE:

No, love to me is a spiritual and physical fusion. Lovers come together creating a unity out of their differences.

MARGARET:

I can't argue with you, George. You're too strong for me.

GEORGE:

You're the one who's strong! You've showed me so many worlds that I never knew, but you guard yourself more and more. You conceal your thoughts!

MARGARET:

You're right . . . I am used to concealing my thoughts. I do appreciate your coming back to Arizona with me. I know you wanted to go to Canada. We enjoy so many things together. But I do conceal my fear of getting ill again. I'm afraid of that and you sense it.

GEORGE:

Forget about being ill. Don't dwell on it so much.

MARGARET:

When we married, we signed an agreement to be independent. Our finances are separate. We have no claims on each other. I'll never be a burden on you. I couldn't stand that.

GEORGE:

Don't you think I feel the same way? We have to trust each other. I'm older than you are. Women live longer than men. Wouldn't Jung tell you that we should live in the present moment?

MARGARET:

Of course . . . Let's live for the sunrise and not worry about the night.

(They stand looking at the sunrise.)

SCENE 6

(The lights come up on GEORGE, *talking to* SHIRLEY *and* ERWIN.*)*

GEORGE:
Sorry you had to come all this way . . . She woke up and complained of feeling dizzy. Her arm was numb. Well, you know the rest. The doctor says she was lucky.

ERWIN:
Is even a slight stroke lucky?

GEORGE:
You know how doctors mean lucky . . . All they see is illness. They think any survivor is lucky.

SHIRLEY:
How long will they keep her in the hospital?

GEORGE:
They want to give her some more tests. There's one problem . . .

ERWIN:
What problem?

GEORGE:
This is not easy to say . . . I'm afraid Margaret is becoming depressed again. She's very difficult to talk to . . .

SHIRLEY:
In what way?

GEORGE *(hesitating):*
She doesn't want to come home.

ERWIN:
She wants to stay in the hospital?

GEORGE:
She wants to visit a friend in California, but I think it's just an excuse.

SHIRLEY:
An excuse for what?

GEORGE:
I don't know . . . Maybe you can find out.

346

ERWIN:

It's funny . . . She kept writing about how glad she was to be back in Arizona . . .

SHIRLEY:

Did she tell you that anything was disturbing her?

GEORGE:

One moment she was dragging me out to watch the sunrise. The next moment she was saying that, if she became ill, she didn't want to be a burden. Of course, I tried to reassure her . . .

SHIRLEY:

She must have had a premonition of her stroke.

ERWIN:

After anything bad happened to her, mother always wanted to travel to change her luck.

GEORGE:

I admit I was hurt. I work hard in the garden, try not to think about us. I can't talk to her. She draws away from me. Can you understand how that makes me feel? I want to shout at her, shake her alive into our former love . . .

SHIRLEY:

Your *former* love?

GEORGE:

Nothing could separate us before. After she left me alone in Germany, despite anything I could do, she kept slipping away from me. It was almost as though she anticipated this stroke . . . I don't want to lose her . . .

(*The lights dim and come up on* MARGARET *sitting in a chair, dressed in a housecoat. She is talking to* ERWIN *and* SHIRLEY, *who stand uneasily, facing her.*)

MARGARET (*trying to smile*):

It's only a little stroke. The doctors say I was lucky! But I feel as if I'm living on the edge of time. (*As music is heard, the* DANCER *appears as Bear Dancer.*) I want to go to California to visit my friend, Elizabeth. George will be all right for a week or two. He's used to shifting for himself . . . Don't look so worried! I'm not depressed. Just apprehensive . . .

347

Why should I be depressed when you young people are here? You know how much I love you . . . Last night I had a dream . . . My old Indian trader friend, Lorenzo Hubbell, was dying . . . A bear came to visit him. If you dream of a bear, the dream may mean you have too much power of the bear. The bear spirit in your life is too aggressive. You need a ceremony said over you to cleanse you. A medicine woman, Woman Singer, came to sit with Lorenzo and me. With one hand, she held my hand. With the other hand, she held Lorenzo's. Her face was serene like the stars on a clear desert night. Without speaking, she sang her inner song. The pain in Lorenzo's face eased. The aggressive force of the bear began to roll away. Singing Woman knew that to love, the soul must remain free. The soul must find its own independence. Dying, I want to become independent. I don't want George to be my loving executioner. A loving executioner is still an executioner, do you understand?

(Blackout.)

SCENE 7

(ERWIN and SHIRLEY are talking across space. Perhaps they are separated temporarily, and are talking across space on the phone, although no phone is visible. Perhaps they are thinking their inner thoughts.)

ERWIN:
Mother doesn't want to go back to Arizona and live with George.

SHIRLEY:
Her stroke has affected Margaret more than she admits.

ERWIN:
She believes that she's dying. She wants to die her own peaceful death.

SHIRLEY:
George is not a peaceful man.

ERWIN:
That's what she meant by calling him a loving executioner.

SHIRLEY:
How can there be a loving executioner?

ERWIN:
We pretend to love old people and push them into rest homes and nursing

348

homes so they don't bother us. Out of sight out of mind. That's how we become loving executioners. We push death out of sight in this country.

SHIRLEY:
Maybe she's right. We don't try to understand death until it's too late. Margaret wants to avoid a death that's just part of the morticians' Better Business world.

ERWIN:
Is their romance really ended?

SHIRLEY:
It's over, I'm afraid. George and Margaret used to laugh together. Suddenly, they stopped. Maybe when we stop laughing we begin to hate.

ERWIN:
That frightens me. How can real love turn to hate? I want to hold you, not talk like this. Are we talking on the telephone or just to ourselves in space?

SHIRLEY:
I like living with you, Erwin. You're my man, but sometimes you're five thousand miles away.

ERWIN:
That's right. Auden said once, "The only thing that distinguishes people today from people in the past is that tomorrow you can be five thousand miles away." Everyone today is on a space trip.

SHIRLEY:
Forget about our space. What about our child?

ERWIN:
It doesn't seem the right time.

SHIRLEY:
Your mother would like a grandchild before she dies.

ERWIN:
Maybe she doesn't have that long.

(*Upstage, the* DANCER *has appeared as a masked kachina clown, dancing to soft, powerful drum music. But his costume is strange, half-comic, half-sinister, an imitation of a mocking death god. As* SHIRLEY *and* ERWIN *continue to speak, they address this dancing figure unconsciously.*)

349

SHIRLEY:

Your mother is an amazing woman. If she can't laugh anymore with George, she wants to laugh with death. A child would help her and you.

ERWIN:

Maybe you're right, but how can you laugh with death? Our youth culture wants to deny death and live forever. Stick in a new gene and live free. Give everyone an instant cure for any illness.

SHIRLEY:

Don't be bitter.

ERWIN:

Sometimes I want to dance old age into oblivion too.

SHIRLEY:

A child will help you dance.

ERWIN:

Let's try. I won't object.

SHIRLEY:

You can be more passionate than that.

ERWIN:

I'll try to improve.

SHIRLEY:

I hope you understand how I feel about Margaret. She's not just my mother-in-law. I love her because she never stops searching for the secret of change.

ERWIN:

Maybe there's no secret of change. What if change just happens to you?

SHIRLEY:

I'd hate to believe that. We Nisei had to learn to adjust to become Americans. We had to change. We're still trying to change the country into more of a democracy.

ERWIN:

I want to see Mother and George laughing again. I don't want them to be alone. Let's never be alone, Shirley. I need you . . .

SHIRLEY:

Don't worry, we won't be alone . . .

(Blackout, as the dancing kachina figure freezes. He does not exit until the end of Scene 8.)

SCENE 8

(SHIRLEY confronts the dancing kachina figure, who is frozen into silence.)

SHIRLEY:

Who are you? *(The DANCER bends over, shaking as if in laughter.)* Are you laughing? Margaret and George have forgotten how to laugh. I'll save Erwin from them. *(The DANCER turns into a new position, challenging her.)* I promise you we won't be alone, Erwin. A child laughs at you. You laugh back. A child makes a family. Our child will be part of a new community. *(The DANCER turns again.)* How can I help Erwin? Create a family, hold a job at the same time? Impossible questions! If I try too many things, I'll do nothing well. *(Gesturing, the DANCER turns to confront her.)* I remember you . . . You visited the relocation camps often. Dancer of death, frozen in silence. Maybe death is the true melting pot. I believe in the melting pot dream. The trouble is every skin must blend into white American. A racist country struggling to change . . . *(The DANCER twists into another position.)* Tell me about community! You came for my parents. My father, an honest storekeeper, helped his neighbors. My mother worked with him in the store. Good Americans when we were sent to the camps, they were forced to sell the store cheap to a white buyer. Branded enemies, they died of loneliness after the war. No time to create a new community . . . *(Slowly, the DANCER exits.)* Speak, death! Give me some answer! You're going to meet Margaret . . .

SCENE 9

(MARGARET is talking to ERWIN and SHIRLEY.)

MARGARET:

Stop worrying about me. It's going to be all right. I'm back in Arizona. George and I made a bargain. As the outside man, he does everything that needs to be done outside. As the inside woman, I do everything inside. At dinner, we talk only about the future. So the present doesn't bother us. We're like two old people bent over a buried treasure map, eagerly tracing the trails to the impossible treasure caves of the future.

ERWIN:

Are you afraid of George?

SHIRLEY:

Is George cruel to you?

MARGARET:

He takes away my peace. Under the pretense of helping me, he taunts me with the sense that I'm not trying hard enough to regain my health. He's not ready to understand death.

SHIRLEY *(aside):*

Who is? In a so-called Rest Home yesterday, I saw wheelchairs that were more real than the skeleton people in them. What if Margaret ends up there?

MARGARET *(continuing):*

Why don't we stop lying that we want to take care of old people? What we really want is to grind up their bones. We want to use their dust to prepare the magical future of eternal youth!

ERWIN *(aside):*

The other night I dreamt that mother and George were dead and I was free . . .

MARGARET *(continuing):*

My mind is torn between the one god of my parents and the many gods of the Navajos. I want peace. I want to go to a peaceful Death Home, not a false Rest Home. I want to understand and live with death. When you're dying, you find it's just as important to die well as to live well. George doesn't want to deal with my doctors and medical expenses. Sometimes I think George is turning into Coyote. He's trying to trick me into living in his active, aggressive world . . .

SCENE 10

(As the light changes, GEORGE *moves into a dominant upstage space for his monologue as he transforms into Coyote.)*

GEORGE:

The landscape is full of family ghosts accusing me. Have I not tried to love and admire them? In my isolation, the radio offers me commercial advice. *Boom or Bust . . . Plan your Option Strategies!* I want to take a torch to this society of greed. It turns language, philosophy, and romance into money! My cynicism festers on my tongue. To please Margaret, I try to turn into Coyote. She listens to me with a growing dislike that she cannot conceal. I want to fly away! . . . One day Coyote was lying by a spring under some cottonwood trees watching a flight of larks. They land on the ground just beyond him. He begs them to teach him how to fly.

I want to be a winged being and soar into space above these human ghosts who mock me! The birds laugh at Coyote. I beg them again to teach me how to fly! Finally, they tell me to hold my feet against my chest and take off in that position. I feel like a grotesque clown. I take a giant leap into the air and fall back with a thud. Margaret, save me! Why is the love I feel turning into hatred? Why am I Coyote, the trickster, growling at you and your children with suspicion? After I keep begging them, the tormenting birds agree to pull some feathers from their wings. They tie the feathers to my legs. The birds have lightning power in their wings. If I show her I can fly, perhaps Margaret will fly with me! The birds say they will try to lift me off the ground three times. On the final try, I stay up in the air. My hairy arms are shining wings! I can change my life! The birds become frightened. Why should a land animal be able to fly? I flap my arms faster and faster, desperately trying to keep up with the birds across a water hole. Suddenly they turn on me. One by one, they snatch back the feathers they have given me. I crash into the water and drown . . . No one can kill Coyote. I resurrect along the trails of life. I am a trail-builder. I cut disease out of plants along the trail. If I am a sullen, bitter animal, I am also a medicine man! I am a white coyote. Look at me, I am good luck! But the people see me as a yellow coyote. They drive Coyote into the wilderness. They trap me, snarling with fear. Don't you understand what isolation does to Coyote?

The other day, Margaret, I got into my old car and started to drive away from you. At the top of a steep hill, I started down towards a sharp curve. I was singing, celebrating my escape from you, Margaret! Suddenly, the brakes went out! Gathering speed, my car headed for a huge cottonwood tree. How can you die, Coyote? I sing and laugh, Margaret, at my ridiculous situation. Swinging the wheel sharply, I angle around the tree. Coyote will escape from you, Margaret! I crash into a haystack in a barn! Stupid Coyote, he can't escape from you, Margaret. It's you who must die. Coyote lives forever!

(Blackout.)

SCENE 11

(MARGARET *enters in a wheelchair, pushed by* GEORGE.)

353

MARGARET:
Where are we going?

GEORGE:
On a voyage, Margaret.

MARGARET:
Where are the children?

GEORGE:
They're coming to see you off.

MARGARET:
You're coming too?

GEORGE:
You need someone to take care of you. I want you to have physical therapy.

MARGARET:
I don't need you. You're rolling me to my death.

GEORGE:
You must struggle to recover your health.

MARGARET *(snapping)*:
Push faster!

GEORGE:
I can't push faster.

MARGARET:
Why is death so slow? When I had my first stroke, I thought one more time will end it, but doctors prolong our lives. With their new technology, they send us slowly into eternity in wheelchairs. Do you know what I call this chair?

GEORGE:
We used to listen to Wagner all the time. You call it *Love-Death*.

MARGARET:
You are a demon, George. Push me faster!

(ERWIN *and* SHIRLEY *enter and stop, as if looking for* MARGARET *and* GEORGE.):

GEORGE:
Your children are here.

354

MARGARET:
So they're my children now . . . You've given up on the family.

GEORGE:
I push the wheelchair . . . *(He calls.)* Erwin! Shirley!

(ERWIN and SHIRLEY move towards them.)

MARARET *(standing up suddenly):*
I will not be seen in a wheelchair! It is too humiliating to be pushed along by an old Coyote, a trickster! You're not fun anymore, George.

SHIRLEY:
I'm glad you're getting away, Margaret. You need a trip.

ERWIN:
Where are you going?

GEORGE:
Your mother has not decided if she wants to live or die.

MARGARET *(throwing up her arms and whirling around):*
I am dancing back into memory! Do you remember, Erwin, when I danced with your father? *(calling)* Lorenzo, I'm coming!

SHIRLEY:
Who's she calling?

ERWIN:
She's calling Lorenzo Hubbell . . .

SHIRLEY:
He's been dead for a long time.

ERWIN:
Mother, you'd better get back in your chair.

MARGARET:
Everyone wants to confine me. Death will not free me! I am waiting for a god to seize me, and he won't come.

SHIRLEY:
I can't believe she's dancing.

(MARGARET gets back into the wheelchair.)

ERWIN:
She's not dancing, she's in a wheelchair with a broken hip.

GEORGE:

I want to take care of her. She needs medical help.

ERWIN:

You can't help her anymore.

MARGARET:

When I grew up, traveling by train was an adventure. Trains conquered the land, selling real estate to eager settlers. A wild, greedy country desired instant conquest, chained to the swift movement of the clock . . . A country that refused to acknowledge the Indian sense of history and time . . . *(calling again)* Lorenzo, take me back into the Navajo world! *(The figure of* HUBBELL, *played by the actor, appears.)*

HUBBELL:

Margaret! Do you want to come with me?

MARGARET:

Yes, Lorenzo, take me to Woman Singer! *(She steps out of the wheelchair.)* I need to be cured. *(She speaks to* ERWIN.*)* It's all right now. Lorenzo will take me to Woman Singer and the Sacred Mountain.

ERWIN:

Mother, please . . .

MARGARET:

George was pushing my chair slower and slower. He wants me frozen in space so I can't move.

ERWIN:

He takes care of you. Why do you think he's so cruel now?

MARGARET:

He can't stand my being ill, my preparing for death. When he speaks to me his voice is full of resentment . . . I know the sound of a trap when I hear it. I won't stay in his trap now that Lorenzo is here.

(As LORENZO *waits,* MARGARET *draws* ERWIN *closer, whispering to him.* SHIRLEY *begins to question* GEORGE.*)*

SHIRLEY:

What's the matter with her?

GEORGE:

She can't die fast enough.

SHIRLEY:
Why does she hate you? What happened?

GEORGE:
Love is movement. In old age, the mind still desires to move, but the flesh is frozen in time.

SHIRLEY:
I don't believe you. Love is also resting silently together.

GEORGE:
Wait till you get old . . .

MARGARET (calling):
Take away the wheelchair, George! I give it to you! Sit in it yourself!

GEORGE (angrily):
Never, Margaret! I'll never need it! (He pushes the wheelchair savagely off-stage so that it crashes with a loud noise.)

MARGARET:
Lorenzo, I am coming! (She walks towards LORENZO.)

HUBBELL:
Ghosts float from the past into the future, living memories. I speak English, Spanish, and Navajo. I love to be with people of all races. When I trade, I am not greedy. A small profit is enough. I know what it means when the Navajos say in their Night Chant, "It shall be finished in beauty." Even ghosts try to help the women they love finish in beauty . . . (MARGARET takes his arm and they begin to move off.)

ERWIN:
I'm sorry, George. This can't go on . . . She can't stand you anymore.

GEORGE:
How do you think I feel about her! (as SHIRLEY stares at him) Don't look at me that way! Margaret and I were lovers! Love passes . . . All of us were never a family! We were the Last Romantics!

MARGARET (turning back, holding LORENZO'S arm):
Goodbye, George . . . Your white hair ripples in the wind. You're like a wind-god sitting on the hero's shoulder and whispering in his ear. You recite to him poems and instruct him about plant diseases. You tell him about the excitement of building secret trails high to the gods. But the wind fades out . . . Silent, the wind waits in bitterness to move again . . . Goodbye, my children! Do not despair. May you wander in the

house of happiness as I too am wandering where the dark rain cloud hangs low before the door. The wheelchair is gone! Be glad! The hypocritical Rest Home is illuminated as a Death Home! I go to see whether the one god or the many gods will create a new world of beauty!

(As the lights dim slowly, she walks out, arm in arm, with LORENZO, *as* GEORGE *is left standing there. Blackout.)*

SCENE 12

(The lights come up to reveal ERWIN *and* SHIRLEY, *as if standing outside of a church from which the end of Bach's B Minor Mass can be heard.)*

SHIRLEY:
I know how you feel, Erwin, but you shouldn't have walked out.

ERWIN:
He made it his own ceremony. It was George's ceremony, not Mother's!

SHIRLEY:
She wanted an Episcopalian ceremony at the end.

ERWIN:
All of the music was George's favorites. Nothing of hers!

SHIRLEY:
You read several of her poems . . .

ERWIN:
The son's last tribute as her childhood church folded her in its forgiving arms! George arranged that!

SHIRLEY:
Don't blame George! You know how every Indian village has a kiva as well as a church for double safety. Margaret never left the church even though she loved the kiva.

ERWIN:
Her spirit wasn't there in church today. When I read her poems, she wasn't there listening to me.

SHIRLEY:
Her spirit went off into the Indian world.

ERWIN:

Only her white friends were here in the church.

SHIRLEY:

She wanted a formal goodbye to the white world of her parents. If you lived in a divided world as she did, you might have arranged two farewells.

ERWIN:

Was this a funeral for the living or the dead? George adored the music as though it redeemed him!

SHIRLEY *(as the music ends):*
Don't argue with George when he comes out. That won't help.

ERWIN:

I'll never forgive him!

SHIRLEY:

Stop acting this way. You'll just make things worse!

(GEORGE enters and looks at them slowly.)

GEORGE:

Margaret loved the Bach B Minor Mass . . . We used to listen to it together.

ERWIN:

She wasn't here today.

GEORGE:

I think she was. She wanted an Episcopalian service out of respect for her family and friends. I chose her favorite music.

ERWIN:

You mean *your* favorite music!

SHIRLEY *(intervening):*
Erwin just thinks it strange, holding a ceremony for Margaret in the church she rejected. That's why he walked out.

GEORGE:

I was wondering . . .

ERWIN:

It seemed so hypocritical. Mother wasn't a hypocrite!

GEORGE *(stiffly):*
I was only doing what she wanted.

ERWIN *(unable to suppress his feelings):*
It's not just this ceremony. It's what you did to her at the end.

SHIRLEY:
Erwin . . .

GEORGE *(trying to contain himself):*
I did my best to take care of her . . . The wheelchair separated us . . .
(suddenly, to SHIRLEY*)* Did she tell you that she hated me at the end?

SHIRLEY *(hesitating):*
What do you mean?

GEORGE:
She was sick. Her whole personality changed! Her medical expenses were
tremendous. I poured my money into her care since she didn't have
enough insurance. She became suspicious that I resented her illness.

ERWIN:
She called you a miser! You know what happened. She was afraid of you!

GEORGE:
What do you really know about us? We were happy once. I thought I had
a new family, but you always resented me!

SHIRLEY:
Don't argue this way. Margaret wouldn't like it.

GEORGE *(to* SHIRLEY*)*:
You don't understand the spectre of old age when it invades! Margaret
and I had a written financial agreement, but she couldn't keep it. I've got
all of the extra expenses I paid for Margaret down on paper. She had no
right to hate me! I can show you the financial details . . .

ERWIN:
Fuck the financial details!

SHIRLEY:
Stop this, both of you! Margaret would hate this quarreling!

GEORGE:
How can you judge unless you feel the cruelty of old age when body and
mind suddenly begin to fail? *(He glares at them for a long moment, then
exits.* ERWIN *starts after him, then stops, burying his face in his hands.)*

SHIRLEY:
I know, it's not over yet. You need to confront George, but it doesn't do

any good to hate him. He's too mixed up. Don't cry. Margaret's spirit is still alive. We know what she wanted. Somewhere her spirit is seeking its own peace . . .

(*Blackout.*)

SCENE 13

(MARGARET *and the actor playing* LORENZO HUBBELL *appear.*)

MARGARET:
I feel as though I'm floating on top of the world!

HUBBELL:
You're on the Sacred Mountain. When the wind blows, we'll float into the valley.

MARGARET:
All those graveyards down there . . . And the ruins . . .

HUBBELL:
Wars, slaughtered civilizations, ghosts wandering in time through the ruins . . .

MARGARET:
So this is resurrection . . .

HUBBELL:
Ghosts learn about endurance.

MARGARET:
If this is eternity, it drifts along . . . What kind of religion prevails?

HUBBELL:
Fragments of many religions . . .

MARGARET:
No priests, medicine men, no prophets?

HUBBELL:
Shadows of what we were . . .

MARGARET:
How do ghosts meet the living?

HUBBELL:

The dead dream of the living, and the living dream of the dead. Their dreams battle forever across time.

MARGARET:

I have to haunt my children . . .

HUBBELL:

You're a strong enough ghost to haunt your children, your husbands, your friends, even people you don't know.

MARGARET *(laughing):*

Dominant ghosts! Do I have any free will in haunting people?

HUBBELL:

Free will is a problem for ghosts too!

MARGARET:

What I like about being a ghost is the feeling of lightness. No deadweight of duty any more . . .

HUBBELL:

Weightless, we're able to surprise people!

(The lights change to focus on another area where ERWIN *and* SHIRLEY *confront each other. The lights give the effect of* MARGARET *and* HUBBELL *floating towards them.)*

ERWIN:

Last night I dreamt of Mother . . .

SHIRLEY:

Funny, so did I.

ERWIN:

She was riding across the desert in an old Ford with Lorenzo Hubbell to deliver a sewing machine to a Navajo woman.

SHIRLEY:

She was trying to tell me something about George. I can't remember what!

MARGARET:

Memory is too repetitious.

HUBBELL:

Ghosts have the same problem as people. They need to be more imaginative!

MARGARET:
How are you, Erwin?

ERWIN *(to* SHIRLEY*)*:
I wish Mother knew about our child.

SHIRLEY:
Our little Margaret . . . She's even beginning to look like your mother.

MARGARET:
I have a grandchild! A ghost can be a proud grandparent too!

HUBBELL:
Why not? Speak to them more directly.

MARGARET:
How do I do that?

HUBBELL:
How does Hamlet's ghost-father speak to Hamlet?

MARGARET *(to* ERWIN *and* SHIRLEY*)*:
Did you two deal with George after my death?

SHIRLEY *(to* ERWIN*)*:
I think I remember my dream . . . Your mother was asking me how we dealt with George after her death . . .

ERWIN:
Ha! She'd turn in her grave if she knew what he wanted. He went crazy!

SCENE 14

(GEORGE, ERWIN *and* SHIRLEY *confront each other.*)

GEORGE *(handing a folder of papers to* ERWIN*)*:
I've prepared a complete list of my expenses in regard to Margaret . . .

SHIRLEY:
How can you talk that way?

GEORGE:
Someone has to be practical in this family. I want it clear how much money I put into Margaret's house as well as her medical expenses.

ERWIN:
You're claiming the house?

SHIRLEY:
It's half Erwin's!

GEORGE:
It's mine legally. You know Margaret and I signed an agreement. Check the papers.

ERWIN:
She left everything to me.

GEORGE:
She had nothing to leave. Those papers will show how recklessly she spent.

SHIRLEY:
Don't call her reckless. You used to admire her courage.

GEORGE:
She became an invalid. Her mind was affected. I don't want to argue with you.

ERWIN:
I want all of mother's manuscripts and sandpaintings.

GEORGE:
You can have the manuscripts. Her Navajo sandpaintings I've given to the Museum in her name.

SHIRLEY:
You could have saved some for Erwin.

ERWIN:
Is it true you want to use some of mother's estate to establish a scholarship at your university in memory of your first wife!

GEORGE:
That's none of your business. From the beginning, Erwin, you were against me. You helped ruin my marriage.

ERWIN:
You ruined your own marriage! I'll fight you in court, George. Mother left me half of her estate.

GEORGE:
There's nothing left. It's all down in those papers.

SHIRLEY:
You'll end up alone, George. You know that.

GEORGE:
I've been alone all my life . . .

SCENE 15

(As the lights change, they flicker to give the effect of GEORGE *floating into the scene with* MARGARET *and* LORENZO. SHIRLEY *and* ERWIN *are present now too.)*

MARGARET:
I feel as if George is around here somewhere. How come you see some ghosts, and others you don't see!

HUBBELL:
I suppose it depends on the power of the presence.

(At first GEORGE *is seen dimly. Then, as his speech progresses in intensity, he is brilliantly illuminated.)*

GEORGE:
I resent my loneliness . . . I resent my invisibility even more! All my life I worked hard. I did unusual things. I traveled a lot to study plants. I helped to translate Theophrastus. I built beautiful mountain trails. I discovered a new plant disease that is named after me. As a teacher, I was conscientious. I tried to teach my students respect for the natural environment. When I think about what happened to me, I don't believe it was all my fault. This was a hell of a difficult family! We loved each other at first . . .

MARGARET *(staring, as* GEORGE *is illuminated brightly):*
I can see George now! He was always a romantic looking person with his beard and his strong body.

HUBBELL:
He's trying very hard to be a powerful looking ghost. There's a lot of frustrated energy . . .

SHIRLEY *(to* ERWIN):
What good does it do to resent George so much? He's dead now.

ERWIN:
I don't give a damn about George, but I keep thinking about him.

MARGARET (to HUBBELL):

Maybe it's the good side of George blazing up. I can remember the romance too. Who would have thought that we enjoyed sleeping together at our age? I wrote love poems to him. He translated Goethe for me. I read my Navajo stories to him. We shared many different rooms together with romantic fires blazing. We made a ceremony out of candles and wine . . . The force of ceremony never dies! (The DANCER appears to music.)

HUBBELL:

Time doesn't heal anything, but it uncovers a kind of balance. Time echoes with a chorus of voices . . .

SHIRLEY:

The ghosts of love linger on in time. Where would we be if they didn't haunt us?

ERWIN:

I wrote a poem about Margaret and George that ends:

"If the Last Romantics fade in time and love leads at last to hate, Love never dies. A joyous love will always be the aim of fate."

GEORGE:

I'm really blazing now, Margaret! I'm burning out all of our bad times! Do you see me?

MARGARET:

I see you, George. I'll never forget our love and hate. If you hear my ghost singing, it's Woman Singer singing her cure—there is a healing if hands can grip across space and time . . .

(Slowly, as if across enormous distances, as the DANCER gestures, the five sets of arms reach out and their hands clasp across space and time.)

THE END

NOTE

The Last Romantics is my most autobiographical play, based on my mother's second marriage to a distinguished plant pathologist. But I didn't want to write a "confessional" play; I wanted the characters and the famous people with whom they were involved to have mythical dimensions. The voyage on which they are embarked does, it seems to me, mark the last stages of nineteenth-century romanticism—hence the title.

Stylistically, the play incorporates strong musical, dance, and visual elements—a search for a new music theatre—to dramatize the conflict between southwestern Indian cultures and the conservative Episcopalian, eastern background that my mother experienced. I am grateful to the composer, John Geist, the Hopi weaver, Ramona Sakiestewa, who has designed the planned 1993 production in San Francisco, the director and producer of Tour de Force Theatre, Andrea Gordon, and the actors, Marjory Panetti, Larry Pisoni, Julian Lopez-Morillas, Terry Lamb, Sharon Omi, and Ken Crow, who helped to develop the play in a series of reading workshops.